Economics, Law, and Institutions in Asia Pacific

The Asia Pacific region is expected to steadily enhance its economic and political presence in the world during the twenty-first century. At the same time, many serious economic and political issues remain unresolved in the region. To further academic enquiry and enhance readers' understanding about this vibrant region, the present series, Economics, Law, and Institutions in Asia Pacific, aims to present cutting-edge research on the Asia Pacific region and its relationship with the rest of the world. For countries in this region to achieve robust economic growth, it is of foremost importance that they improve the quality of their markets, as history shows that healthy economic growth cannot be achieved without high-quality markets. High-quality markets can be established and maintained only under a well-designed set of rules and laws, without which competition will not flourish. Based on these principles, this series places a special focus on economic, business, legal, and institutional issues geared towards the healthy development of Asia Pacific markets. The series considers book proposals for scientific research, either theoretical or empirical, that is related to the theme of improving market quality and has policy implications for the Asia Pacific region. The types of books that will be considered for publication include research monographs as well as relevant proceedings. The series show-cases work by Asia-Pacific based researchers but also encourages the work of social scientists not limited to the Asia Pacific region. Each proposal and final manuscript is subject to evaluation by the editorial board and experts in the field.

All books and chapters in the Economics, Law and Institutions in Asia Pacific book series are indexed in Scopus.

Rachita Gulati · Dil B. Rahut · Sunil Kumar ·
Tetsushi Sonobe
Editors

Emerging Challenges in Banking in Asia and the Pacific

Crises, Innovation, Inclusion, and Resilience for a Sustainable Future

ADBInstitute

Springer

Editors
Rachita Gulati
Asian Development Bank Institute
Tokyo, Japan

Indian Institute of Technology Roorkee
Uttarakhand, India

Sunil Kumar
Faculty of Economics
South Asian University
New Delhi, Delhi, India

Dil B. Rahut
Asian Development Bank Institute
Tokyo, Japan

Tetsushi Sonobe
National Graduate Institute for Policy Studies (GRIPS)
Tokyo, Japan

Asian Development Bank Institute
Tokyo, Japan

ISSN 2199-8620 ISSN 2199-8639 (electronic)
Economics, Law, and Institutions in Asia Pacific
ISBN 978-981-92-2143-1 ISBN 978-981-92-2144-8 (eBook)
https://doi.org/10.1007/978-981-92-2144-8

This work was supported by Asian Development Bank Institute.

This Springer imprint is published by the registered company Springer Nature Singapore Pte Ltd.
The registered company address is: 152 Beach Road, #21-01/04 Gateway East, Singapore 189721, Singapore

Foreword

Asia and the Pacific has emerged as the primary engine of global economic expansion, marked by diversity, rapid urbanisation, and technological adaptability. As economies across the region continue on their growth trajectories, the banking systems underpinning this prosperity face an array of challenges. The interconnected nature of global financial markets, emerging risks from climate change, technological disruption, and inequalities in financial inclusion create a need to reimagine how banking institutions operate, regulate, and serve society. From the lessons of the Asian financial crisis to the disruptive shocks of the COVID-19 pandemic, the imperative for the region's banking sector has shifted. The goal is no longer merely growth at any cost, but rather a strategic move toward quality growth that is resilient, inclusive, productive, and environmentally sustainable.

This book comes at a moment when policymakers, regulators, and financial institutions are grappling with these unprecedented transformations. The rapid digitalisation of financial services, the emergence of fintech innovators, and the exploration of central bank digital currencies (CBDCs) are reshaping the foundations of banking. Alongside this, the urgency of addressing climate change and advancing financial inclusion adds layers of complexity to an already challenging policy landscape. These are not isolated issues, but interconnected challenges that require comprehensive, forward-thinking responses.

A central theme of this volume is the period of "creative destruction" that is currently reshaping monetary and banking systems. The rapid proliferation of fintech and the exploration of CBDCs offer opportunities to bridge the financing gap for micro, small, and medium-sized enterprises and marginalised populations, but they also introduce unprecedented implications for stability. Within this evolving landscape, crisis preparedness, technological innovation, financial inclusion, and sustainability are mutually reinforcing dimensions of a resilient financial system. Drawing on lessons from past crises, the volume provides practical guidance for navigating future uncertainties. Its chapters examine critical policy issues related to the effectiveness of monetary policy and prudential regulation, the role of CBDCs in financial architecture, the management of associated risks, and the potential of fintech and digitalisation to advance financial inclusion without undermining stability. These themes reflect the dilemmas policymakers presently confront, and the evidence-based analysis presented in this book offers clarity.

Through case studies, such as those on Brunei Darussalam, the authors highlight the gap between access and meaningful usage: high internet penetration does not automatically translate into financial inclusion when structural barriers continue to exclude the unbanked. This is vital for policymakers, as building digital infrastructure alone is not enough. Beyond digitalisation, the volume also examines the structural impediments to private-sector credit. In several developing Asian economies, excessive government borrowing, rather than prudential regulation, limits private lending by crowding out productive investment. Finally, the book aligns the trajectory of the banking sector with the global sustainability agenda. It documents a shift in central banking in which policy shocks have accelerated the integration of the Sustainable Development Goals, particularly climate action, into supervisory mandates. The transition to a green economy is now framed not as a peripheral corporate responsibility concern, but as a core element of financial stability and risk management.

I commend the editors and contributors for this timely contribution. This book serves as an essential knowledge product for central bankers, regulators, policymakers, and academic scholars. As Asia and the Pacific navigates a rapidly evolving financial landscape, the analyses and evidence presented in this book will be an essential resource for strengthening the region's financial systems so that they remain resilient to future shocks while being inclusive enough to expand opportunities and shared prosperity for all.

Bambang Brodjonegoro
Dean and CEO
Asian Development Bank Institute
Tokyo, Japan

Acknowledgments

This volume is the result of scholarly contributions submitted in response to a Call for Papers on "From Crisis to Resilience: shaping the Future of Banking in Asia and the Pacific", and the subsequent virtual conference co-hosted by the Asian Development Bank Institute (ADBI) and South Asian University on 30–31 January 2025. The rich discussions, insightful observations, and diverse research perspectives shared during the event provided the intellectual foundation for this book.

The editors extend their sincere gratitude to all keynote speakers, paper presenters, and participants for their valuable engagement. Special appreciation is offered to our plenary speakers for sharing their insightful and thought provoking perspectives: Jennifer Elliott (International Monetary Fund); Ashima Goyal (Emeritus Professor, Indira Gandhi Institute of Development Research, India); Barbara Casu (Professor of Banking and Finance & Director of Centre for Banking Research, Bayes Business School, University of London, United Kingdom); M. Kabir Hassan (Professor, University of New Orleans, United States); Arup Mitra (Professor, Faculty of Economics, South Asian University, New Delhi, India); Sureka Ketawala (Additional Director, Central Bank of Sri Lanka, Sri Lanka); and Yong Tan (Associate Professor, University of Bradford, United Kingdom).

The editors are also deeply grateful to Arief Ramayandi (Senior Research Economist, ADBI), Daniel Suryadarma (Senior Economist, ADB), John Beirne (Principal Economist, ADB), Kinga Tshering (Founder and CEO, Institute of Happiness, Kingdom of Bhutan), and Siong Hook Law (Professor, Universiti Putra Malaysia, Malaysia) for skillfully chairing the conference sessions.

We appreciate the anonymous reviewers for their constructive comments and suggestions, which greatly enhanced the quality of the volume. We also wish to acknowledge the invaluable support of Jie Mi (former Research Associate, ADBI), Nilaphy Phommachanh (Research Associate, ADBI) in coordinating the conference, and Dean Irvine, Adam Majoe, Juno Kawakami and Amala Gobiraman in assisting throughout the production process.

Finally, we extend our sincere appreciation to all contributors to this publication for their cooperation, dedication, and generous investment of time in bringing this publication to fruition.

Praise for *Emerging Challenges in Banking in Asia and the Pacific*

"This timely book offers critical insights into navigating the complex landscape of banking in Asia and the Pacific. By integrating lessons from past crises with emerging challenges—from fintech disruption to climate risks and uneven access to finance—it provides policymakers with actionable frameworks for building resilient and inclusive financial systems. Through its comprehensive analysis of regulatory approaches, monetary policy tools, and governance practices, combined with an emphasis on regional cooperation, the book is essential reading for policymakers seeking to strengthen banking stability in an era of unprecedented transformation and uncertainty."

—Prof. M.K.Hassan, *University of New Orleans*

"This volume provides an exploration of the twin imperatives reshaping Asian banking systems: the digital revolution and the sustainability transition. By rigorously analyzing the stability implications of central bank digital currencies and fintech alongside the integration of climate risk into supervisory frameworks, the authors offer a forward-looking guide. It is a vital resource for understanding how the region can navigate digital disruption while steering financial systems toward a resilient, net-zero future."

—Prof. Barbara Casu, *Director of the Centre for Banking Research & Professor of Banking and Finance, Bayes Business School*

"This volume navigates the complex nexus of historical legacies and emerging macro-financial risks to offer a vital roadmap for restoring and maintaining banking soundness and sustainability. By thoroughly examining the relationship between crisis resilience and structural challenges, such as the sovereign bank nexus, digital disruptions and governance, the authors emphasize strengthening governance and institutional defense lines. This book is an excellent resource for central bankers and regulators seeking to leverage robust policy frameworks to ensure systemic stability and sustainable recovery amidst global volatility."

—Mrs. Sureka Ketawala, *Additional Director, Bank Supervision Department, Central Bank of Sri Lanka*

Contents

Contributors

Rishman Jot Kaur Chahal Department of Humanities and Social Sciences, Indian Institute of Technology Roorkee, Roorkee, Uttarakhand, India; Mehta Family School of DS and AI, Indian Institute of Technology Roorkee, Roorkee, Uttarakhand, India

Avik Ghosh Reserve Bank of India, Kanpur, India

Rachita Gulati Asian Development Bank Institute, Tokyo, Japan; Department of Humanities and Social Sciences, Indian Institute of Technology Roorkee, Roorkee, Uttarakhand, India

Garima Gupta Department of Humanities and Social Sciences, Indian Institute of Technology Roorkee, Roorkee, Uttarakhand, India

Hazwan Haini Centre for Strategic and Policy Studies, Bandar Seri Begawan, Brunei Darussalam

Anwar Hashim Centre for Strategic and Policy Studies, Bandar Seri Begawan, Brunei Darussalam

Ploypailin Kijkasiwat Faculty of Business Administration and Accountancy, Khon Kaen University, Khon Kaen, Thailand

Niraj Koirala California State University, Los Angeles, CA, USA

Sunil Kumar Faculty of Economics, South Asian University, New Delhi, India

Muhammad Ayub Khan Mehar Employers' Federation of Pakistan, Karachi, Pakistan

Dil B. Rahut Asian Development Bank Institute, Tokyo, Japan

Tetsushi Sonobe National Graduate Institute for Policy Studies (GRIPS), Tokyo, Japan;
Asian Development Bank Institute, Tokyo, Japan

Long Yang College of Graduate Study in Management, Khon Kaen University, Khon Kaen, Thailand

Chapter 1
Emerging Challenges in Banking in Asia and the Pacific: Crises, Innovation, Inclusion, and Resilience for a Sustainable Future

Rachita Gulati, Dil B. Rahut, Sunil Kumar, and Tetsushi Sonobe

Abstract This introductory chapter outlines the central themes for analyzing the evolving banking landscape across the Asia-Pacific region. It examines how financial systems are navigating persistent vulnerabilities from past crises, rapid digital transformation, and emerging macro-financial threats, such as climate change. The chapter previews the book's interconnected themes: crisis response and financial governance, the balance between FinTech adoption and banking stability, and the adoption of central bank digital currencies (CBDCs). Finally, it provides a foundational framework for building crisis-ready, digitally inclusive, and sustainability-driven banking systems to drive quality growth.

Keywords Banking crisis · Financial resilience · Digital transformation · Asia

1.1 Context and Motivation

Banking systems across Asia and the Pacific region have long played a pivotal role in driving economic growth, promoting financial inclusion, and supporting sustainable development. These systems have been tested by three watershed crises: the Asian financial crisis (AFC) of 1997, which exposed vulnerabilities in corporate

R. Gulati · D. B. Rahut · T. Sonobe
Asian Development Bank Institute, Tokyo, Japan

R. Gulati (✉)
Department of Humanities and Social Sciences, Indian Institute of Technology Roorkee, Roorkee, Uttarakhand, India

S. Kumar
Faculty of Economics, South Asian University, New Delhi, India

T. Sonobe
National Graduate Institute for Policy Studies (GRIPS), Tokyo, Japan

R. Gulati et al. (eds.), *Emerging Challenges in Banking in Asia and the Pacific*, Economics, Law, and Institutions in Asia Pacific,
https://doi.org/10.1007/978-981-92-2144-8_1

governance, exchange rate management, and foreign debt exposure; the global financial crisis (GFC) of 2007–2009, which highlighted improved resilience but persistent liquidity risks; and the coronavirus disease (COVID-19) pandemic of 2020, which accelerated digital transformation while straining loan portfolios. Each episode prompted regulatory reforms and deepened regional cooperation, underscoring the need for continued vigilance in the face of emerging threats, such as climate change, cyber risks, and geopolitical tensions.

Today, the rapid pace of digital transformation, the rise of fintech innovations, and increasingly complex regulatory environments demand innovative and inclusive approaches to bank regulation and supervision. The integration of new technologies, exploration of central bank digital currencies (CBDCs), and expansion of sustainable finance initiatives are reshaping the role of banks and financial institutions. As the region navigates economic shifts, geopolitical pressures, and technological advancements, assessing the resilience of its banking systems remains crucial. Past crises, whether economic, financial, or political, have exposed vulnerabilities and served as catalysts for reform. They compel regulators and policymakers to adopt new measures to strengthen systemic resilience and safeguard financial stability.

Despite its dynamic and high-growth economies, the Asia and the Pacific region remains highly vulnerable to external shocks and emerging threats, particularly because of its growing interconnectedness with non-bank financial institutions (NBFIs) and global financial markets. Climate change, digital disruptions, and widening inequalities further exacerbate systemic vulnerabilities in the region. The painful lessons learned from the 1997 AFC, where high levels of foreign debt, unmanaged exchange rate risks, and excessive leverage led to a surge in non-performing loans (NPLs) and widespread financial collapse, helped the region better withstand the 2008–2009 GFC. Measures such as the accumulation of foreign reserves proved critical in averting a currency crisis, although liquidity shortages, especially in US dollars, still posed challenges. More recently, the coronavirus disease (COVID-19) pandemic and the 2023 United States (US) banking crisis have underscored the fragility of financial systems and the urgent need to build adaptable and future-ready institutions. In an increasingly interconnected global economy, regional and global shocks can destabilize banking systems quickly. As geopolitical tensions intensify and uncertainty in global trade persists, Asian economies face a growing imperative to establish forward-looking protocols and robust crisis preparedness frameworks.

Recent technological advancements in the banking sector, such as digitalization and fintech, have the potential to improve financial access for underserved populations. These innovations can help integrate more people into the financial system, support economic growth, reduce inequality, and provide low-cost credit and payment solutions for the poor. However, these developments also pose significant risks to the banking sector. Cybersecurity threats, data privacy and protection concerns, operational risks, and regulatory and compliance challenges are often at the center of the debate. In many cases, regulatory frameworks struggle to keep pace with the rapid adoption of new technologies, leading to gaps in oversight. Furthermore, limited financial and digital literacy among marginalized groups may prevent them from fully benefiting from these advancements, potentially leaving them further behind.

Climate change also poses a significant threat to banking stability. Climate-related risks can affect the financial system through both physical and transition risks. Physical risks refer to asset losses or business disruptions caused by climate-related events such as floods, wildfires, droughts, and storms. These events can damage assets used as collateral or interrupt business activities, leading to income loss. Consequently, businesses may struggle to repay their loans, leading to an increase in NPLs of banks. Transition risks, on the other hand, stem from the shifting of the economy away from fossil fuels toward a low-carbon society. Policy changes, regulatory adjustments, and technological advancements may negatively affect the performance of fossil fuel-dependent firms, potentially reducing their profitability and debt repayment capacity. Both risks undermine the stability of the banking system.

To navigate this complex landscape, it is essential to assess the resilience of banking systems in the face of crises, uncertainties, and ongoing transformations. Learning from past experiences, particularly how banks adapt to external and internal shocks, is crucial. Equally important is identifying successful strategies that have proven effective in maintaining stability while reforming or discarding ineffective ones. Recognizing emerging risks, such as cyber threats, information technology (IT) vulnerabilities, climate-related risks, and geopolitical tensions, enables timely strategy development. In the current phase of post-pandemic economic recovery, banking systems face growing stress in maintaining financial sustainability amid the digital disruption caused by new non-banking entrants challenging traditional institutions. This evolving landscape makes it imperative to examine regulatory responses that protect financial stability while balancing competition and facilitating the benefits of technological innovations.

Against this backdrop, this book addresses interconnected concerns that provide an analytical framework for understanding how banking systems in Asia and the Pacific can achieve resilience, inclusion, and sustainability. In particular, the book deals with the following key concerns.

- How have national, regional, and global financial governance mechanisms evolved in response to past crises, and are they adequate to address future shocks?
- What is the relationship between fintech adoption, financial inclusion, and banking stability, and under what conditions does digital transformation enhance or threaten financial resilience?
- How should central banks design and deploy digital currencies, such as CBDCs, to complement monetary policy objectives without destabilizing traditional banking systems?
- What role do policy shocks, both positive (such as the Sustainable Development Goals and the Millennium Development Goals) and negative (such as financial crises), play in shaping central banks' orientation toward sustainable development?
- How can monetary policy and prudential regulations be calibrated to support private sector credit flows while maintaining banking stability?

These questions guide the empirical investigations and policy analyses presented in the chapters that follow, culminating in a synthesis of lessons learned and the strategic imperatives for the banking systems of the region.

1.2 Significance of the Book

This book offers critical insights into the lessons learned and reforms implemented by policymakers, regulators, and international organizations in response to past crises in Asia and the Pacific. It makes several distinctive contributions to the literature on banking and financial stability. While most studies on banking resilience and digital transformation focus on advanced Western economies, this volume centers on perspectives from Asia and the Pacific, offering insights from a region that accounts for approximately 46% of global gross domestic product (GDP) and comprises a diverse mix of advanced and emerging economies. The volume addresses post-pandemic recovery challenges, recent CBDC pilot programs in India and China, the 2023 US banking crisis, and emerging climate-related financial risks, which are issues at the forefront of current policy discussions. The collected chapters examine past experiences and policy responses to major regional and global crises. The volume also explores the expanding role of new technology developments, particularly in creating a digital ecosystem and its role in advancing financial inclusion. The emerging issue of CBDCs and their implications for banking stability has also been investigated, along with other relevant issues. Overall, the book provides a forward-looking perspective on enhancing financial inclusion and presents evidence of how monetary policy tools and prudential regulations shape banks' lending and investment practices amid ongoing challenges.

1.3 Organization of the Book

The chapters in this volume are organized around interconnected themes that collectively address the research questions outlined above.

The volume begins with the first theme on Crisis Response and Financial Governance by examining how economies have strengthened financial governance in response to successive crises, exemplifying the cases of Southeast and East Asia.

In Chapter 2, Long Yang and Ploypailin Kijkasiwat lay the foundational framework by examining how Southeast and East Asia have responded to financial crises by enhancing financial governance mechanisms at the national, regional, and global levels. Triggered by the Asian financial crisis of 1997 and reinforced by the global financial crisis of 2008, these regions implemented significant reforms to address systemic weaknesses in governance and prevent future crises. At the national level, countries such as Thailand and Indonesia have introduced regulatory frameworks to stabilize their financial sectors, improve corporate governance, and enhance transparency. Regionally, initiatives such as the Chiang Mai Initiative Multilateralization and the ASEAN+3 framework have strengthened financial cooperation and created a collective safety net to mitigate liquidity risks. Globally, Southeast and East Asian economies have played a vital role in shaping multilateral financial governance through participation in G20-led initiatives and the establishment of alternative institutions, such as the New Development Bank, created by BRICS countries (Brazil, the Russian Federation, India, the People's Republic of China, and South Africa). This chapter establishes the "three lines of defense" framework—national, regional, and global—that subsequent chapters build upon when examining specific policy interventions.

Building on this governance context, the book addresses a critical contemporary challenge: harnessing digital transformation to advance financial inclusion while maintaining stability. Chapters 3 and 4 explore how technological innovation can bridge access gaps, while examining the trade-offs between rapid digital adoption and banking sector resilience.

In Chapter 3, Hazwan Haini and Anwar Hashim focus on the future of financial inclusion in Brunei Darussalam, offering a detailed case study of the "access-usage gap" that characterizes many economies in Asia and the Pacific. Brunei Darussalam has made significant progress in expanding mobile and internet connectivity, placing it ahead of many Association of Southeast Asian Nations (ASEAN) peers. However, financial inclusion remains moderate, with gaps in banking usage, digital transactions, and financial depth. The results highlight that only 65.7% of the population holds bank accounts, with even lower adoption rates for online banking and debit cards. Although the digital payment market has expanded, disparities in adoption are evident, with declining average transaction values per user. The authors emphasize the need to bridge digital infrastructure gaps, particularly in underserved rural areas; enhance financial literacy to build awareness and confidence; create an adaptive regulatory framework that encourages innovation, inclusion, and security; promote public–private partnerships to drive fintech adoption; and address data gaps.

Building on the access-usage gap identified in Chapter 3, Chapter 4 by Niraj Koirala empirically explores the relationship between financial inclusion, fintech, and their interactions with banking stability. Using an unbalanced panel dataset from 21 economies in Asia and the Pacific—including the People's Republic of China, India, Japan, the Republic of Korea, and several ASEAN and South Asian countries—spanning 2000 to 2021, the study constructs financial inclusion and fintech indices using principal component analysis and employing panel fixed effects and instrumental variable methods. The findings reveal that financial inclusion enhances banking stability by diversifying credit portfolios and increasing access to stable retail deposits. However, the study finds that fintech adoption is likely to decrease banking stability in the region, perhaps due to regulatory gaps in overseeing rapidly expanding fintech operations or the risks associated with rapid credit expansion without adequate risk assessments. Critically, fintech is found to exert negative pressure on the positive effects of financial inclusion on banking stability—a "speed-stability trade-off," whereby rapid fintech adoption, while enhancing credit accessibility, can weaken borrower repayment discipline and increase overleveraging. The study also finds that foreign bank assets and capitalization positively influence stability, while higher monetary policy rates negatively affect stability. Finally, this study identifies two key channels, operational efficiency (proxied by the cost-to-income ratio) and risk management (proxied by the non-performing loan ratio), through which fintech and financial inclusion affect banking stability. This chapter emphasizes the need for strong regulatory frameworks and effective risk management practices to harness the benefits of fintech and financial inclusion while mitigating the associated risks. These insights are particularly relevant for policymakers in the region's fastest-growing fintech markets.

The final thematic cluster investigates how central bank policies and innovations shape banking stability and credit allocation. From sustainable development orientations to CBDC design and monetary-prudential coordination, the subsequent chapters analyze the policy levers available to policymakers navigating an evolving financial landscape.

Chapter 5, by Avik Ghosh, investigates the role of financial inclusion and central bank policies in achieving the SDGs in Asia and the Pacific. Drawing on data from 15 economies over 31 years and employing fixed-effects panel regression and instrumental variable techniques, this study demonstrates that financial inclusion alone is insufficient to achieve the SDG targets. This chapter underscores the pivotal role of policy shocks, such as the MDGs, SDGs, the 1997 Asian financial crisis, and the 2007–2009 global financial crisis, in driving sustainable development. Innovatively, by applying the topic modelling technique of Natural Language Processing to 1815 central bank documents from 2000 to 2022, this chapter reveals a growing emphasis on sustainable macroeconomic development in response to these shocks. The findings highlight a shared commitment among the region's central banks to align their policies with the national SDG objectives.

While Chapter 5 examines central banks' policy orientations, Chapter 6, by Garima Gupta, Rachita Gulati, and Rishman Jot Kaur Chahal, investigates the impact of CBDC adoption on bank stability in India and the PRC, with particular attention to the role of monetary policy as a moderating factor. Using a multidimensional stability index encompassing capital adequacy, profitability, asset quality, liquidity, and efficiency, the authors employ dynamic panel models to analyze bank-level data from 74 banks from 2013 to 2022. The results reveal that CBDC adoption significantly enhances bank stability, with more pronounced effects in India, a difference attributed to variations in economic structures, digital ecosystems, and monetary policy frameworks between the two nations. Critically, the findings reveal that accommodative monetary stances amplify the stability benefits of CBDCs by improving liquidity and transparency, whereas tighter policies reduce these benefits because of competition between traditional deposits and CBDC holdings. This finding has significant implications for how central banks should coordinate CBDC implementation with their monetary policy. The policy recommendations emphasize the need for careful CBDC design to balance digital currency adoption with traditional banking systems and minimize potential disruption.

Complementing the focus on central bank innovations, Chapter 7 by Muhammad Ayub Khan Mehar examines the impact of monetary policy tools and prudential regulations on commercial banks' lending and investment capacity in Pakistan. Using panel data from 33 Pakistani commercial banks over five years and utilizing the random effects model and seemingly unrelated regression estimation technique, this study assesses how regulatory instruments such as the capital adequacy ratio, statutory liquidity ratio, and cash reserve ratio influence bank advances, deposits, liquidity, and profitability. The findings reveal that prudential regulations encourage bank investment and lending, with equity requirements particularly enhancing investment, advances, deposit mobilization, and liquidity. Importantly, the study reveals a phenomenon of fiscal dominance, whereby monetary and fiscal policies, rather than prudential regulations, act as the primary constraints on private-sector credit growth, as excessive government borrowing from commercial banks crowds out lending to the private sector. Policy recommendations call for a balanced regulatory approach that maintains financial stability while facilitating an adequate private-sector credit flow.

The book concludes with a synthesis chapter that integrates the findings from all the preceding contributions to present a forward-looking roadmap for the region. Chapter 8, by Rachita Gulati, Dil B. Rahut, Sunil Kumar, and Tetsushi Sonobe, synthesizes the book's findings to present a forward-looking roadmap for banking systems that support resilience, inclusion, innovation, and sustainability in Asia and the Pacific. Drawing systematically on the empirical evidence and policy insights from Chapters 2–7, the chapter examines five critical challenges: macroeconomic volatility and crisis risks, digital disruption and cybersecurity threats, financial inclusion gaps between access and meaningful usage, climate and sustainability pressures on bank balance sheets, and regulatory complexity from blurred institutional boundaries. The authors then propose four strategic imperatives: strengthening macroprudential frameworks, promoting digital public infrastructure and secure CBDC design, advancing inclusive finance for underserved populations, and integrating climate risk into supervision. This chapter provides actionable recommendations for governments, regulators, and development partners, serving as a practical guide for building crisis-ready, digitally inclusive, and climate-conscious banking systems across the region.

Overall, this book aims to advance policy discussions on strengthening resilience, fostering innovation, and advancing sustainable finance in banking systems. The collective contributions presented in the chapters offer strategic insights into addressing global challenges by promoting digital financial inclusion and sustainable financial practices. The book emphasizes the importance of encouraging the development of policies to foster collaboration between traditional banks and fintech firms, building regulatory sandboxes to evaluate technologies, and formulating actionable policy recommendations. These discussions support the development of robust and future-ready banking systems across the Asia and the Pacific region. Together, these contributions demonstrate that building a banking system that is crisis-ready, digitally inclusive, climate-conscious, and innovation-enabled is central to shaping Asia's prosperity through quality growth. The region's ability to convert disruption into opportunity will depend on coordinated action across governments, regulators, financial institutions, and development partners.

Chapter 2
Ready for the Next Financial Crisis? Strengthening Financial Governance Mechanisms

Long Yang and Ploypailin Kijkasiwat

Abstract In recent years, currency volatility among Southeast and East Asian economies has fueled concerns about the possible occurrence of another financial crisis in Asia and the Pacific Region. The Asian financial crisis in 1997 and the global financial crisis in 2008 revealed some serious deficiencies in global financial governance systems. In particular, the International Monetary Fund's crisis resolution mechanisms were widely criticized. In the context of this history, this paper studies the development of national, regional and global financial governance in the aftermath of the Asian and global financial crises. The discussion examines how individual economies as well as regional and global governance actors have strengthened their financial systems, promoted financial cooperation, reformed key financial institutions and established alternative institutions. Although the development of financial governance mechanisms at national, regional and global levels have created these three lines of defence, policymakers in Asia and the Pacific need to prepare for the next financial crisis in an increasingly interconnected world economy. This paper's authors propose some policy measures to improve the vigilance and adaptability of financial governance mechanisms in the face of ongoing challenges and uncertainties.

Keywords: Financial crisis · Financial governance · Financial institutions

---

The Global Financial Stability Report is a survey by the IMF staff published twice a year, in the spring and fall. The report draws out the financial ramifications of economic issues highlighted in the IMF's World Economic Outlook. The report was prepared by IMF staff and has benefited from comments and suggestions from Executive Directors following their discussion of the report on April 3, 2024. The views expressed in this publication are those of the IMF staff and do not necessarily represent the views of the IMF's Executive Directors or their national authorities.

L. Yang
College of Graduate Study in Management, Khon Kaen University, Khon Kaen, Thailand

P. Kijkasiwat (✉)
Faculty of Business Administration and Accountancy, Khon Kaen University, Khon Kaen, Thailand

R. Gulati et al. (eds.), *Emerging Challenges in Banking in Asia and the Pacific*, Economics, Law, and Institutions in Asia Pacific,
https://doi.org/10.1007/978-981-92-2144-8_2

2.1 Introduction

There has been growing concern among central bankers, monetary policymakers, and institutional investors that a financial crisis might be brewing in the Asia and the Pacific region. It is noteworthy that Southeast Asian currencies have been struggling against a strong US dollar over the past few years, and according to Jean et al. (2024), the Indonesian rupiah, Thai baht, Malaysian ringgit, Vietnamese dong, and Philippine peso depreciated by about 5% in the first half of 2024. In the previous period, from early 2023 to mid-2024, these currencies had depreciated by up to 10% (Jean et al. 2024). As a major Asian currency, the value of the Japanese yen has decreased significantly since 2020, plunging to about 160 yen per US dollar in April 2024, and the Bank of Japan had to intervene in the market after the yen had dropped to its lowest level against the US dollar since 1990 (Yerushalmy 2024). Although the US Federal Reserve cut interest rates by half a percentage point in September 2024, the US interest rates remained relatively high because monetary policymakers predicted that a two-percentage point rate cut would take place gradually between the end of 2024 and early 2026 (Myers 2024).

The next financial crisis could be triggered by a slump in the value of some currencies. This was the case in July 1997 when the Asian financial crisis struck after the Bank of Thailand had announced the floating of the baht, and the value of the Thai baht decreased immediately by 20% due to foreign speculative investment (Punyaratabandhu 1998). In the first 6 months of the crisis, the value of the ringgit and the baht decreased by 45% and more than 50%, respectively, while the rupiah plunged by 80% (Suhaidi 2022). The Asian economies witnessed a significant drop in their capital inflows (more than $100 billion) in the first year of the crisis (Suhaidi 2022), and in 1998, Thailand and Indonesia suffered from an annual GDP contraction of 10.5% and 13.1%, respectively (Sundich 2024). The Asian financial meltdown eventually escalated into a global crisis, contributing to the Russian ruble crisis in 1998 and the collapse of the Brazilian real in 1999. In the contemporary globalized economy, a new round of financial meltdowns would inevitably lead to an economic decline, which would not only be devastating for the economic output of the nations and the region involved, but would also have a deleterious global impact.

The severe consequences of the Asian financial crisis in the late 1990s, along with the outbreak of a more devastating global financial crisis one decade later, highlighted serious deficiencies in the global financial governance (GFG) system. Germain (2001, 2010) conceptualized GFG as a set of rules for governing international financial institutions (IFIs) and the establishment of mechanisms to enforce these rules. Importantly, the main purpose of the GFG system is to provide financial stability, promote financial cooperation, and support financial markets at three governance levels, namely national, regional, and global (Alexander et al. 2006; Moloney 2017; Woo et al. 2016). During the Asian and global financial crises, the inability of relevant GFG actors to provide "credible crisis prevention and crisis management mechanisms" (Jędrzejowska 2020, p. 103) had compelled policymakers to create new measures and consolidate existing mechanisms to strengthen the resilience of financial systems.

It is these efforts to establish more effective global financial mechanisms that are the focus of the current discussion. This chapter addresses the following research question: How have individual economies, as well as regional and global governance actors, consolidated their financial systems and promoted financial cooperation? Correspondingly, this chapter examines the historical trajectory of national, regional, and global financial governance development in the aftermath of the Asian and global financial crises. The Sect. 2.2 starts with an overview of the crisis management of Southeast and East Asian countries during the Asian and global financial crises. In Sects. 2.3 and 2.4, the development of national and regional financial governance in Southeast and East Asia is documented. Section 2.5 discusses the development of multilateral global financial governance led by the Group of 20 (G20) and the alternative GFG mechanisms created by BRICS.[1] In the Sect. 2.6, some policy measures are proposed by the authors.

2.2 The Asian and Global Financial Crises

The Asian financial crisis, or the Tom Yum Kung crisis, originated in Thailand. The Thai government immediately requested financial assistance from the IMF, especially after becoming insolvent (in terms of its insufficient foreign currency reserves) and consequently unable to meet its foreign currency obligations. At that time, the IMF crisis resolution measures were largely determined by the US Treasury and the Federal Reserve Bank, which were widely criticized by many economists and scholars in the aftermath of the crisis (Haggrad 2010; Sussangkarn 2002, 2011). The reasons for the dissatisfaction with the IMF programs can be summarized as follows: (1) the failure to differentiate between the economic, political, and sociocultural contexts of the various nations; (2) the harsh nature of the tight fiscal and monetary policies; (3) the unwillingness to allow nonmarket-based interventions (e.g., controlling capital flows); (4) the imposition of full guarantees for creditors (mostly foreign) of financial institutions; (5) the imposition of rapid structural reform measures (e.g., privatization of state-owned enterprises and the selling of key assets at "fire sale" prices) (Feldstein 1998; Sachs 1997; Stiglitz 1998, 2002).

At the height of the crisis, many Southeast and East Asian economies had no option but to request financial support from the IMF, but as one of the most important actors in governing the global financial system, the IMF was not prepared for the outbreak of the Asian financial crisis (Grimes and Kring 2020). In December 1997, the IMF started a "drain watch" by monitoring how the Bank of Korea "was being forced to relinquish precious reserves to meet the demands of foreign banks for repayment on their loans" (Blustein 2003, p. 8). The IMF even encouraged Asian countries

[1] BRICS is an acronym for a group of five major emerging economies: Brazil, the Russian Federation, India, the People's Republic of China, and South Africa.

to rely on themselves to stabilize their equity markets (Dobson and Chen 2015). According to Chen and Granville (2000), the crisis revealed the IMF's inadequacy in controlling cross-border capital flows. In addition, the IMF had never provided sufficient funds to tackle the Asian financial meltdown, partially because the US (as the largest IMF shareholder) lacked the "enthusiasm" to manage the crisis (Sheng 2009). For instance, the Fund only provided a rescue package of $21 billion for the Republic of Korea and compelled the country to further open its economy to foreign investors and products (Kim 2017).

The poor preparation for crisis management significantly undermined the Bretton Woods institutions (the IMF and the World Bank) and the US-dominated financial governance legitimacy from the perspective of many Southeast and East Asian countries. Albeit minimally, the IMF programs during the crisis had contradictory effects on the Bretton Woods financial system (Gavin 2020). Blustein (2003) pointed out that "the failure of the IMF's rescue of [the Republic of] Korea in early December 1997 was one of the scariest moments in the series of crises that rocked the world economy in the late 1990s". This crisis was ultimately costly to the IMF, because "its response led developing economies to implement strategies to escape its orbit through self-insurance programs" (Grabel 2022, pp. 129–130).

The global financial crisis resulted in the most severe worldwide economic crisis since the Great Depression of the 1930s. In 2007, this crisis began with the bursting of the real estate bubble and the mortgage loans emergency in the US. One year later, the bankruptcy of the Lehman Brothers investment bank shocked the global financial markets. The massive government bailout programs from the US and Europe helped other major financial institutions to survive the crisis (Helleiner 2011; Stiglitz 2010). Unlike the Asian financial crisis, the global financial meltdown hit developed economies and spilled over to developing ones (Lane 2013).

At this point in time, problems with the IMF were again apparent. Before the 2008 financial crisis, the IMF had been marginalized as its loan portfolio fell to only $10 billion (Helleiner 2016). Further, the IMF failed to predict this crisis, and it was unwilling and/or unable to act on early warning signs (Rajan 2010). When the crisis broke out, many economies in Southeast and East Asia were very reluctant to borrow from the IMF, because the Fund's loan conditions for addressing the Asian financial crisis were widely criticized for being "overly intrusive, unhelpful, and excessively influenced by US policy goals" (Helleiner 2016, p. 4). For example, the finance minister of the Republic of Korea explained that his country had a negative attitude towards the IMF, and thus he refused to ask for financial assistance from this institution (Chey 2012).

As with the Asian financial crisis, the 2008 financial crisis exposed the vulnerability or resilience of financial institutions and the effectiveness of all nations' financial crisis management (Huotari and Hanemann 2014). Compared to the developed economies in North America and Europe, most economies in Southeast and East Asia were well prepared to tackle the global financial crisis, largely due to the economic and financial reforms at both national and regional levels that they had undertaken in the aftermath of the Aian financial crisis (Woo et al. 2016). In particular, many Southeast and East Asian governments had successfully improved their regulatory systems to implement remedial actions, whereas policymakers and financial elites from the US and UK failed to undertake financial regulatory measures by promoting neoliberal principles in economic development (Baker 2010; Drezner and McNamara 2013). Moreover, Asian countries had accumulated vast foreign exchange reserves through persistent current account surpluses (James et al. 2008). At the height of the global financial crisis, three financial soundness indicators, namely nonperforming loans, risk-weighted capital adequacy ratios, and bank return on assets, had demonstrated systematic improvement in the health of the Asian banking system (James et al. 2008).

2.3 National Financial Governance

Thailand experienced a macroeconomic miracle between the mid-1960s and mid-1990s. In 1993, the World Bank described it as one of the high-performing economies in the world (Birdsall et al. 1993); however, fueled by its "uncontrolled financial sector," which adopted financial liberalization to enable the free flow of capital as well as encouraging excessive and careless investments in the property market, Thailand eventually became "the weak link in the Asian financial chain" (Lauridsen 1998, p. 1575). Thailand's financial governance reforms following the Asian financial crisis provide valuable lessons for other nations in the Asia and the Pacific region, especially contemporary fastest-growing economies such as Indonesia, the Philippines, and Viet Nam.

2.3.1 Thailand's Crisis Management

Thailand took several critical measures to address the Tom Yum Kung crisis from July to October 1997. The crisis management began with the decision made by the Bank of Thailand to float the baht, ending its fixed exchange rate with major trading partners from 2 July 1997 (Bank of Thailand 2022). This step successfully halted the depletion of Thailand's foreign reserves, and thus the nation could regain control over its currency. One month later, Thailand entered into loan negotiations with the IMF by agreeing to stringent conditions to secure financial assistance amounting, in total, to $17.2 billion (Sussangkarn 2002). Another crucial measure was the release of an economic recovery plan on 13 October 1997 to restore public confidence in Thailand's financial system. More specifically, this plan enforced the suspension of 58 financial institutions that were required to clean up both their own and their borrowers' balance sheets. The Plan also established the Financial Sector Restructuring Authority (FSRA) to oversee the liquidation process of the 58 suspended institutions and created the Asset Management Corporation (AMC) financial institution to manage nonperforming loans from those financial companies (Charoenseang and Manakit 2002; Siamwalla 2005).

In the subsequent phase of crisis management (from November 1997 to December 2000), the Thai government continued to implement measures to stabilize and restore the financial sector. For example, capital control measures and higher interest rates were used to control inflation, prevent capital outflow, and attract capital inflows, resulting in regaining stability in the exchange rate from October 1998 (Krongkaew 1999). Additionally, the FSRA announced a restoration plan for the suspended financial institutions. They allowed only two out of the 58 closed financial institutions to reopen, while the others eventually entered the process of selling their nonperforming loans to the AMC (Bank of Thailand 2022). In August 1998, the FSRA issued a plan to raise capital for financial institutions in line with the standards of the Bank for International Settlements (BIS), involving public savings, foreign investments, and bond sales (Hoontrakul and Karnchanasai 2010). In March 1999, an economic stimulus package was introduced, which included a significant loan from Japan under the Miyazawa plan, tax reductions, and measures to support small and medium enterprises (SMEs) and housing loans (Scott 2002). Furthermore, the government implemented various supportive measures through negotiating with the IMF and enacting relevant laws to facilitate smooth policy operations (Overholt 1999).

The reforms and measures have resulted in substantial improvements to financial governance in Thailand. For example, various bank governance reforms have led to banks performing better, and corporate governance has been enhanced through stricter regulations and improved internal mechanisms (Jongsureyapart et al. 2012; Pathan et al. 2008). The Bank of Thailand has continually updated its regulations to align with international standards, thus contributing significantly to the nation's financial stability (Hoontrakul and Karnchanasai 2010). Despite these advances, ongoing challenges remain, such as political interference and the need for further transparency and regulatory enforcement (Sussangkarn and Vichyanond 2007). In addition, measures to improve corporate financing structures and enhance investor protection have been recommended to reduce vulnerability to economic shocks (Alba et al. 1998). Overall, Thailand's concerted efforts towards financial governance reform have laid a robust foundation for economic stability and growth since the 2000s.

The Thai financial system was not significantly affected during the 2008 financial crisis because their financial institutions had become more risk-averse due to the painful experiences that they had undergone during the Asian financial crisis. In particular, the Thai financial sector avoided debt instruments such as collateralized debt obligations, which triggered the US mortgage loans crisis (Chandoevwit 2010). The Thai financial system had kept nonperforming loans and risk exposure to the real estate sector at low levels before the crisis (Nidhiprabha 2010)—for example, the proportion of nonperforming loans declined from 45% in 1998 to under 10% in 2005 (Jitsuchon and Sussangkarn 2009). In 2008, Thailand had accumulated more than $100 billion in gross foreign reserves, which meant that they could manage capital outflow and address depreciation pressure on the exchange rate when financial markets confronted liquidity challenges in developed economies and massive capital outflow occurred in developing ones (Jitsuchon and Sussangkarn 2009).

Although the Thai financial system remained sound at the height of the global financial meltdown, the Thai economy suffered from a significant decline in exports and tourism. The contraction in GDP began in the last quarter of 2008, and the economic slump lasted until the third quarter of 2009 (Asian Development Bank 2010). Therefore, the Thai government responded to the economic recession with both fiscal stimulus programs and monetary easing and expansionary fiscal policies. In January 2009, the first stimulus package, worth B116.7 billion (or $3.3 billion), was announced (Sangsubhan and Basri 2012). According to Doraisami (2014), this program was issued as a mid-year supplement budget aimed at adding stimulus checks to improve consumption expenditure, increase government expenditure via investment programs, stimulate SMEs and community-based investment, and promote exports and tourist industries. In mid-2009, the government introduced a larger stimulus package worth B1.43 trillion ($41.9 billion) to increase domestic demand and improve Thailand's long-term economic and social strength (Sangsubhan and Basri 2012). This package invested around B1 trillion in Thailand infrastructure projects, such as road, railway, and irrigation systems (Doraisami 2014).

Before the outbreak of the global financial crisis, the Thai monetary authorities chose to hold or raise interest rates to address potential inflation, which could have been caused by the increasing energy and food prices that had occurred since early 2008 (Jitsuchon and Sussangkarn 2009). When the domestic economic downturn happened in the fourth quarter of 2008, the Bank of Thailand dropped the policy rates to only 1.25% through cutting rates four times for a total of 250 basis points between December 2008 and April 2009 (Grenville and Ito 2010). Furthermore, the Thai government implemented a fast-track fiscal policy to provide liquidity for large corporations, SMEs, and as personal credit to households (Doraisami 2014). More specifically, the Ministry of Finance ordered six special financial institutions (Thai state banks) to provide an extra targeted loan of B301.5 billion (Jitsuchon 2010). These policy measures for crisis management appeared to be effective. The Thai economy recovered from crisis from the fourth quarter of 2009 onwards, and its GDP growth reached 10.6% in the first half of 2010 (Asian Development Bank 2010). Figure 2.1 outlines the development of financial governance in Thailand starting from the 1997 financial crisis.

2.3.2 *Comparative Insights*

In addition to Thailand, the crisis management strategies of Indonesia, Malaysia, and the Republic of Korea offer complementary lessons. Severely affected by the Asian financial crisis, Indonesia experienced a significant economic decline, a dramatic devaluation of its currency, and a deep political crisis in the late 1990s. The collapse of the Indonesian economy was closely associated with its problematic banking sector between 1997 and 1998 (Hill 1999; Soesastro and Basri 1998; Stiglitz and Greenwald 2003). In 1997, the loan-to-deposit ratio surpassed 100% and the ratio

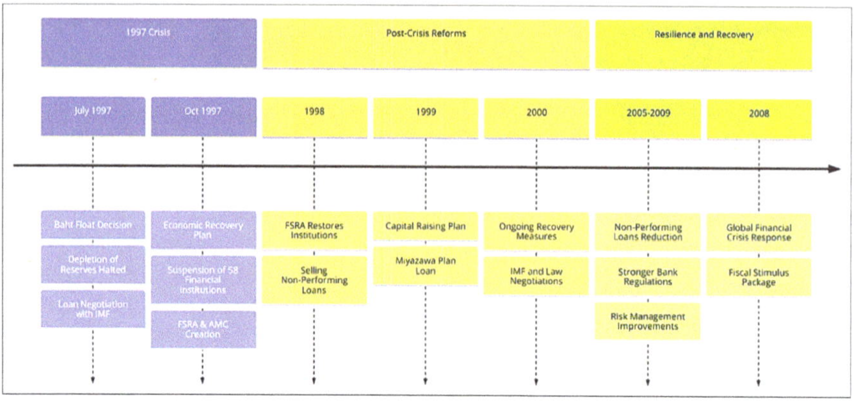

Fig. 2.1 Development of financial governance in Thailand. *Note* Authors' illustration

of nonperforming loans to total loans was approximately 27%, indicating that the Indonesian banking sector was highly leveraged (Basri 2018). Indonesia's crisis management was driven by IMF strategies (Sato 2005), and between November 1997 and August 1998 the IMF introduced four programs to implement banking restructuring and financial institution reforms (IMF 2003). Those reforms, designed by the IMF, focused on the creation of an Indonesian Bank Restructuring Agency and a banking safety net, as well as the improvement of the Indonesian central bank's independence (Basri 2018).

Malaysia's crisis management differed from the strategies adopted by Indonesia and Thailand. For example, the Malaysian government implemented capital controls to tackle the Asian financial crisis, rather than seeking financial assistance from the IMF (Doraisami 2005, 2014). To halt the depreciation of the ringgit, the Malaysian government initially adopted macroeconomic stability policies, such as increasing interest rates and reducing government spending (Bhattacharya 2001); however, the ringgit continued to decline when "offshore institutions (mainly in Singapore) borrowed ringgit at premium rates (double or triple the prevailing interest rates in Malaysia) to purchase dollars and bet in favor of the ringgit's collapse" (Kaplan and Rodrik 2002, p. 399). In September 1998, capital control measures were introduced to ban offshore trading in the ringgit. These measures, including the freezing of external accounts and a ban on ringgit transactions among foreigners, enabled Malaysia to peg the ringgit at RM3.80 per US dollar (Bhattacharya 2001; Doraisami 2005; Kaplan and Rodrik 2002).

During the Asian financial crisis, the Republic of Korea was another seriously affected economy in Asia and the Pacific. Importantly, Korean crisis management adopted the IMF-sponsored corporate restructuring programs that targeted the big chaebols (Korean industrial conglomerates). Since the 1960s, the role of the chaebol had been justified as an economic engine for fast economic growth in the Republic of Korea (Lee 2000). However, the chaebol-driven economy suffered from serious problems during the 1997 crisis—in particular, the collapse of the Hanbo Group in early 1997 led to a chain of chaebol bankruptcies, which shook public confidence in August 1997 (IMF 2003). The Government of the Republic of Korea aimed to improve the capital structure of the big four chaebols (Haley 2000), and their policy measures included "the ban of intra-group transactions, the imposition of a de facto numerical cap on debt-equity ratios, strengthening of minority shareholder rights, improvement of account transparency, introduction of outside directorship, and so on" (Chang and Shin 2002, p. 246).

An important Thai innovation was strategic default during the Asian financial crisis. Overholt (1999) noted that Thai bankruptcy law failed to protect investors, because "creditors effectively had no way to seize assets that had been placed as collateral for loans to debtors who subsequently defaulted" (1021). In reality, solvent Thai companies faced two options: (1) pay the loans and go bankrupt; or (2) do not pay the loans and keep their business alive (Overholt 1999). At that time, it became advantageous for Thai businesses not to pay, and thus those borrowers turned their loans into so-called "strategic nonperforming" ones (Overholt 1999). Vongvipanond (2007) argues that the Thai government adopted "a market-based decentralized approach to financial restructuring". Eventually, this approach allowed most Thai family businesses (80% of court cases) to regain their previously insolvent companies if they could work with creditors (Vongvipanond 2007). Table 2.1 summarizes key strategies from Indonesia, Malaysia, the Republic of Korea, and Thailand.

The impact of the global financial crisis on the Indonesian economy was limited. Although the 2008 crisis reduced export demand across Asian nations, Indonesia had a relatively small share of exports in its GDP. Sangsubhan and Basri (2012, p. 250) pointed out that "the share of Indonesia's total exports in GDP amounted to 29% in 2008 compared with 76% for Thailand (45% in the Republic of Korea, and 234% in Singapore)." Moreover, the Indonesian banking sector had become more resilient before the global financial meltdown. In 2008, the loan-to-deposit ratio was maintained at under 80% and the ratio of nonperforming loans to total loans was less than 4% (Basri 2018). Similarly to other countries' key policy responses to the crisis, the Indonesian government launched a fiscal stimulus package in early 2009 valued at Rp73.3 trillion ($7 billion) or 1.4% of the GDP (Resosudarmo et al. 2021). Compared to its neighboring economies including Australia, Malaysia, and Thailand, the size of Indonesia's stimulus package was modest (Sangsubhan and Basri 2012).

Malaysia was relatively unaffected by the global financial crisis in the first half of 2008; it had strengthened its domestic banking system after the Asian financial crisis

Table 2.1 Key strategies for managing the Asian financial crisis

Country	Key measures	Lessons for financial governance
Indonesia	IMF-led banking reform	Policy integration with global norms
Malaysia	Capital controls	Sovereign decision-making
Rep. of Korea	Corporate restructuring	Corporate governance
Thailand	Strategic default	Decentralised financial restructuring

Source Author's own illustration

and kept the percentage of nonperforming loans to total loans to less than 3% in 2008 (Khoon and Hui 2010). However, triggered by a sharp decline in exports and foreign direct investment, the contraction of the Malaysian economy began in the last quarter of 2008 and lasted throughout 2009 (James et al. 2008). The Malaysian government implemented two fiscal stimulus packages to address the 2008 crisis. In November 2008, the government introduced the first package of RM7 billion (or 1% of GDP), aimed at financing infrastructure projects (Doraisami 2014), with the second and much larger stimulus package of RM60 billion being announced in March 2009. Doraisami (2014) noted that this package provided RM25 billion as bank guarantees for SMEs.

The Republic of Korea was one of the Asian nations most severely affected by the global financial crisis. Between 2008 and the first half of 2009, the Korean won suffered from the sharpest devaluation worldwide (Shin 2014). In 2008, the Korean stock market and exports both plunged, resulting in large-scale capital outflows similar to those in the 1997 crisis (Lee and Rhee 2012; Pirie 2016). In order to manage the 2008 crisis, the Korean government introduced two massive fiscal stimulus packages from 2008 to 2009. The government carried out the largest fiscal expansion among the G20 countries, with crisis-related policy measures amounting to 3.6% of GDP in 2009 (Horton et al. 2009). Korean SMEs received direct transfers amounting to 1% of GDP (OECD 2010). Importantly, such a timely fiscal stimulus during the global financial meltdown contributed greatly to the Republic of Korea's fast economic recovery in the 2010s (Hong 2010).

2.4 Regional Financial Governance

Southeast and East Asian nations learned from the financial crisis of the late 1990s, recognizing that they had to collectively consolidate their regional financial mechanisms to tackle any crises in the future. It had become apparent that the strongest financial governance mechanisms, particularly at the national level, can sometimes prove insufficient (Jędrzejowska 2020; McNamara 2016). This led these nations to develop regional financial arrangements (RFAs) based on the model established in the first generation of RFAs in the 1970s. In order to counter the collapse of the Bretton Woods system and the economic difficulties triggered by the first oil crisis, the first generation of RFAs) emerged during this period (Rhee et al. 2013). At that time, emerging and developing economies created RFAs, including the Arab Monetary Fund and the Latin American Reserve Fund. Likewise, in the aftermath of the Asian financial crisis, a new generation of RFAs was born in the Asia and the Pacific region (Rhee et al. 2013).

2.4.1 Evolution of ASEAN+3 Mechanisms

Established by 13 Southeast and East Asian economies (and Hong Kong, China) in the early 2000s, the key alternative mechanism (arising from the Asian financial crisis) for enhancing regional financial governance is the Chiang Mai Initiative Multilateralization (CMIM) (Ocampo 2006; Pitakdumrongkit 2015; Posen and Rhee 2010). As a multilateral currency swap arrangement with a total size of $240 billion, it currently includes the 10 member states of the Association of Southeast Asian Nations (ASEAN) and the "Plus Three" nations, namely the People's Republic of China (PRC), Japan, and the Republic of Korea (AMRO 2024; ARIC 2024). There were two main stages in the evolution of the CMIM between 1997 and 2014, which are discussed below.

As the largest Asian economy in the 1990s, Japan initially proposed the establishment of an Asian Monetary Fund (AMF), which aimed to provide urgent financial support for Thailand (Manupipatpong 2002). Such a timely proposal "raised temporary hopes among the crisis-ridden economies of Asia but elicited a stringent rebuke from the IMF and the US Treasury, and ultimately fell to the wayside in favor of a more IMF-centered approach" (Lipscy 2003, p. 93). At that time, the IMF was preparing to release a rescue package for Thailand, and this Japanese proposal did not receive enough support in Southeast Asia (Sussangkarn 2011). Hence, the AMF idea failed to materialize. However, it only took a few months for the other ASEAN+3 nations to propose further plans for creating regional financial mechanisms. After these suggested ideas had been widely discussed over the following years, the Chiang Mai Initiative (CMI) was finally agreed by all ASEAN+3 countries in 2000 (Siregar and Miyaki 2015), resulting in the most tangible outcome in the first stage of regional financial governance.

The evolution of the CMI into the CMIM marked a more tangible and substantive stage of financial cooperation in Southeast and East Asia. After all, the original CMI was "a network of bilateral agreements that were not even extended to all of the organization's purported members," and thus it lacked any "supranational" governance structures (Haggrad 2010, p. 265). Furthermore, Sussangkarn (2011) noted that the CMI could only be viewed as a "symbolic initiative" during its first stage, because the size of the fund (in the middle 2000s) was still too small. He further explained that if the CMI had been available before the Asian financial crisis, "Thailand would have been able to draw about $2 billion from the CMI swap arrangement prior to asking for IMF assistance" (Sussangkarn 2011, p. 208). Hence, the potential funds that could have been provided by the original CMI would have been insignificant compared to the IMF's actual rescue package for Thailand in 1997 (which amounted to $17.2 billion).

Before the outbreak of the global financial crisis, the urgency for Asia and the Pacific to consolidate their regional governance mechanisms declined as the region gradually recovered from the crisis of the late 1990s. However, the collapse of Lehman Brothers in 2008 warned Southeast and East Asian economies that they had to prepare for a potential financial meltdown in their own regions (Siregar and

Miyaki 2015). Hence, the ASEAN+3 nations considered upgrading the RFAs through promoting a multilateralization of the CMI and then increased the foreign exchange reserves pool to $120 billion in 2009 (AMRO 2024). Five years later, these nations agreed on the amended CMIM by doubling its total size to $240 billion from $120 billion, introducing the CMIM precautionary line and increasing the IMF delinked portion from 20% to 30% (ARIC 2024). Table 2.2 summarizes the ten key milestones in the development of the CMIM.

The CMIM has never been tapped, despite being formed more than two decades ago. Compared with some well-established RFAs, this evolving regional mechanism has been confronted by serious implementation challenges due to its relatively narrow mandate and complicated decision-making process. The CMIM mandate has been largely limited to tackling the region's balance-of-payments and short-term liquidity difficulties. By contrast, other RFAs have more diverse objectives. For example, in 2020, the Arab Monetary Fund and the Latin American Reserve Fund provided fiscal support to address the impacts of the COVID-19 pandemic in their own regions (Han 2022). In 2011, the ASEAN+3 Macroeconomic Research Office (AMRO) was created to analyze the ASEAN+3 economies and their financial risks, with a view to managing surveillance and organizing the CMIM's lending programs (Grimes and Kring 2020). Importantly, AMRO is not the decision-making authority to activate the CMIM, whose governance structure is based on the annual rotation of co-chairs, the Ministerial-Level Decision-Making Body and the Executive-Level Decision-Making Body (AMRO 2025). This complicated arrangement has significantly hindered the efficient implementation of this RFA FRA.

2.4.2 Complementary Institutions and Forums

Established in 1966, the Asian Development Bank (ADB) is one of the key financial institutions that contribute to socioeconomic development in Asia. This regional institution aims to maximize "the development impact of its assistance by facilitating policy dialogues, providing advisory services, and mobilizing financial resources through cofinancing operations that tap official, commercial, and export credit sources" (Asian Development Bank 2024, para. 3). During the Asian financial crisis, the ADB worked with the IMF and the World Bank by supporting financial sector development for the region (Nehru 2014). Between 1997 and 1999, this institution provided loan programs totaling $7.1 billion to Indonesia, the Republic of Korea, and Thailand, helping to avoid a further deterioration of the economic conditions of those member states (Asian Development Bank 2009). One decade later, the ADB took "additional proactive measures" to help developing member countries (DMCs) to deal with the global financial crisis (Ruiz-Brunschwig et al. 2011). In 2009, the ADB established the Countercyclical Support Facility and provided $2.5 billion to five DMCs, namely Bangladesh, Indonesia, Kazakhstan, the Philippines, and Viet Nam (Ruiz-Brunschwig et al. 2011).

Table 2.2 Milestones of the Chiang Mai Initiative Multilateralization

Time	Milestones	Description
September 1997	The Asian Monetary Fund (AMF)	Japan initiated the AMF idea at the Group of 7 (G7)'s meeting held in Hong Kong, China
November 1997	The Manila Framework	Asian finance and central bank deputies discussed a new financial cooperation framework at Manila, Philippines
December 1997	Endorsement of the Manila Framework	Finance ministers from the ASEAN nations; Australia; the People's Republic of China; Hong Kong, China; Japan; the Republic of Korea; and the United States endorsed the Manila Framework at the meeting in Kuala Lumpur, Malaysia
May 2000	Agreement of the CMI	At the Asian Development Bank meeting held in Chiang Mai, Thailand, the ASEAN+3 nations' finance ministers confirmed: (1) the ASEAN Swap Arrangement (ASA); a regional currency swap mechanism had existed since 1977; (2) the new network of bilateral swap arrangements (BSAs) among the ASEAN+3 nations
October 2003	Conclusion of 13 BSAs	The CMI successfully extended the ASA to include the BSAs with the Plus 3 nations. The conclusion of 13 BSAs enabled the reserves pool to reach the total size of $35 billion. The ASEAN+3 nations also agreed that 10% of the amount could be utilized, without any linkage to an IMF program
May 2005	Increase of the CMI currency swap amount	The amount of swap arrangements under the CMI grew to $90 billion. In addition, the amount of money a CMI member could draw from any 'de-linked' IMF programs increased from 10% to 20%
May 2007	Formation of the multilateral reserves pooling	At the tenth ASEAN+3 finance ministers' meeting, the principle of converting the bilateral schemes of the CMI into a multilateral reserves pooling scheme was agreed
May 2009	Agreement of the CMIM	At the 12th ASEAN+3 finance ministers' meeting, two core objectives of the CMIM were declared: (1) to address short-term liquidity difficulties in the region; (2) to supplement existing international financial arrangements
May 2010	The CMIM became effective	The CMIM agreement came into effect from March, 2010. Later, it was also agreed that the total size of CMIM would be $120 billion, with 80% contributed by Plus 3 nations and the rest by the ASEAN nations
July 2014	The amended CMIM	The amended CMIM agreement came into effect. It aimed to strengthen the regional financial safety net for the CMIM participants in responding to potential or actual balance-of-payments and short-term liquidity difficulties

Source Created by the authors based on a synthesis of the relevant literature

Focused on supporting infrastructure development, the Asian Infrastructure Investment Bank (AIIB) is another important multilateral development bank (MDB) in the region. In October 2014, the AIIB was launched to enhance connectivity among member states and meet infrastructural challenges through financing road, port, and airfield development projects in the least developed Asian economies (Mishra 2016). This regional institution began operations in 2016 and had grown to 110 approved members worldwide. Between 2016 and 2024, it collaborated with 37 member states by approving 303 projects, contributing to about $59 billion in sectors such as energy, transportation, economic resilience, and finance/liquidity (Asian Infrastructure Investment Bank 2024). Moreover, the AIIB has promoted financial cooperation and partnership to tackle regional development challenges by working with other MDBs. For example, the AIIB and ADB cofinanced 12 infrastructure projects and COVID-19 response programs in 2020, providing a total of $4.7 billion for 11 nations in Asia and the Pacific (Asian Development Bank 2020).

Widely recognized as the highest-level intergovernmental forum in Asia and the Pacific, the Asia-Pacific Economic Cooperation (APEC) has 21 members. More specifically, APEC is "a regional economic forum established in 1989 with the purpose of promoting free trade and investment and enhancing e cooperation in social and development areas to advance prosperity, sustainable, and inclusive economic growth in the region" (Bank of Thailand 2023, para. 1). In the late 1990s, APEC was not "a policy co-ordinating and rule-making body with a capacity for crisis management" (Cheng 1998, p. 26). Therefore, it played "a negligent role" in addressing the Asian financial crisis, despite most APEC member states having high expectations that this regional forum would actively cope with the crisis (Cheng 1998). One decade later, APEC leaders addressed the global financial crisis by providing capacity-building and technical cooperation to strengthen regional economic integration. For instance, APEC launched the Investment Facilitation Action Plan to improve the investment environment and initiated the Ease of Doing Business Action Plan to reduce behind-the-border barriers in the region (APEC 2024; Nixon 2009).

As an important economic forum in Southeast and East Asia, the ASEAN+3 finance ministers and central bank governors meeting (AFMGM+3) represented another collective effort to strengthen regional financial cooperation. The 1997 crisis warned Asian economies that they lacked effective financial governance mechanisms for crisis prevention and management (Hamilton-Hart 2003). Hence, the leaders of ASEAN member states and the PRC, Japan, and the Republic of Korea proposed the AFMGM+3 mechanism at the ASEAN+3 summit in December 1998 (AMRO 1999). The first AFMGM+3 was held in March 1999 and enabled Asian government officials to discuss and exchange views on financial and macroeconomic matters of concern to the region (AMRO 1999). At the most recent AFMGM+3 in 2024, this forum supported a transition of the CMIM by including a new "paid-in capital structure" to enhance the effectiveness of the regional financial safety net, which would further complement the global financial safety net (ASEAN 2024). Table 2.3 lists the main functions of key financial institutions and economic forums in Asia and the Pacific.

Table 2.3 Functions of regional financial institutions and economic forum

Financial institution/economic forum	Main function
Asian Development Bank (ADB)	Facilitate socioeconomic development in Asia
Asian Infrastructure Investment Bank (AIIB)	Support infrastructure development in Asia
Asia-Pacific Economic Cooperation (APEC)	Promote regional economic integration
ASEAN+3 Finance Ministers' and Central Bank Governors' Meeting (AFMGM+3)	Strengthen the regional financial cooperation

Source Author's own illustration

There is a need to meet the various financial requirements of developing counties in Asia and the Pacific. As the most important financial institution, the IMF provides financial assistance to developing and developed nations experiencing economic difficulties, thus contributing to international economic cooperation and stability (Feldstein 1998). However, the IMF needs to adapt to the social and economic realities of many emerging economies (Niyonkuru 2016). For instance, Zaman (2023) proposed the establishment of a Regional Monetary Fund (RMF) to address the financial requirements of developing nations. In particular, there was a proposal for an Islamic Monetary Fund (ISMF) that takes into consideration the Muslim-majority nations' cultural, economic, and religious characteristics (Zaman 2023) and could help ASEAN countries such as Brunei Darussalam, Indonesia, and Malaysia to obtain more effective regional financial support.

2.5 Global Financial Governance

The Asian and global financial crises triggered various reforms in the global financial system. For instance, the establishment of the Financial Stability Board and the Group of 20 underscored the importance of multilateral financial cooperation. However, the IMF and the World Bank have remained pivotal to the global financial governance system. The 2010 governance reform of the Bretton Woods institutions improved the inclusivity of the GFG system, but the impact remained limited (for example, the Global South was still underrepresented). These limitations eventually spurred the BRICS nations to create alternative financial governance institutions, including the Contingent Reserve Arrangement and the New Development Bank, thus enhancing the multilateral development of the GFG system.

2.5.1 The G20-Led Financial Stability Board

In the aftermath of the Asian financial crisis, two new international bodies, namely the Financial Stability Forum (FSF) and the Group of 20 (G20), were forged by the G7 to strengthen multilateral financial cooperation. In early 1999, the FSF was created by the G7 finance ministers and central bank governors to further regulate the global financial system (Porter 2000). At that time, the FSF rallied "national authorities responsible for financial stability in significant international financial centres, international financial institutions, sector-specific international groupings of regulators and supervisors, and committees of central bank experts" (Financial Stability Forum 2009, para. 16). According to Jordan (2010), the key objective of this intergovernmental organization was to promote global financial stability and create an early warning system, thus identifying any potential weaknesses of particular financial systems at the national level and preventing a recurrence of the 1997 financial crisis.

However, the FSF played a marginal role in promoting global financial cooperation. Until the outbreak of the global financial crisis, the FSF had only published some status reports and regular risk evaluations of the global financial system (Helleiner 2010). This organization failed to "carve out a distinctive position, integrating the various perspectives of the diverse membership, as was originally hoped" (Davies and Green 2008, p. 116). In March 2009, the G20 leaders agreed to expand the FSF membership (to all G20 countries as well as Spain and the European Commission) and establish the Financial Stability Board (FSB). As the FSB's main decision-making authority, the Plenary not only had national or regional representation for enhancing global financial stability but also included the chairs of the main standard-setting bodies and central bank committees as well as representatives of the IMF, the World Bank, the Bank for International Settlements (BIS), and the Organisation for Economic Co-operation and Development (OECD) (Financial Stability Forum 2009). In order to improve the FSB's regulatory standards, the G20 invited key international rule-makers, such as the Basel Committee on Banking Supervision (BCBS) and the International Organization of Securities Commissions (IOSCO), to join the FSB board (Gadinis 2013).

The emergence and evolution of the G20 was closely associated with the growing need to enhance multilateral financial cooperation between the Global North and South. Comprising ten developing economies, nine developed economies, and the European Union, the finance ministers and central bankers of the G20 countries first met at the end of 1999 (Dadush and Suominen 2012). The aim of the G20 meeting (at the ministerial level) at that time was to establish an economic forum to improve global financial cooperation between developed and developing nations in relation to the Asian financial crisis (Kirton 2013, 2017). Almost one decade after the first G20 meeting, the G20 took on a leadership role when the existing governance institutions and clubs, including the IMF, the World Bank, the G7, and the G20 at the ministerial level, failed to coordinate an adequate response to address the 2008 financial meltdown (Smith 2011).

The G20 and the FSB have together coordinated the reform of the global financial system. Emerging as a coordinating executive among global governance institutions, the G20 has worked through the FSB to coordinate with other intergovernmental governance institutions and networks (e.g., the IMF, OECD, BCBS, and IOSCO) to set standards, monitor enforcement and compliance, and assist with p recovery (Cho and Kelly 2012). In addition to other international financial rule-makers, the FSB reports to the G20 leaders, with such accountability providing the FSB with greater authority in shaping international financial rule-making, even though this organization was initially designed to act as a loose network of G20 government officials (Helleiner 2010). The deep connection between the G20 and the FSB has empowered G20 governments to effectively intervene in international financial regulation by adding specific amendments to the existing rule-making standards, proposing new policymaking initiatives, and monitoring compliance with international rules at the national level (Gadinis 2013).

2.5.2 Reform of Bretton Woods Institutions

The Bretton Woods institutions largely reinforced the dominating role of the US in the GFG system. In the 1940s, the aim of creating the IMF was to provide "short-term finance" for international economic stability, whereas the purpose behind the creation of the World Bank was to provide "long-term development finance" for reducing global poverty (Rana and Pacheco Pardo 2018, p. 233). In reality, based on the convertibility of the dollar to gold and a pegged exchange rate between the US dollar and other currencies (Cesarano 2006), the Bretton Woods monetary system strengthened American global leadership in the postwar economic recovery and established a dollar-dominated global financial architecture (Steil 2013). Although the Bretton Woods system collapsed after the US decided to delink the dollar and gold in 1971 (Costigan et al. 2017), the institutional legacies, including the IMF and the World Bank, sustained their influence in governing the international financial and monetary systems (Helleiner 2019). It is argued that the US-led GFG system was aimed at perpetuating the "benefits and costs in favor of the Global North, large firms, and other privileged actors" (Grabel 2022, p. 141).

The American unipolar GFG system faced serious challenges from the Global South in the aftermath of the Asian and global financial crises. The emergence of the G20 reflected a shift towards multilateralism and decentralization in contemporary GFG development (Helleiner 2016; Rana and Pacheco Pardo 2018). As an enlarged global governance club consisting of major developed and developing economies, the G20 implemented the reform of the Bretton Woods twins. At the Pittsburgh summit in September 2009, the G20 leaders agreed to redistribute the IMF quota, which resulted in a shift of 6.2% quota shares from the developed to the developing nations (Lesage et al. 2013, 2015). According to the IMF (2016), four emerging market economies, namely Brazil, the PRC, India, and the Russian Federation, joined the US, Japan, France, Germany, Italy, and the UK to become the IMF's 10 largest shareholders after the governance reform in 2010. At the same time, the World Bank implemented two-phase governance reforms by shifting 4.59% of voting from the developed to developing nations, increasing the voting share of southern countries to 47.19% in the World Bank (Vestergaard and Wade 2013, 2015).

However, after the 2010 reforms, the US and the Global North still maintained their dominating roles in governing the IMF and the World Bank. For instance, the US still held more than 15% of voting shares in the Bretton Woods twins, which meant that the US had successfully kept its sole veto power within the governance structure (Larionova and Shelepov 2019). In reality, the BRICS nations merely had 12.9% of voting shares in the World Bank, whereas the G7 held a much larger voting share of 46.8% (Suchodolski and Demeulemeester 2018). The combined voting shares of the BRICS countries in the IMF increased to 14.2%, while the G7 nations retained a significant voting share of 41.3% (Merking and Kring 2023). More than 5 years after the initial agreement, the IMF reform became effective when it received formal verification from the US Congress (Berger et al. 2019; Nelson and Weiss 2014). In order to prevent the PRC from gaining more voting power, another round of the IMF quota increase and voting share redistribution was blocked by the Trump administration in 2019 (Bretton Woods Project 2019).

2.5.3 Emergence of BRICS-Led Mechanisms

Unsurprisingly, the Global South began to create alternative financial governance mechanisms because the North-led GFG reform did not effectively enhance multilateralism in 2010. Outside the Bretton Woods twins, the five BRICS founding members (Brazil, the Russian Federation, India, the PRC, and South Africa) established the Contingent Reserve Arrangement (CRA) and the New Development Bank (NDB). These new South-led financial governance institutions attempted to provide developing nations with liquidity to meet short-term payment pressures and mobilize resources to support long-term development projects (Luo and Yang 2021). As alternative institutions designed to finance the developing world, the formation of the CRA and the NDB has been widely regarded as a key milestone for the Global South's cooperation in initiating and facilitating their own GFG mechanisms (Liu 2016; Morozkina 2018; Wang 2019).

The twin governance institutions of the BRICS nations attempt to promote the multilateral development of a GFG system at the global level. These alternative GFG mechanisms directly challenge the North-dominated financial governance structure (Cooper and Farooq 2013; Xu and Liu 2022). In 2012, the BRICS leaders started to discuss the possibility of setting up the CRA (BRICS 2014), and 2 years later, the five founding BRICS members established it (BRICS 2014). In 2015, $100 billion was committed by the BRICS nations to the CRA Fund, which can be drawn upon by member states in cases of emergency. This BRICS Fund "parallels the IMF's role of providing short-term liquidity to address financial crises" (Helleiner and Wang 2018, p. 575). According to Shahrokhi et al. (2017), the CRA is only around 13% of the

IMF's fund size. It focuses on "providing liquidity through currency swaps to mitigate balance-of-payments pressures" between the five BRICS nations, while the IMF has a much larger "global financial reach" (Shahrokhi et al. 2017, p. 2). It is argued that in order to improve the effectiveness of this South-led financial governance institution, the Fund should consider establishing a research facility, expanding its membership size, and creating more specific crisis response mechanisms (Cattaneo et al. 2015).

At the same time, the BRICS nations proposed the creation of a new multilateral development bank, and the agreement for establishing the NDB was signed in 2014 (NDB 2024). One year later, the BRICS nations held the inaugural meeting for the NDB board of governors and appointed the first president (NDB 2024). Leslie Maasdorp, Vice President of the NDB, stated that the BRICS Bank aimed to serve developing countries of the Global South (Maasdorp 2019). More specifically, the NDB provides long-term financial support for infrastructure and sustainable development projects, not only in the BRICS countries but also in the developing world (Helleiner and Wang 2018). Apart from the World Bank and other MDBs, the NDB's initial fund of $100 billion was equally distributed among the BRICS founding members, thus eliminating the possibility of a single member state gaining a veto right (Wang 2017, 2019) and enhancing genuine multilateralism in GFG development. This BRICS bank has achieved some tangible successes during its first decade. For example, it became fully operational when the five members deposited the first two installments of paid-in capital from 2016 to 2017 (Chin 2024). In 2021, four developing nations, namely Bangladesh, Egypt, the United Arab Emirates, and Uruguay, joined the Bank as new or prospective members (Ye 2023). To date, the NDB has approved 96 projects in providing $32.8 billion to mainly finance transport infrastructure and COVID-19 emergency assistance in southern nations (NDB 2025).

The BRICS nations have attempted to promote an alternative GFG system to better reflect changes in the contemporary global economic and geopolitical landscape. The BRICS members have encouraged the use of their own currencies in global trade and reduced their reliance on dollar financing by establishing and using the NDB (Liu and Papa 2022). In addition, BRICS nations such as the PRC and India have created alternative international payment systems, namely the Cross-Border Interbank Payment System (CIPS) and the Structured Financial Messaging System (SFMS), respectively (Freidin 2024), with the aim of avoiding potential sanctions and breaking away from the North-led financial order. More recently, BRICS Pay has been initiated as a way of challenging the dominance of the dollar in global trade and the traditional financial systems (e.g., SWIFT), thus contributing to an increasingly multipolar global financial system (Krause 2024; Valamontes 2024). Drawing on the key points, challenges/limitations, and impacts/outcomes of the three global-level mechanisms discussed in this section, the GFG development is presented in Table 2.4.

Table 2.4 The multilateral development of financial governance mechanisms

Mechanisms	Key points	Challenges and limitations	Impacts and outcomes
Financial Stability Board (FSB)	1. In 1999, the G7 established FSF to promote financial stability and provide early warnings. 2. The 2009 expansion included all G20 members and became the FSB. 3. The G20 coordinated reforms through the FSB with global rule-making bodies like the IMF, OECD, and BCBS.	1. The FSF's initial impact was limited, producing only status reports and evaluations. 2. The FSB was initially a loose network with limited enforcement power. 3. Governance remains influenced by the Global North dominance.	1. Enhanced global financial coordination. 2. Strengthened the G20's leadership in financial governance. 3. Integrated developing economies into financial stability discussions through expanded membership.
Bretton Woods Institutions	1. The IMF and World Bank historically dominated by the US. 2. The 2010 reforms shifted some voting shares to Global South. 3. The G20 implemented quota redistribution by increasing emerging markets' influence.	1. The US had maintained veto power in the IMF. 2. The BRICS and Global South are still underrepresented in the World Bank and IMF. 3. Further reforms blocked by the US in 2019.	1. Incremental increase in the Global South's influence in Bretton Woods institutions. 2. Highlighted limitations of existing governance structures, spurring alternative mechanisms.
BRICS-Led Mechanisms	1. In 2015, the BRICS established the CRA for short-term liquidity and the NDB for long-term development finance. 2. The NDB has funded infrastructure and sustainable projects globally with $100 billion in equal contributions from members. 3. Aimed to counter the Global North-dominated governance.	1. Limited scale and scope compared to IMF and World Bank. 2. The CRA mirrors the IMF but focuses on the BRICS nations. 3. NDB faces challenges in competing with well-established IFIs.	1. Promoted multilateralism cooperation. 2. Created alternatives to the IMF and World Bank for developing nations. 3. Enhanced focus on sustainable development and infrastructure in the Global South.

Source Created by the authors based on a synthesis of the relevant literature

2.6 Discussion and Conclusion

The evolution of financial governance mechanisms in response to the Asian financial crisis and the global financial crisis underscores the critical need for robust and resilient financial systems. The historical trajectory outlined in this chapter demonstrates that national, regional, and global financial governance structures have undergone significant reforms aimed at enhancing stability and mitigating future risks. It appears that the readiness of Asian countries for a potential financial crisis has been enhanced as a result of these reforms. For instance, the current real estate crisis in the PRC, triggered by the collapse of property giants like Evergrande, has threatened the stability of domestic and global financial markets. However, the PRC's Lehman moment did not happen (Liu 2024). The PRC's financial authority managed the housing bubble burst and prevented massive bank failures. Furthermore, the yen plummeted around 60% between the second half of 2020 and the first half of 2024. Given Japan's prominent role in global financial markets, such a major currency depreciation had sparked worldwide concerns. In August 2024, the yen went through a sudden appreciation after the Bank of Japan raised the interest rate and reduced investors' rising concerns about possible financial market turmoil (Schnabl 2024). It can be argued, therefore, that the PRC and Japan, two major financial governance actors in Asia and the Pacific, have improved their crisis preparedness by strengthening the resilience of financial institutions.

Nevertheless, in an increasingly interconnected global economy, Southeast and East Asian nations must prepare for the next financial crisis. In the past two and a half decades, the development of financial governance mechanisms at national, regional, and global levels has consolidated the three lines of defense in addressing any future financial crises, and each individual nation's financial system stands as the first line of this defense. In the aftermath of the Tom Yum Kung crisis, comprehensive financial policy measures and economic reforms were introduced and implemented to prevent financial turmoil and stabilize the Thai economy. These measures and reforms attempted to improve Thai bank governance, corporate governance, and overall financial sector stability (Charoenseang and Manakit 2002; Pathan et al. 2008). These initiatives followed the Asian financial crisis, which had revealed many weaknesses in the Thai financial system during the 1990s and significantly shaped the development of financial governance in Thailand (Sussangkarn and Vichyanond 2007). Consequently, the more risk-averse Thai financial system performed well in dealing with the 2008 financial crisis. Moreover, Asian economies, including Indonesia, Malaysia, and the Republic of Korea, had reflected on the hard lessons of the Asian financial meltdown, thus adopting expansionary fiscal policies to regain GDP growth in the aftermath of the global financial crisis.

Regional financial arrangements can provide a second line of defense when individual nations require financial support. In the late 1990s, the controversial crisis resolution of the IMF not only reduced the domination of an American unipolar GFG system but also forged a consensus among Southeast and East Asian nations to establish pluripolar and alternative financial institutions and governance mechanisms

(Grabel 2022 Pitakdumrongkit 2015). The establishment and evolution of the Chiang Mai Initiative Multilateralization (CMIM) highlights the importance of enhancing regional financial governance for preventing or mitigating financial crises in Asia and the Pacific, as the development of the CMIM strengthens the region's commitment to collective financial security and the creation of alternative governance mechanisms that can act independently of existing regional and global financial arrangements (Kim and Rhee 2014). In addition, some key financial institutions, and economic forums such as the ADB, AIIB, APEC, and AFMGM+3, can collectively strengthen the regional financial safety net for economies in Asia and the Pacific.

The third line of defense is comprised of the most powerful global financial institutions and mechanisms, attempting to resolve crises at both national and regional levels. The G20 and the FSB were established to address some of the deficiencies of the North-dominated GFG system, since the IMF and all of the G7 nations had failed to provide timely crisis resolutions during the Asian and global financial crises. The Bretton Woods institutions, despite their significant roles, have faced criticism and challenges about their ability to manage crises effectively in developed and developing economies. The rise of the G20's role in improving global financial cooperation between developed and developing nations and the creation of alternative financial institutions by the BRICS nations, such as the Contingent Reserve Arrangement (CRA) and the New Development Bank (NDB), signify a shift towards a more multilateral and inclusive financial governance system, and these new mechanisms and alterative institutions can provide more tailored support to developing countries and enhance global financial resilience (Kozul-Wright and Poon 2015). Table 2.5 summarizes policy recommendations at each level of financial governance.

Table 2.5 Recommendations to strengthen financial governance

Governance level	Key recommendations
National	1. Enhance financial regulations and corporate governance standards. 2. Improve disclosure standards to create transparency and adopt financial technologies to reinforce risk management. 3. Promote sustainable economic practices, such as Thailand's sufficiency economy principle.
Regional	1. Expand the objectives of CMIM beyond liquidity support. 2. Foster collaboration among regional institutions and forums such as ADB, AIIB, APEC and AFMGM+3. 3 Establish clearer rules for activating regional financial safety nets.
Global	1. Emphasise a leadership role of the G20 in promoting a multilateral and inclusive financial governance system. 2. Advocate for further IMF and World Bank governance reforms to eliminate veto powers and increase representation for developing nations. 3. Support the growth of BRICS-led initiatives to diversify global financial governance.

Source Author's own illustration

To further strengthen the resilience of financial systems in Asia and the Pacific, several policy measures should be considered. At the national level, enhancing financial regulations and corporate governance standards remains crucial. First, Asian corporate governance such as in matters of disclosure and transparency could be improved by implementing the OECD corporate governance principles (Lu and Batten 2023). In addition, more effective financial governance needs to include the adoption of advanced financial technologies to improve risk management and embrace sustainable and inclusive economic development principles to foster long-term resilience. In Thailand, the economic disaster of the late 1990s put an end to the hyper-growth era and led to a shift in macroeconomic policy. The King's philosophy of sufficiency economy le serves as a Thai model for sustainable development by integrating ecological and social dimensions into economic planning, and thus supports sustainable practices at both community and national levels, fostering resilience against economic shocks and environmental challenges.

Regionally, the development of financial safety nets and reserve pooling arrangements, such as the CMIM, should be continued and reinforced to support financial stability and economic growth among Southeast and East Asian nations. For instance, the CMIM needs to further clarify rules and procedures to activate lending. At the height of the global financial crisis, the CMI was not activated due to the inherent weaknesses of its institutional setting at that time (Kawai 2015). In 2020, the CMIM did not respond to the COVID-19 pandemic because it focused only on "addressing urgent short-term liquidity and/or balance-of-payment difficulties in the region and to supplementing IMF lending" (Han 2022, p. 754). Thus, the CMIM needs to collaborate with other well-established institutions and forums, and hence enhance financial cooperation and economic integration in Asia and the Pacific.

On the global stage, major governance actors should empower the G20's leadership role of strengthening the multilateral governance mechanisms, thereby further improving financial cooperation between the developed and developing economies. In addition, further governance reforms in the Bretton Woods institutions are necessary to enhance the multilateral development of the GFG system. Policymakers in Asia and the Pacific should work together to prohibit any member states of the IMF and the World Bank from keeping veto powers and increase the representation and voice of the Global South in these institutions. At the IMF, developing countries hold 41% of the votes while generating 58% of the global GDP (in terms of purchasing power parity) and have 86.4% of the world population, whereas developed economies have just 13.6% of the global population and yet have 59% of the votes (UNCTAD 2024). Therefore, supporting the growth and influence of alternative financial governance institutions, including the CRA and the NDB, will also be essential. Importantly, fostering a more balanced and equitable global financial system that addresses the needs of all nations is paramount in order to prevent fragmentated financial governance.

The chapter's suggested policy measures are aimed at improving the vigilance and adaptability of financial governance mechanisms. However, it lacks empirical evidence to support the recommendations. To the best of the author's knowledge, most financial governance-related studies have relied on conceptual analysis. Therefore, future studies could include primary data and adopt a quantitative approach to examine how measures proposed in this chapter might strengthen financial governance at different levels. Researchers should pay close attention to the impact of ongoing challenges and uncertainties, particularly AI, cybersecurity, and climate change, on shaping financial governance and crisis preparedness. These emerging risks introduce new complexities into regulatory oversight, risk management, and financial stability. AI-driven financial decision-making raises concerns about transparency, algorithmic biases, and systemic risks. Cybersecurity threats pose challenges to the resilience of financial institutions, necessitating stronger regulatory frameworks. Climate risks, including financial exposure to extreme weather events and the transition to a low-carbon economy, demand more robust governance mechanisms. While empirical studies (see Chen et al. 2024; Gigante and Zago 2023; IMF 2024; Mohsen et al. 2024; Ng and Kwok 2017; Zhang et al. 2022) have analyzed the influence of these factors on financial stability, institutions, regulations, and green finance, their direct implications for financial governance mechanisms remain underexplored. Future research should investigate how governance frameworks can adapt to these evolving risks and enhance crisis preparedness.

References

Alba, P., S. Claessens, and S. Djankov. 1998. Thailand's corporate financing and governance structures. Policy Research Working Paper, World Bank Group, Washington, D.C.

Alexander, K., R. Dhumale, and J. Eatwell. 2006. *Global governance of financial systems: The international regulation of systemic risk*. Oxford: Oxford University Press.

AMRO. 1999. The joint statement of the 1st ASEAN+3 deputy finance ministers and deputy central bank governors' meeting. The ASEAN+3 Macroeconomic Research Office (AMRO), March 17. Available from https://amro-asia.org/the-joint-statement-of-the-1st-asean3-deputy-finance-ministers-and-deputy-central-bank-governors-meeting-march-18-1999-afdcm-3-ha-noi-vietnam/. Accessed on 9 December 2024.

AMRO. 2024. About us. The ASEAN+3 Macroeconomic Research Office (AMRO). Available from https://amro-asia.org/history/. Accessed on 10 December 2024.

AMRO. 2025. Supporting RFAs and the implementation of the CMIM. The ASEAN+3 Macroeconomic Research Office (AMRO). Available from https://amro-asia.org/about-us/regional-financing-arrangements/. Accessed on 10 December 2024.

APEC. 2024. APEC Ease of Doing Business (EoDB) action plan. Asia-Pacific Economic Cooperation. Available from https://www.apec.org/groups/economic-committee/toolkit-for-structural-reform/eodb-action-plan. Accessed on 11 December 2024.

ARIC. 2024. Chiang Mai Initiative [Multilateralisation]. Asia Regional Integration Center (ARIC). Available from https://aric.adb.org/initiative/chiang-mai-initiative. Accessed on 6 June 2024.

ASEAN. 2024. Joint statement of the 27th ASEAN+3 finance ministers' and central bank governors' meeting. Association of Southeast Asian Nations, May 3. Available from https://asean.org/joint-statement-of-the-27th-asean3-finance-ministers-and-central-bank-governors-meeting/. Accessed on 18 December 2024.

Asian Development Bank. 2009. Lessons from the Asian Development Bank's responses to financial crises. Asian Development Bank. Available from https://www.adb.org/sites/default/files/evaluation-document/35964/files/eib-2009-02-0.pdf. Accessed on 29 December 2025.

Asian Development Bank. 2010. *Asian development outlook 2010 update: The future of growth in Asia*. Manila: Asian Development Bank.
Asian Development Bank. 2020. Partnership report 2020. Asian Development Bank. Available from https://www.adb.org/multimedia/partnership-report2020/partners/multilateral/asian-infrastructure-investment-bank/. Accessed on 1 July 2024.
Asian Development Bank. 2024. About ADB. Asian Development Bank. Available from https://www.adb.org/who-we-are/about. Accessed on 15 December 2024.
Asian Infrastructure Investment Bank. 2024. Project summary. Asian Infrastructure Investment Bank. Available from https://www.aiib.org/en/projects/summary/index.html. Accessed on 25 December 2024.
Baker, A. 2010. Restraining regulatory capture? Anglo-America, crisis politics and trajectories of change in global financial governance. *International Affairs* 86 (3): 647–663. https://doi.org/10.1111/j.1468-2346.2010.00903.x.
Bank of Thailand. 2022. Lessons learnt from the Asian financial crisis. Bank of Thailand. Available from https://www.bot.or.th/en/our-roles/special-measures/Tom-Yum-Kung-lesson.html. Accessed on 2 June 2024.
Bank of Thailand. 2023. Asia-Pacific Economic Cooperation. Bank of Thailand. Available from https://www.bot.or.th/en/our-roles/international-cooperation/regionalfora/apec.html. Accessed on 20 December 2024.
Basri, M. C. 2018. Twenty years after the Asian financial crisis. In *Realizing Indonesia's economic potential*, edited by L. E. Breuer, J. Guajardo, and T. Kinda, 21–45. Washington, DC: International Monetary Fund.
Berger, A., A. F. Cooper, and S. Grimm. 2019. A decade of G20 summitry: Assessing the benefits, limitations and future of global club governance in turbulent times. *The South African Journal of International Affairs* 26 (4): 493–504. https://doi.org/10.1080/10220461.2019.1705889.
Bhattacharya, A. K. 2001. The Asian financial crisis and Malaysian capital controls. *Asia Pacific Business Review* 7 (3): 181–193.
Birdsall, N. M., et al. 1993. *The East Asian miracle: Economic growth and public policy*. Washington, D.C.: World Bank Group.
Blustein, P. 2003. *The chastening: Inside the crisis that rocked the global financial system and humbled the IMF*, 1st ed. New York: Public Affairs.
Bretton Woods Project. 2019. US blocks IMF voting rights redistribution. Bretton Woods Project, December 12. Available from https://www.brettonwoodsproject.org/2019/12/imf-voting-rights-redistribution-blocked-by-the-us/. Accessed on 9 December 2024.
BRICS. 2014. Treaty for the establishment of a BRICS contingent reserve arrangement. BRICS Information Centre, University of Toronto, July 16. Available from http://www.brics.utoronto.ca/docs/140715-treaty.html. Accessed on 30 May 2024.
Cattaneo, N., M. Biziwick, and D. Fryer. 2015. The BRICS contingent reserve arrangement and its position in the emerging global financial architecture. *Policy Insights* 10:1–7.
Cesarano, F. 2006. *Monetary theory and Bretton Woods: The construction of an international monetary order*. Cambridge: Cambridge University Press.
Chandoevwit, W. 2010. The impact of the global financial crisis and policy responses in Thailand. *TDRI Quarterly Review* 25 (1): 12–24.
Chang, H., and J. Shin. 2002. Evaluating the post-crisis corporate restructuring in Korea. *Seoul Journal of Economics* 15 (2): 245–276.
Charoenseang, J., and P. Manakit. 2002. Financial crisis and restructuring in Thailand. *Journal of Asian Economics* 13 (5): 597–613. https://doi.org/10.1016/S1049-0078(02)00175-6.
Chen, E. K., and B. Granville. 2000. The Asian financial crisis of 1997–8: A case of market failure, government failure or international failure. In *Essays on the world economy and its financial system*, edited by B. Granville and S. Ostry, 49–65. London: The Royal Institute of International Affairs.
Chen, F., X. Zeng, and X. Guo. 2024. Green finance, climate change, and green innovation: Evidence from China. *Finance Research Letters* 63:105283.

Cheng, T. J. 1998. APEC and the Asian financial crisis: A lost opportunity for institution-building? *Asian Journal of Political Science* 6 (2): 21–32.
Chey, H. K. 2012. Why did the US Federal Reserve unprecedentedly offer swap lines to emerging market economies during the global financial crisis? Can we expect them again in the future? GRIPS Discussion Papers, 11–18, National Graduate Institute for Policy Studies, Tokyo.
Chin, G. T. 2024. Introduction—The evolution of New Development Bank (NDB): A decade plus in the making. *Global Policy* 15 (2): 368–382.
Cho, S., and C. R. Kelly. 2012. Promises and perils of new global governance: A case of the G20. *Chicago Journal of International Law* 12 (2): 491–562.
Cooper, A. F., and A. B. Farooq. 2013. BRICS and the privileging of informality in global governance. *Global Policy* 4 (4): 428–433. https://doi.org/10.1111/1758-5899.12077.
Costigan, T., D. Cottle, and A. Keys. 2017. The US dollar as the global reserve currency: Implications for US hegemony. *World Review of Political Economy* 8 (1): 104–122. https://doi.org/10.13169/worlrevipoliecon.8.1.0104.
Dadush, U., and K. Suominen. 2012. Is there life for the G20 beyond the global financial crisis? *Journal of Globalization and Development* 2 (2): 1–14.
Davies, H., and D. Green. 2008. *Global financial regulation: The essential guide.* Cambridge: Polity.
Dobson, W., and E. K. Y. Chen. 2015. Introduction: Financial development in Asia—Work in progress. In *Financial development and cooperation in Asia and the Pacific*, edited by E. K. Y. Chen and W. Dobson, 1st ed., 1–10. London: Routledge. https://doi.org/10.4324/9781315885216-1.
Doraisami, A. 2005. The political economy of capital flows and capital controls in Malaysia. *Journal of Contemporary Asia* 35 (2): 249–263.
Doraisami, A. 2014. Macro-economic policy responses to financial crises in Malaysia, Indonesia and Thailand. *Journal of Contemporary Asia* 44 (4): 581–598.
Drezner, D. W., and K. R. McNamara. 2013. International political economy, global financial orders and the 2008 financial crisis. *Perspectives on Politics* 11 (1): 155–166. https://doi.org/10.1017/S1537592712003660.
Feldstein, M. 1998. Refocusing the IMF. *Foreign Affairs* 77 (2): 20–33.
Financial Stability Forum. 2009. Press Release. Financial Stability Forum, April 2. Available from https://www.fsb.org/2009/04/financial-stability-forum-re-established-as-the-financial-stability-board/. Accessed on 28 December 2024.
Freidin, E. 2024. BRICS Pay as a challenge to SWIFT network. Lowy Institute, December 31. Available from https://www.lowyinstitute.org/the-interpreter/brics-pay-challenge-swift-network. Accessed on 19 March 2025.
Gadinis, S. 2013. The Financial Stability Board: The new politics of international financial regulation. *Texas International Law Journal* 48 (2): 157–175.
Gavin, F. J. 2020. California dreaming: The crisis and rebirth of American power in the 1970s and its consequences for world order. In *The downfall of the American order?* Edited by P. J. Katzenstein and J. Kirshner, 86–104. Ithaca: Cornell University Press. http://www.jstor.org/stable/10.7591/j.ctv1sfsf3t.11.
Germain, R. D. 2001. Global financial governance and the problem of inclusion. *Global Governance* 7 (4): 411–423. https://doi.org/10.1163/19426720-00704006.
Germain, R. D. 2010. *Global politics and financial governance.* Basingstoke and New York: Palgrave Macmillan.
Gigante, G., and A. Zago. 2023. DARQ technologies in the financial sector: Artificial intelligence applications in personalized banking. *Qualitative Research in Financial Markets* 15 (1): 29–57.
Grabel, I. 2022. Post-American moments in contemporary global financial governance. In *The downfall of the American order?* Edited by P. J. Katzenstein and J. Kirshner, 124–143. Cornell University Press. http://www.jstor.org/stable/10.7591/j.ctv1sfsf3t.11.

Grenville, S., and T. Ito. 2010. An independent evaluation of the Bank of Thailand's Monetary Policy under the inflation targeting framework, 2000–2010. Bank of Thailand Evaluation Paper. Available from https://www.bot.or.th/content/dam/bot/documents/th/our-roles/monetary-policy/about-monetary-policy/GI04-GrenvilleItoV10.pdf. Accessed on 6 June 2024.

Grimes, W. W., and W. N. Kring. 2020. Institutionalizing financial cooperation in East Asia: AMRO and the future of the Chiang Mai Initiative Multilateralization. *Global Governance* 26 (3): 428–448. https://doi.org/10.1163/19426720-02603005.

Haggrad, S. 2010. Regional responses to financial crises: The Americas, East Asia, and Europe. In *Responding to financial crisis: Lessons from Asia then, the United States and Europe now*, edited by A. S. Posen and C. Rhee, 249–276. Washington: Peterson Institute for International Economics.

Haley, U. C. 2000. Corporate governance and restructuring in East Asia: An overview. *Seoul Journal of Economics* 13 (3): 225–252.

Hamilton-Hart, N. 2003. Co-operation on money and finance: How important? How likely? *Third World Quarterly* 24 (2): 283–297.

Han, B. 2022. The CMI and CMIM. In *Trauma to triumph: Rising from the ashes of the Asian financial crisis*, edited by H. E. Khor, D. C. Guinigundo, and M. Kawai, 711–762. World Scientific Publishing. https://doi.org/10.1142/9789811253560.

Helleiner, E. 2010. What role for the new financial stability board? The politics of international standards after the crisis. *Global Policy* 1 (3): 282–290.

Helleiner, E. 2011. Understanding the 2007–2008 global financial crisis: Lessons for scholars of international political economy. *Annual Review of Political Science* 14 (1): 67–87. https://doi.org/10.1146/annurev-polisci-050409-112539.

Helleiner, E. 2016. Legacies of the 2008 crisis for global financial governance. *Global Summitry: Politics, Economics and Law in International Governance* 2 (1): 1–12. https://doi.org/10.1093/global/guw006.

Helleiner, E. 2019. The life and times of embedded liberalism: Legacies and innovations since Bretton Woods. *Review of International Political Economy* 26 (6): 1112–1135. https://doi.org/10.1080/09692290.2019.1607767.

Helleiner, E., and H. Wang. 2018. Limits to the BRICS' challenge: Credit rating reform and institutional innovation in global finance. *Review of International Political Economy* 25 (5): 573–595.

Hill, H. 1999. *The Indonesian economy in crisis: Causes, consequences, and lessons*. New York: Palgrave Macmillan.

Hong, K. 2010. Fiscal policy issues in Korea after the current crisis. ADBI Working Paper 225, Asian Development Bank Institute, Tokyo.

Hoontrakul, P., and C. Karnchanasai. 2010. The evolution of corporate governance in banking industry of Thailand from the 1997 Asian crisis to the 2008 global credit crisis. *CGN: Case Studies (Topic)*. https://doi.org/10.2139/SSRN.1555423.

Horton, M., M. S. Kumar, and P. Mauro. 2009. *The state of public finances: A cross-country fiscal monitor*. Washington, DC: International Monetary Fund.

Huotari, M., and T. Hanemann. 2014. Emerging powers and change in the global financial order. *Global Policy* 5 (3): 298–310. https://doi.org/10.1111/1758-5899.12133.

IMF. 2003. *Evaluation report: The IMF and recent capital account crises: Indonesia, Korea and Brazil*. Washington, DC: Independent Evaluation Office.

IMF. 2016. IMF annual report 2016: Finding solutions together. International Monetary Fund. Available from https://www.imf.org/external/pubs/ft/ar/2016/eng/index.htm. Accessed on 9 June 2024.

IMF. 2024. Global financial stability report: The last mile: Financial vulnerabilities and risks. Washington, DC.

James, W. E., D. Park, S. Jha, J. Jongwanich, A. Terada-Hagiwara, and L. Sumulong. 2008. The US financial crisis, global financial turmoil, and developing Asia: Is the era of high growth at an end. ADB Economics, Working Paper Series No. 139. Asian Development Bank, Manila, Philippines.

Jean, X., M. A. Low, N. Gopalakrishnan, M. Hoang, S. Wong, and S. Park. 2024. Credit FAQ: A look at why South and Southeast Asian firms are standing up to a strong dollar. S&P Global, May 16. Available from https://www.spglobal.com/ratings/en/research/articles/240516-credit-faq-a-look-at-why-south-and-southeast-asian-firms-are-standing-up-to-a-strong-dollar-13105063. Accessed on 25 May 2024.

Jędrzejowska, K. 2020. From global to regional financial governance? The case of Asia-Pacific. In *The future of global economic governance: Challenges and prospects in the age of uncertainty*, edited by M. Rewizorski, K. Jędrzejowska, and A. Wróbel, 1st ed., 103–118. Springer International Publishing AG. https://doi.org/10.1007/978-3-030-35336-0.

Jitsuchon, S. 2010. Fiscal policy issues in Thailand after the current economic crisis. *Public Policy Review* 6 (4): 741–767.

Jitsuchon, S., and C. Sussangkarn. 2009. Thailand's growth rebalancing. ADBI Working Paper 154, Asian Development Bank Institute, Tokyo.

Jongsureyapart, C., V. Wise, and A. Yaftian. 2012. Post-crisis corporate governance and the Thailand banking Sector. *Banks and Bank Systems* 7 (1): 40–49.

Jordan, C. 2010. The dangerous illusion of international financial standards and the legacy of the financial stability forum. *San Diego International Law Journal* 12:333–337.

Kaplan, E., and D. Rodrik. 2002. Did the Malaysian capital controls work? In *Preventing currency crises in emerging markets*, edited by S. Edwards and J. A. Frankel, 393–440. Chicago: University of Chicago Press.

Kawai, M. 2015. From the Chiang Mai Initiative to an Asian Monetary Fund. ADBI Working Paper Series, No. 527. Asian Development Bank Institute, Tokyo.

Khoon, G. S., and L. M. Hui. 2010. *The impact of the global financial crisis: The case of Malaysia.* Penang: Third World Network.

Kim, S. 2017. South Korea 20 years after the IMF rescue package. Koren Economic Institute of America (KEIA), December 4. Available from https://keia.org/the-peninsula/south-korea-20-years-after-the-imf-rescue-package/. Accessed on 10 June 2024.

Kim, S., and C. Rhee. 2014. The Chiang Mai Initiative Multilateralization: Perspectives and prospects. *Asian Economic Policy Review* 9 (2): 145–167.

Kirton, J. J. 2013. *G20 Governance for a globalized world*. Ashgate. https://doi.org/10.4324/9781315583747.

Kirton, J. J. 2017. Governing together: The Gx future. *Studia Diplomatica* 68 (3): 7–28.

Kozul-Wright, R., and D. Poon. 2015. Development financing: The rise of alternative financial institutions. *Global Policy* 6 (1): 59–66.

Krause, D. 2024. The future of global payments: BRICS Pay and the evolving financial order. https://doi.org/10.2139/ssrn.5043142. Accessed on 18 Jun 2025.

Krongkaew, M. 1999. Capital flows and economic crisis in Thailand. *Developing Economies* 37 (4): 395–416.

Lane, P. R. 2013. Financial globalisation and the crisis. *Open Economies Review* 24 (3): 555–580. https://doi.org/10.1007/s11079-012-9266-0.

Larionova, M., and A. Shelepov. 2019. The G7 and BRICS in the G20 economic governance. *International Organizations Research Journal* 14 (4): 48–66.

Lauridsen, L. S. 1998. The financial crisis in Thailand: Causes, conduct and consequences? *World Development* 26 (8): 1575–1591.

Lee, H., and C. Rhee. 2012. Lessons from the 1997 and the 2008 crises in the Republic of Korea. ADB Economics Working Paper Series, 298, Asian Development Bank, Manila, Philippines.

Lee, P. S. 2000. Economic crisis and chaebol reform in Korea. Discussion Paper Series, 14, APEC Study Centre, Columbia Business School, New York.

Lesage, D., P. Debaere, S. Dierckx, and M. Vermeiren. 2013. IMF reform after the crisis. *International Politics (Hague, Netherlands)* 50 (4): 553–578. https://doi.org/10.1057/ip.2013.17.

Lesage, D., P. Debaere, S. Dierckx, and M. Vermeiren. 2015. Rising powers and IMF governance reform. In *Rising powers and multilateral institutions*, edited by D. Lesage and T. van de Graaf, 153–174. Basingstoke: Palgrave Macmillan.
Lipscy, P. Y. 2003. Japan's Asian Monetary Fund proposal. *Stanford Journal of East Asian Affairs* 3 (1): 93–104.
Liu, M. 2016. BRICS development: A long way to a powerful economic club and new international organization. *The Pacific Review* 29 (3): 443–453. https://doi.org/10.1080/09512748.2016.1154688.
Liu, Z. Y. 2024. Does Evergrande's collapse threaten China's economy? Council on Foreign Relations, February 13. Available from https://www.cfr.org/in-brief/does-evergrandes-collapse-threaten-chinas-economy. Accessed on 16 March 2025.
Liu, Z. Z., and M. Papa. 2022. *Can BRICS de-dollarize the global financial system?* Cambridge: Cambridge University Press.
Lu, J., and J. Batten. 2023. The implementation of OECD corporate governance principles in post-crisis Asia. In *Australasian perspectives on corporate citizenship*, edited by D. Birch, 47–62. London: Routledge.
Luo, H., and L. Yang. 2021. Equality and equity in emerging multilateral financial institutions: The case of the BRICS institutions. *Global Policy* 12 (4): 482–508. https://doi.org/10.1111/1758-5899.13003.
Maasdorp, L. 2019. BRICS' New Development Bank turns four: What has it achieved? World Economic Forum, September 20. Available from https://www.weforum.org/agenda/2019/09/brics-new-development-bank-four-sustainability/. Accessed on 12 June 2024.
Manupipatpong, W. 2002. The ASEAN surveillance process and the East Asian Monetary Fund. *ASEAN Economic Bulletin* 19 (1): 111–122. https://doi.org/10.1355/AE19-1H.
McNamara, K. R. 2016. Regional monetary and financial governance. In *The Oxford handbook of comparative regionalism*, edited by T. Risse and T. A. Börzel, 351–373. Oxford: Oxford University Press.
Merking, L., and W. N. Kring. 2023. The International Monetary Fund and quota reform: Background and key considerations. Global Development Policy Center, Boston University, April 26. Available from https://www.bu.edu/gdp/files/2023/04/GEGI_WP_060_FIN.pdf. Accessed on 5 July 2024.
Mishra, R. 2016. Asian Infrastructure Investment Bank: An assessment. *India Quarterly* 72 (2): 163–176.
Mohsen, S. E., A. Hamdan, and H. M. Shoaib. 2024. Digital transformation and integration of artificial intelligence in financial institutions. *Journal of Financial Reporting and Accounting*. https://doi.org/10.1108/JFRA-09-2023-0544.
Moloney, N. 2017. The European Union in international financial governance. *RSF: Russell Sage Foundation Journal of the Social Sciences* 3 (1): 138–152. https://doi.org/10.7758/rsf.2017.3.1.08.
Morozkina, A. 2018. The New Development Bank in the global financial and economic architecture. In *BRICS and global governance*, edited by M. Larionova and J. J. Kirton, 1st ed., 89–105. Routledge. https://doi.org/10.4324/9781315569925-5.
Myers, J. 2024. US Fed cuts interest rates and other economics news to read, September 20. Available from https://www.weforum.org/agenda/2024/09/us-federal-reserve-interest-rates-cut-economy-news-20-september/. Accessed on 20 December 2024.
NDB. 2024. History. New Development Bank. Available from https://www.ndb.int/about-ndb/history/. Accessed on 8 December 2024.
NDB. 2025. Projects. New Development Bank. Available from https://www.ndb.int/projects/. Accessed on 12 March 2024.
Nehru, V. 2014. The World Bank and the Asian Development Bank: Should Asia have both? In *New global economic architecture: The Asian perspective*, edited by M. Kawai, P. J. Morgan, and P. B. Rana, 197–214. Cheltenham: Edward Elgar Publishing.

Nelson, R. M., and M. Weiss. 2014. IMF reforms: Issues for Congress. Congressional Research Service (CRS) reports and issue briefs, April 9. Available from https://sgp.fas.org/crs/misc/R42844.pdf. Accessed on 27 May 2024.

Ng, A. W., and B. K. Kwok. 2017. Emergence of fintech and cybersecurity in a global financial centre: Strategic approach by a regulator. *Journal of Financial Regulation and Compliance* 25 (4): 422–434.

Nidhiprabha, B. 2010. Effectiveness of Thailand's macroeconomic policy response to the global financial crisis. *ASEAN Economic Bulletin* 27 (1): 121–135. https://doi.org/10.1355/ae27-1g.

Nixon, R. 2009. APEC investment facilitation action plan. Asia-Pacific Economic Cooperation, January 31. Available from https://www.apec.org/press/features/2009/0201_apec_investment_facilitation_action_plan. Accessed on 12 December 2024.

Niyonkuru, F. 2016. Failure of foreign aid in developing countries: A quest for alternatives. *Business and Economics Journal* 7 (3): 1–9.

Ocampo, J. A. 2006. Regional financial cooperation: Experiences and challenges. In *Regional financial cooperation*, edited by J. A. Ocampo, 1–39. Baltimore, MD: United Nations Economic Commission for Latin America and the Caribbean, Brookings Institution Press.

OECD. 2010. *OECD economic surveys: Korea 2010*. Paris: Organisation of Economic Co-operation and Developments.

Overholt, W. H. 1999. Thailand's financial and political systems: Crisis and rejuvenation. *Asian Survey* 39 (6): 1009–1035.

Pathan, S., M. Skully, and J. Wickramanayake. 2008. Reforms in Thai bank governance: The aftermath of the Asian financial crisis. *International Review of Financial Analysis* 17 (2): 345–362. https://doi.org/10.1016/j.irfa.2006.05.002.

Pirie, I. 2016. Korea and the global economic crisis. *The Pacific Review* 29 (5): 671–692.

Pitakdumrongkit, K. 2015. Co-chairing international negotiations: The case of the Chiang Mai Initiative Multilateralization. *The Pacific Review* 28 (4): 577–605. https://doi.org/10.1080/09512748.2015.1012540.

Porter, T. 2000. The G-7, the Financial Stability Forum, the G-20, and the politics of international financial regulation. In *International Studies Association Annual Meeting*, Los Angeles, California. International Studies Association.

Posen, A. S., and C. Rhee. 2010. Global and regional financial safety nets: Lessons from Europe and Asia. In *Responding to financial crisis: Lessons from Asia then, the United States and Europe now*, edited by A. S. Posen and C. Rhee, 213–248. Washington: Peterson Institute for International Economics.

Punyaratabandhu, S. 1998. Thailand in 1997: Financial crisis and constitutional reform. *Asian Survey* 38 (2): 161–167. https://doi.org/10.1525/as.1998.38.2.01p0329w.

Rajan, R. 2010. *Fault lines: How hidden fractures still threaten the world economy*. Princeton: Princeton University Press.

Rana, P. B., and R. Pacheco Pardo. 2018. Rise of complementarity between global and regional financial institutions: Perspectives from Asia. *Global Policy* 9 (2): 231–243.

Resosudarmo, B. P., A. A. Abdurohman Yusuf, and D. Hartono. 2021. Spatial impacts of fiscal stimulus policies during the 2009 global financial crisis in Indonesia. *Asia-Pacific Journal of Regional Science* 5 (1): 305–326.

Rhee, Ch., L. Sumulong, and S. Vallée. 2013. Global and regional financial safety nets: Lessons from Europe and Asia. Bruegel, November 20. Available from https://www.bruegel.org/working-paper/global-and-regional-financial-safety-nets-lessons-europe-and-asia. Accessed on 26 December 2024.

Ruiz-Brunschwig, S., B. Carrasco, T. Hayashi, and H. Mukhopadhyay. 2011. The global financial crisis: Impact on Asia and emerging consensus. ADB South Asia Working Paper Series, 3, Asian Development Bank, Manila, Philippines.

Sachs J. D. 1997. The wrong medicine for Asia. *New York Times*, November 3. Available from https://www.nytimes.com/1997/11/03/opinion/the-wrong-medicine-for-asia.html. Accessed on 29 May 2024.

Sangsubhan, K., and M. C. Basri. 2012. Global financial crisis and ASEAN: Fiscal policy response in the case of Thailand and Indonesia. *Asian Economic Policy Review* 7 (2): 248–269.
Sato, Y. 2005. Bank restructuring and financial institution reform in Indonesia. *The Developing Economies* 43 (1): 91–120.
Schnabl, G. 2024. Exchange rate uncertainty endangers Japan's economic stability. East Asia Forum, October 25. Available from https://eastasiaforum.org/2024/10/25/exchange-rate-uncertainty-endangers-japans-economic-stability/. Accessed on 20 March 2025.
Scott, D. F. 2002. A practical guide to managing systemic financial crises: A review of approaches taken in Indonesia, the Republic of Korea, and Thailand. SSRN, May 9. Available from https://papers.ssrn.com/sol3/papers.cfm?abstract_id=636191. Accessed on 22 December 2024.
Shahrokhi, M., H. Cheng, K. Dandapani, A. Figueiredo, A. M. Parhizgari, and Y. Shachmurove. 2017. The evolution and future of the BRICS: Unbundling politics from economics. *Global Finance Journal* 32:1–15. https://doi.org/10.1016/j.gfj.2017.03.002.
Sheng, A. 2009. *From Asian to global financial crisis: An Asian regulator's view of unfettered finance in the 1990s and 2000s*. Cambridge: Cambridge University Press.
Shin, J. S. 2014. *The global financial crisis and the Korean economy*. London: Routledge.
Siamwalla, A. 2005. Anatomy of the crisis. In *Thailand beyond the crisis*, edited by P. Warr, 82–120. London: Routledge. https://doi.org/10.4324/9780203402399-7.
Siregar, R. Y., and K. Miyaki. 2015. The Chiang Mai Initiative and the future of East Asian regional macroeconomic and financial cooperation. In *Financial development and cooperation in Asia and the Pacific*, edited by E. K. Y. Chen and W. Dobson, 1st ed., 118–142. Routledge. https://doi.org/10.4324/9781315885216-6.
Smith, G. S. 2011. *G7 to G8 to G20: Evolution in global governance*. Ontario: Centre for International Governance Innovation.
Soesastro, H., and M. C. Basri. 1998. Survey of recent developments. *Bulletin of Indonesian Economic Studies* 34 (1): 3–54.
Steil, B. 2013. *The battle of Bretton Woods: John Maynard Keynes, Harry Dexter White, and the making of a new world order*. Princeton: Princeton University Press.
Stiglitz J. 1998. Must financial crises be this frequent and this painful? McKay Lecture, Pittsburgh, Pennsylvania, September 23. Available from https://www.kleinteilige-loesungen.de/globalisierte_finanzmaerkte/texte_abc/s/stiglitz_financial_crises.pdf. Accessed on 20 May 2024.
Stiglitz, J. 2002. *Globalization and its discontents*. New York: W. W. Norton & Company.
Stiglitz, J., and B. Greenwald. 2003. *Towards a new paradigm in monetary economics*. Cambridge: Cambridge University Press.
Stiglitz, J. E. 2010. *Freefall: America, free markets, and the sinking of the world economy*. New York: W. W. Norton & Company.
Suchodolski, S. G., and J. M. Demeulemeester. 2018. The BRICS coming of age and the New Development Bank. *Global Policy* 9 (4): 578–585.
Suhaidi, N. 2022. 25 Years on—Are we facing another Asian financial crisis? *The Malaysian Reserve*, November 7. Available from https://themalaysianreserve.com/2022/11/07/25-years-on-are-we-facing-another-asian-financial-crisis/. Accessed on 8 June 2024.
Sundich, N. 2024. Is there another Asian financial crisis brewing? How would stocks be impacted? Stocks down under, May 3. Available from https://stocksdownunder.com/article/another-asian-financial-crisis/. Accessed on 7 June 2024.
Sussangkarn, C. 2002. Economic crisis and recovery in Thailand: The role of the IMF. In *Asian economic recovery: Policy options for growth and stability*, edited by K. Y. Tan, 204–221. Singapore: The Institute of Policy Studies, Singapore University Press.
Sussangkarn, C. 2011. Chiang Mai Initiative Multilateralization: Origin, development, and outlook. *Asian Economic Policy Review* 6 (2): 203–220. https://doi.org/10.1111/j.1748-3131.2011.01196.x.
Sussangkarn, C., and P. Vichyanond. 2007. Ten years after the financial crisis in Thailand: What has been learned or not learned? *Asian Economic Policy Review* 2 (1): 100–118. https://doi.org/10.1111/j.1748-3131.2007.00055.x.

UNCTAD. 2024. Third South Summit: Statement by Rebeca Grynspan, Secretary-General of UNCTAD. United Nations Conference on Trade and Development, January 22. Available from https://unctad.org/osgstatement/third-south-summit. Accessed on 19 December 2024.

Valamontes, A. P. 2024. BRICS new payment system: A challenge to the US dollar's dominance. *Demokritos Scientific Journal* 1 (12): 1–6.

Vestergaard, J., and R. H. Wade. 2013. Protecting power: How Western states retain the dominant voice in the World Bank's governance. *World Development* 46:153–164.

Vestergaard, J., and R. H. Wade. 2015. Still in the woods: Gridlock in the IMF and the World Bank puts multilateralism at risk. *Global Policy* 6 (1): 1–12.

Vongvipanond, P. 2007. *Asian insolvency systems: The Thai perspective.* Paris: OECD Publishing.

Wang, H. 2017. New multilateral development banks: Opportunities and challenges for global governance. *Global Policy* 8 (1): 113–118. https://doi.org/10.1111/1758-5899.12396.

Wang, H. 2019. The New Development Bank and the Asian Infrastructure Investment Bank: China's ambiguous approach to global financial governance. *Development and Change* 50 (1): 221–244. https://doi.org/10.1111/dech.12473.

Woo, J. J., M. Ramesh, M. Howlett, and M. K. Coban. 2016. Dynamics of global financial governance: Constraints, opportunities, and capacities in Asia. *Policy & Society* 35 (3): 269–282. https://doi.org/10.1016/j.polsoc.2016.10.002.

Xu, Y., and H. Liu. 2022. The power of building parallel institutions: How China's new strategy advances global governance reform. *Asian Perspective* 46 (4): 707–731. https://doi.org/10.1353/apr.2022.0028.

Ye, F. 2023. The New Development Bank and the structure of the multilateral development financial system. *Review of Development Economics* 27 (3): 1957–1972.

Yerushalmy, J. 2024. Why has the yen fallen to a decade's low and what does it mean for Japan's economy? *The Guardian*, April 30. Available from https://www.theguardian.com/world/2024/apr/30/japan-economy-yen-currency-value-falling-low-impact. Accessed on 30 May 2024.

Zaman, K. 2023. The future of financial support for developing countries: Regional and Islamic monetary funds. *Politica* 1 (1): 1–8.

Zhang, D., M. Mohsin, and F. Taghizadeh-Hesary. 2022. Does green finance counteract the climate change mitigation?: Asymmetric effect of renewable energy investment and R&D. *Energy Economics* 113:106183.

Chapter 3
The Future of Digital Financial Inclusion in Brunei Darussalam

Hazwan Haini and Anwar Hashim

Abstract This study explores the future of digital financial inclusion in Brunei, emphasizing the interplay between technological advancement and financial access. It provides an overview of Brunei's financial technology landscape and outlines future scenarios for digital financial inclusion. Brunei presents a unique case as a small, open, and resource-rich economy grappling with an uneven digital divide. Despite a high internet penetration rate of 95% and universal 4G coverage, digital financial inclusion remains limited by structural and socio-economic barriers. Although the government has introduced various policies to promote digital financial inclusion, adoption rates and transaction values remain low.

Our analysis reveals that only 65.7% of Brunei's population holds a bank account, with even lower rates of online banking and debit card ownership. Although the digital payment market has expanded significantly, the average transaction value per user has declined, underscoring disparities in adoption. The study also highlights connectivity gaps, particularly in rural areas, where only 70% of households have reliable internet access. We identify five key drivers of change to build inclusive digital ecosystems and offer policy recommendations for economies grappling with an uneven digital divide. Future research should further explore how inclusive digital ecosystems can advance full financial inclusion.

Keywords Financial inclusion · FinTech · Digital banking · Brunei · Digitalisation · Future scenario

3.1 Introduction

Financial inclusion is a key policy objective for both advanced and developing economies, as it supports economic growth, advances social goals, and reduces inequalities by expanding access to affordable financial services and payment systems. Digitalization, particularly through digital payment services, has emerged

H. Haini (✉) · A. Hashim
Centre for Strategic and Policy Studies, Bandar Seri Begawan, Brunei Darussalam

R. Gulati et al. (eds.), *Emerging Challenges in Banking in Asia and the Pacific*, Economics, Law, and Institutions in Asia Pacific,
https://doi.org/10.1007/978-981-92-2144-8_3

as a crucial tool in addressing financial exclusion. However, despite its potential, significant challenges persist, including the digital divide, regulatory gaps, and the risk of marginalizing vulnerable groups who lack access to technology or digital literacy.

This study explores the role of technology in advancing financial inclusion in Brunei Darussalam, using a futures scenario approach based on descriptive analysis and conditional correlations of selected financial access indicators. Financial inclusion and technological innovation remain key policy priorities for Brunei Darussalam, as they are for many advanced and emerging economies. We argue that traditional measures of financial inclusion[1] and financial depth[2] are no longer sufficient, especially with the growing shift toward online transactions and digital financial applications replacing conventional financial channels. While Brunei Darussalam is well positioned to leverage digital technologies with its near full 4G internet coverage, the limited use of banking services and the lack of diverse financial applications continue to hinder progress toward digital financial inclusion.

While our study is rooted in practical policy considerations, it offers several innovations to the existing literature. First, it extends the limited body of research on futures studies by providing new evidence and policy insights. To the best of our knowledge, most futures studies on financial inclusion have focused on larger economies, particularly India (see Kapoor 2014), so our study contributes a fresh perspective by examining Brunei Darussalam—a small, open economy grappling with an uneven digital divide—thus broadening the geographical and contextual scope of the literature.

Second, Brunei Darussalam remains a relatively understudied economy in the literature. While the mechanisms of financial inclusion and technological adoption are broadly similar across many Southeast Asian economies, Brunei Darussalam's experience is distinct, as its policies are largely driven by government initiatives in collaboration with the private sector. Our study offers practical policy recommendations aimed at better understanding the future of financial inclusion and technology in Brunei Darussalam.

3.2 Theoretical Considerations

3.2.1 Financial Inclusion

Financial inclusion refers to the provision of financial services to all segments of the population, including both the privileged and the marginalized, with a view to ensuring that no one is excluded from the formal financial system (Ozili 2020). These

[1] Number of bank branches, ATMs, and regional indicators.

[2] Credit from banks and private institutions.

services encompass access to savings, loans, insurance, and payment and remittance services, delivered affordably and sustainably (Iqbal and Sami 2017). While various theories explain the drivers of financial inclusion, several emphasize the crucial role of governments in expanding access to formal financial services. Notable examples include public good theory, public services theory, and public money theory, which advocate proactive government intervention to promote financial inclusion (Ozili 2020).

Financial inclusion is widely recognized as a driver of economic growth and development, based on the premise that the greatest benefits accrue to those previously excluded from the financial system (Demirgüç-Kunt and Klapper 2013). Research also underscores its role in addressing persistent income inequality by expanding financial access (Beck et al. 2009). Furthermore, financial inclusion can indirectly foster growth by improving the allocation of credit to firms (Johnson and Arnold 2012). It also contributes to financial system stability by lowering nonperforming loan rates and reducing default risks, as broader access to deposits helps diversify funding sources (Morgan and Pontines 2014; José and García 2016).

Consequently, financial inclusion has become a key policy objective for many governments (Ozili 2021), and the World Bank has developed a framework to guide countries in expanding financial access and inclusion (World Bank 2022).[3] However, several barriers continue to limit individuals' access to formal financial services, including the cost of services, the physical distance to financial institutions, and stringent documentation requirements, which are often imposed to uphold financial stability through regulatory standards (Hawkins 2006; Demirgüç-Kunt and Klapper 2013).

For example, rural areas are often underserved, particularly in developing countries (Mahadeva 2011). Additionally, a lack of education and understanding can prevent potential users from accessing financial services (Beck et al. 2009). Advocates of financial inclusion emphasize the need for a holistic approach that addresses both supply and demand issues (Dev 2006). Supply-side challenges include gaining access to credit and physical financial services through branches or automated teller machines (ATMs), while demand-side issues involve awareness, financial literacy,[4] and the productivity of agents.

[3] There are five pillars for countries to achieve financial inclusion according to the World Bank framework, namely: Pillar 1: National Financial Inclusion & Fintech Policy and Strategy; Pillar 2: Financial Products and Providers for Underserved Segments; Pillar 3: Financial Consumer Protection; Pillar 4: Financial Capability and Behavioural Insights; Pillar 5: Micro, Small and Medium Enterprise (MSMS) Finance (see more at: https://www.worldbank.org/en/topic/financialinclusion/overview). [Accessed 30 Sept 2025].

[4] Financial literacy is the ability to understand and effectively apply various financial skills, including budgeting, saving, investing, and managing debt, to make informed decisions that enhance personal financial well-being.

These solutions address the root causes of financial exclusion by incorporating a range of mechanisms in a systematic manner. However, recent innovations and technological advancements have further enhanced opportunities to improve financial inclusion. Financial innovation[5] and technology are particularly valuable in overcoming existing structural and infrastructural barriers, allowing access to underserved market segments (Ozili 2021). Generally speaking, digitalization lowers the cost of information technology infrastructure, facilitates organizational and business transformation, and can potentially increase transaction volumes and capital flow between agents (Haini and Wei Loon 2022).

3.2.2 *The Role of Technology in Financial Inclusion*

The use of technology in finance is often referred to as FinTech, which involves the application of technology to deliver financial solutions, or TechFins, which are technology and data companies that integrate financial services into their value chains (Yap and Borhan 2021). While there are distinctions between the two, Southeast Asia has witnessed rapid growth in the adoption of technology in finance, as evidenced by the large number of internet users and the proliferation of FinTech and TechFin companies (Ozili 2021). While this trend can be beneficial, it also risks exacerbating financial exclusion in two key ways: First, low-skilled and financially illiterate users may struggle to adapt to new technological advancements (Sarma and Pais 2011); and second, banks and tech companies face growing regulatory and compliance burdens, which could further marginalize excluded groups (Yap and Borhan 2021).

There is reason to question the assumption that poor individuals benefit directly from financial inclusion (Mader 2018). It is argued that for-profit actors delivering inclusive services are often driven more by market incentives and policy agendas than by pro-poor development objectives, which can lead to increased inequality and exclusion, as the distribution of financial capital becomes a competitive process. Similarly, some studies suggest that excessive financial inclusion can be harmful, as it may create a moral hazard. With all agents gaining access to the formal financial sector, including those engaged in criminal activities, the risks increase (Ozili 2020). In this context, extreme financial inclusion refers to universal participation in the formal financial market, regardless of an individual's risk profile or income level.

[5] Financial innovation refers to the development of new financial instruments, technologies, products, and services aimed at enhancing the efficiency and effectiveness of financial service delivery.

3.2.3 *Traditional Financial Inclusion and Technology Adoption in Brunei Darussalam*

Brunei Darussalam's financial landscape, as shown in Table 3.1, demonstrates a moderate level of financial access relative to its regional peers, particularly regarding traditional banking channels. With 17.6 bank branches and 73.96 ATMs per 100,000 adults, Brunei Darussalam outperforms ASEAN neighbors such as Cambodia and Myanmar. However, its domestic credit to the private sector, at 35.71% of GDP, remains lower than that of countries like Malaysia and Singapore, suggesting that there is room for growth in private sector lending. The underdeveloped stock market indicates that Brunei Darussalam relies heavily on traditional banking and lacks significant capital markets, pointing to the need for greater diversification within its financial sector. These factors highlight the importance of enhancing financial inclusion while addressing gaps in financial depth and capital market development to fully realize its economic potential.

Table 3.1 Selected indicators of financial access and development—cross comparison 2021

	Number of bank branches (per 0.1 million adults)	Number of ATMs (per 0.1 million adults)	Domestic credit to private sector (% of GDP)	Stocks traded, total value (% of GDP)	Market capitalization of listed domestic companies (% of GDP)
Brunei Darussalam	16.24	73.10	36.27	–	–
Cambodia	12.40	31.61	166.26	–	–
Indonesia	15.92	48.09	36.99	17.09	48.77
Lao PDR	3.07	28.06	–	–	–
Malaysia	8.46	54.28	127.24	54.67	110.82
Philippines	8.99	29.37	49.94	9.10	72.43
Singapore	6.94	54.33	–	–	152.82
Thailand	9.37	108.14	164.08	118.11	118.30
Viet Nam	2.91	27.05	124.28	51.89	76.07
PRC	8.78	81.44	177.27	226.48	81.02
Japan	33.69	116.94	193.74	125.99	129.99
UAE	8.13	51.70	75.15	28.82	133.69
Qatar	9.36	52.41	123.32	17.28	103.04
Kuwait	12.68	81.21	–	28.01	96.36
Saudi Arabia	7.43	62.04	–	67.87	305.59

GDP = gross domestic product, Lao PDR = Lao People's Democratic Republic, PRC = People's Republic of China, UAE = United Arab Emirates
Source World Development Indicators, World Bank (various years)

Table 3.2 highlights the uneven distribution of financial services across Brunei Darussalam's districts, revealing significant disparities. The capital district, Brunei-Muara, is the best served, with 36 branches and 85 single-function machines, while remote areas like Temburong have only two branches and no multifunction machines. This stark contrast underscores a clear urban-rural divide, with access to financial and digital services concentrated in the capital, leaving rural populations underserved.

On a positive note, Table 3.3 highlights Brunei Darussalam's robust ICT infrastructure, which plays a critical role in advancing both financial inclusion and economic development. With 12.37 fixed broadband subscriptions and 19.77 fixed telephone subscriptions per 100 people, Brunei Darussalam's connectivity surpasses that of countries like Cambodia and Myanmar, though it still lags behind leaders like Singapore and the Republic of Korea. The country boasts a high rate of mobile cellular subscriptions at 131.22 per 100 people, which supports the adoption of mobile banking and eWallets—key tools for reaching underserved populations. Additionally, with 95% of the population using the internet and a high GDP per capita ($30,313.41), Brunei Darussalam demonstrates both the capacity and the potential for widespread adoption of digital financial services. While Brunei Darussalam has made significant progress in terms of technological readiness, continued efforts to enhance digital literacy and infrastructure will be essential to fully harness technology with a view to greater financial inclusion.

Thus, Brunei Darussalam's financial system, while equipped with a relatively strong banking infrastructure, shows limited financial depth with a low domestic credit to private sector ratio and an underdeveloped capital market. This indicates the need for diversification beyond traditional banking to boost financial inclusion, especially for SMEs. In terms of technology, Brunei Darussalam is well positioned to expand digital financial services with high internet penetration and mobile adoption.

Table 3.2 Traditional financial access indicators in Brunei Darussalam (2023)

District	Branches (including head office)	Single-function machines onsite	Single-function machines offsite	Multifunction machines onsite	Multifunction machines offsite
Brunei-Muara	36	85	59	32	13
Temburong	2	4	0	0	0
Tutong	3	4	7	3	0
Belait	10	19	8	6	6
Total	51	112	74	41	19

Source Brunei Darussalam Central Bank (2023)

Table 3.3 Selected indicators of economic development and ICT sector—cross comparison 2021

	Fixed broadband subscriptions (per 100 people)	Fixed telephone subscriptions (per 100 people)	Mobile cellular subscriptions (per 100 people)	Individuals using the internet (% of population)	GDP per capita (constant 2015 $)
Brunei Darussalam	17.58	24.90	135.50	95.62	29,673.17
Cambodia	1.98	0.24	119.96	55.60	1429.94
Indonesia	4.49	3.26	133.65	62.10	3892.96
Lao PDR	2.02	17.40	64.96	62.00	2566.28
Malaysia	10.89	24.10	140.59	96.75	10,605.68
Philippines	8.51	4.13	143.44	63.40	3328.04
Singapore	27.52	34.30	147.48	96.92	67,638.65
Thailand	17.32	6.46	168.78	85.27	6133.29
Viet Nam	19.54	3.16	138.87	74.21	3408.76
PRC	37.56	12.70	121.54	73.05	11,223.26
Japan	35.94	48.90	160.88	82.91	35,701.45
UAE	36.50	22.90	194.73	100.00	42,715.44
Qatar	11.08	16.30	144.20	100.00	61,022.50
Kuwait	1.62	–	162.78	99.70	26,452.97
Saudi Arabia	33.80	21.10	126.36	100.00	20,237.71

GDP = gross domestic product, Lao PDR = Lao People's Democratic Republic, PRC = People's Republic of China, UAE = United Arab Emirates.
Source World Development Indicators, World Bank (various years)

3.3 The Financial Technology Landscape in Brunei Darussalam

3.3.1 Digital Finance Policies and Regulation in Brunei Darussalam

Brunei Darussalam has implemented several policies to promote technological adoption and financial development, including fiscal consolidation programs aimed at corporatizing its communications and technology sector (Centre for Strategic and Policy Studies 2024). This includes the *Brunei Darussalam Financial Sector Blueprint (2016–2025)* (Brunei Darussalam Central Bank 2016), a strategic framework designed to enhance the financial services sector. The Central Bank recognizes the growing importance of the sector and its steady contribution to the economy.

In the past, much of the effort expended by the government, the Brunei Darussalam Central Bank,[6] and the financial industry focused on enhancing financial literacy (Pg Hj Md Salleh and Baha 2020).[7] However, in recent years, there has been a shift toward promoting technological adoption in the financial landscape. In 2017, the Central Bank established a FinTech office to encourage the use of digital and innovative financial technologies, products, and services aimed at increasing financial inclusion while improving efficiency, reducing costs, and enhancing customer experience (Brunei Darussalam Central Bank 2019).

In 2019, the Brunei Darussalam Central Bank released the *Digital Payment Roadmap for Brunei Darussalam 2019–2025* (Brunei Darussalam Central Bank 2019). The roadmap outlines strategies advocating the adoption of technologies such as QR codes, biometric solutions, and integration with ASEAN payment systems for cross-border transactions, all while maintaining consumer data security and trust in digital payments. It reflects the Central Bank's early commitment to developing a comprehensive digital payment ecosystem by providing a regulatory framework and common standards for digital payments. The roadmap also emphasizes educating the public about the benefits of digital payments in order to build trust and ensure these systems are accessible to all segments of society.

In 2020, the Brunei Darussalam Central Bank published a review, *The State of FinTech in Brunei Darussalam* (Brunei Darussalam Central Bank 2020), which emphasized the need for an integrated ecosystem of FinTech and TechFin organizations in a business environment that benefits consumers through various innovations. One key development highlighted was the introduction of a Regulatory Sandbox by the Central Bank, designed to enhance the accessibility, efficiency, and security of new financial products and services. The report also noted the growing demand for innovations to address the high costs of interbank fees (e.g., real-time gross settlement and automated clearing house systems) and remittance solutions, given Brunei Darussalam's large foreign worker population.

The report also emphasized the government's role in driving Brunei Darussalam's digital agenda, particularly through the Digital Economy Council (DEC).[8] In June 2020, the DEC introduced the *Digital Economy Masterplan 2025*,[9] aligning with the vision of His Majesty Sultan Haji Hassanal Bolkiah Mu'izzaddin Waddaulah for Brunei Darussalam to become a Smart Nation. The Masterplan supports the objectives of Wawasan Brunei 2035, focusing on creating a digital, future-ready society, fostering a vibrant and sustainable economy, and establishing a digitally conducive ecosystem. As part of this vision, the government aims to promote international

[6] Previously known as the Autoriti Monetari Brunei Darussalam (AMBD).

[7] The National Savings Day in Brunei was set for 28 May, and the Financial Planning Association of Brunei Darussalam was established in 2016.

[8] The Digital Economy Council (DEC) took over the roles of the Brunei Darussalam National IT Council (BIT Council) and the e-Government Leadership Forum (EGLF) in providing direction and guidance on digital economy initiatives for Brunei Darussalam.

[9] https://www.mtic.gov.bn/de2025/index.html#page=1. [Accessed 08 Oct 2025].

connectivity, with a cashless society driven by electronic payments and an advanced financial infrastructure.

His Majesty Sultan Haji Hassanal Bolkiah Mu'izzaddin Waddaulah has continued to emphasize the importance of the digital economy, recently announcing plans to establish the *Digital Payment Hub* (The Star 2024). The aim of the hub is to develop modern financial infrastructure to further promote cashless transactions. In conjunction with this, the *National Information Hub* will serve as a centralized platform for digital sharing, complementing the *Digital Payment Hub* by strengthening digital infrastructure and using digital identity for security and verification (Digital Brunei n.d.). This initiative also includes programs aimed at enhancing consumers' technological skills and supporting micro-, small, and medium-sized enterprises (MSMEs) in adopting these technologies.

The recent *Brunei Digital Economy Forum 2024*, organized by the ASEAN and APEC Business Advisory Councils in collaboration with the Ministry of Finance and Economy, marked a significant milestone in the evolution of Brunei Darussalam's digital payment landscape. The forum, themed "*The Future of Digital Trade in Brunei*," highlighted the transformative potential of the *National Digital Payment Hub*, a key element of Brunei Darussalam's *Digital Economy Masterplan 2025*. Haslina Taib, Chair of the ASEAN Business Advisory Council Brunei, emphasized that the hub would not only streamline local transactions but also create new opportunities for entrepreneurs to expand internationally.

Additionally, the forum highlighted the anticipated launch of a national QR payment system, which was expected to further integrate Brunei Darussalam into the regional economy and pave the way for a more connected ASEAN marketplace by late 2025. The developments discussed at the forum signaled a continued proactive approach toward establishing a robust digital economy in Brunei Darussalam, where collaboration between government initiatives and private sector innovation will be pivotal in achieving sustainable growth and competitiveness in an increasingly interconnected world.[10]

3.3.2 The Current State of Digital Finance in Brunei Darussalam

In recent years, Brunei Darussalam's digital payments have shown encouraging growth, with the digital payments market increasing from $123.7 million in 2017 to an estimated $267.8 million in 2023, reflecting improvements even before the pandemic (AMRO 2023). While the COVID-19 pandemic played a significant role in accelerating the adoption of contactless payment methods, AMRO projects that the transaction value will rise to $380.6 million by 2027. The AMRO Annual Consultation Report for Brunei Darussalam 2023 also notes that digital commerce drives the

[10] https://thebruneian.news/2024/09/27/brunei-digital-economy-forum-2024-paving-the-way-for-a-digital-future/. [Accessed 08 Oct 2025].

majority of Brunei Darussalam's digital payment market, accounting for around 90% of all transactions. This aligns with findings from the ICT Market Study Survey by the Authority for Info-communications Technology Industry of Brunei Darussalam (AITI) and the Center for Strategic and Policy Studies (CSPS), which discovered that over 90% of small businesses have adopted a limited number of digital applications.[11]

Brunei Darussalam's financial technology landscape has been evolving rapidly, with both public and private sector initiatives playing a key role in enhancing financial services and promoting cashless transactions. The country has seen a surge in FinTech and TechFin products and services, reflecting a broader trend toward digitalization in the financial sector. These developments are aimed at streamlining financial processes, increasing accessibility, and encouraging more efficient and secure transactions across the nation.

The banking sector in Brunei Darussalam has embraced a variety of FinTech solutions to enhance customer experience and boost operational efficiency. Key offerings include BIBD QuickPay, which enables users to make fast cashless payments via QR codes, and Baiduri Qpay, integrated into the Baiduri b.Digital Personal mobile app for seamless QR code-based purchases. Another notable addition is TAIB Scan to Pay, which also utilizes cashless QR code technology. These services are part of a broader initiative aimed at modernizing Brunei Darussalam's payment systems, driving the country towards a more digital and cashless financial ecosystem.

In addition to traditional banks, Telco-branded wallets have emerged as significant players in Brunei Darussalam's FinTech ecosystem. Progresif Ding offers a digital wallet that enables cashless transactions without the need for a bank account, making it accessible to a broader audience. Similarly, the MyDST SuperApp provides a variety of functionalities, including money transfers, bill payments, and online shopping, thereby further enhancing user convenience. These Telco-branded wallets are also subject to the financial regulations established by the Central Bank, thus ensuring that they operate within a secure and compliant framework.

Independent FinTech operators have also played a crucial role in shaping Brunei Darussalam's evolving financial landscape. Beep Digital Solutions specializes in innovative payment solutions designed to boost customer engagement for businesses. Meanwhile, MoneyMatch, although based in Malaysia, is actively disrupting traditional financial services with its creative approaches. Other noteworthy players include BruPay, which has ceased operations, and Pocket, a mobile application aimed at simplifying money management for users by enabling instant payments via QR codes. Additionally, Jana Kapital stands out as Brunei Darussalam's first Shariah-compliant peer-to-peer crowdfunding platform, offering alternative financing options for MSMEs and opening up investment opportunities for the public.

The regulatory environment in Brunei Darussalam is evolving to support the growth of FinTech. The introduction of the FinTech Regulatory Sandbox in 2017 has provided startups with an opportunity to test their innovations within a controlled framework, fostering an environment that is conducive to experimentation and growth

[11] http://www.csps.org.bn/2022/02/18/csps-aiti-conclude-ict-market-study/. [Accessed 08 Oct 2025].

(Brunei Darussalam Central Bank 2020). This initiative has been successful, with digital payment transactions reportedly increasing by 87.8% since its implementation. The Brunei Darussalam Central Bank plays a crucial role in facilitating this progress, ensuring user safety, and maintaining competitive fairness among providers. However, the BDBC Regulatory Sandbox is currently the only regulatory framework in place that covers the development of FinTech in Brunei Darussalam. Table 3.4 summarizes the digital financial products available in Brunei Darussalam.

Overall, Brunei Darussalam's FinTech landscape is shaped by a collaborative effort among traditional banks, telecommunications companies, independent operators, and regulatory bodies. The aim of this synergy is to modernize financial services while promoting economic growth through enhanced accessibility to, and more efficient, financial transactions. As Brunei Darussalam progresses toward becoming a cashless society, ongoing advancements in technology and regulatory support will be crucial in shaping its future financial ecosystem.

Table 3.4 Summary of digital financial products

Institution	Financial product	Description
Bank Islam Brunei Darussalam	Quick Pay	Cashless payments. Bank account required
Baiduri Bank	Qpay	Cashless payments. Bank account required
TAIB Bank	Scan to Pay	Cashless payments. Bank account required
Progresif	Ding	Cashless payments. Mobile line required and top-up using cash or card
DST	MyDST SuperApp	Cashless payments. Mobile line required and top-up using cash or card
Beep Digital Solutions	Beep+, Digital Payment Solutions	Merchant solutions for e-commerce
MoneyMatch	International Money Transfer	Remittances and foreign currency
Pocket	Pocket App	Cashless payments. Bank card required
Jana Kapital	Crowdfunding	Not in operation. Currently under sandbox regulation
BruPay	BruPay App	Ceased operation

Source Authors' compilation

3.3.3 Risks of, and Barriers to, Adoption

The financial technology landscape in Brunei Darussalam is still in its early stages, yet its potential to catch up with other developing countries is significant. However, there are several challenges to be faced. Brunei Darussalam's relatively small population[12] limits the scale of financial innovation in terms of product and service offerings, and while the country boasts a high level of internet penetration and a large user base, digital literacy remains low due to a lack of awareness and limited adoption of these products and services (International Monetary Fund 2023). Additionally, as well as small enterprises, key sectors—particularly the agriculture industry—have struggled to integrate digitalization into their operations (AMRO 2023). This has led to low levels of digital engagement in the private sector and the eventual closure of some organizations, such as BruPay.

Barriers to adopting FinTech in Brunei Darussalam, particularly in regard to eWallets, have been identified in recent studies examining the perspectives of the younger population. Research using the Unified Theory of Acceptance and Use of Technology (UTAUT) model found that traditional predictors of behavioral intention were less significant than individual attitudes towards technology and anxiety levels (Arine et al. 2020). This indicates that, despite young people's familiarity with various technologies and the benefits of improved internet connectivity, these factors alone have not been enough to drive widespread adoption of eWallets.

Additionally, challenges such as limited vendor acceptance, concerns over financial management and security, and a reluctance to transition from traditional payment methods contribute to the discontinuation intentions among previous users (Sait et al. 2024). Technical issues, such as unreliable internet connectivity and operational functionality, further complicate the landscape, and addressing these barriers is essential for stakeholders seeking to enhance user experiences and foster broader acceptance of digital payment solutions within Brunei Darussalam's evolving financial ecosystem.

Moreover, several key projects remain incomplete despite being in progress for years. Flagship initiatives such as the *National Information Hub*, Digital Identity, and the *Digital Payment Hub* are ongoing, with unclear completion timelines. On a broader scale, Brunei Darussalam ranks relatively low in the *Global Innovation Index*, currently sitting at 87th in the 2023 rankings, reflecting the country's struggle to translate high levels of internet penetration and GDP per capita into meaningful innovation.

Finally, there appears to be a lack of international exposure in Brunei Darussalam's financial technology sector, as MoneyMatch, a FinTech organization from Malaysia, seems to be the only international player currently operating in the market. This is concerning, as international firms bring valuable expertise that could accelerate the development of the financial technology landscape. The broader financial sector in Brunei Darussalam has also seen the exit of two major international banks—Citibank in 2014 and HSBC in 2017 (Bhattacharyay and Bhattacharyay 2022)—along with United Overseas Bank (UOB) selling its retail division to Baiduri. The absence of

---

[12] 450,500 as of 2023 (Department of Economic Planning and Statistics 2024).

international FinTech firms may be hindering the growth and potential of Brunei Darussalam's financial technology ecosystem.

Overall, Brunei Darussalam's financial technology landscape is witnessing significant growth, fueled by government initiatives and strategic frameworks designed to enhance digital payments and financial services. The Brunei Darussalam Central Bank has introduced several key policies, including the *Digital Payment Roadmap* and the creation of a dedicated FinTech office, aimed at driving the adoption of technology and improving financial literacy. However, despite these advancements, challenges persist, including low digital literacy levels among the population, limited vendor acceptance of eWallets, and a general reluctance to transition from traditional payment methods.

Additionally, ongoing flagship projects such as the *National Information Hub* and *Digital Payment Hub* have faced delays, contributing to Brunei Darussalam's relatively low ranking in the Global Innovation Index. The absence of significant international financial innovation also presents a challenge, as seen in the exit of major banks and the limited presence of foreign FinTech firms, and overcoming these barriers is crucial for building a more resilient and dynamic digital economy in Brunei Darussalam.

3.4 Future Scenarios and Drivers of Change

3.4.1 Conditional Correlations

As Brunei Darussalam continues to advance its digital transformation agenda, the future of financial inclusion will be increasingly shaped by the interaction between technology adoption, regulatory frameworks, and the broader socioeconomic environment. Understanding how these factors correlate with financial depth and access is crucial for forecasting potential developments, so this section explores future scenarios for Brunei Darussalam's financial inclusion landscape, focusing on key drivers such as internet penetration, income levels, and the depth of the financial sector. By examining these elements, we aim to identify potential pathways for the country's financial evolution, highlighting both the opportunities and challenges that may arise as Brunei Darussalam works towards achieving greater financial inclusivity.

Figure 3.1 illustrates the relationship between internet penetration, financial depth, and income levels (real GDP per capita in parentheses) across various countries, including Brunei Darussalam. The chart highlights the critical role of digital connectivity in driving financial inclusion and shows that higher internet penetration rates are generally linked to more developed financial sectors and higher income levels, suggesting that enhanced digital infrastructure can facilitate access to financial services and contribute to economic growth.

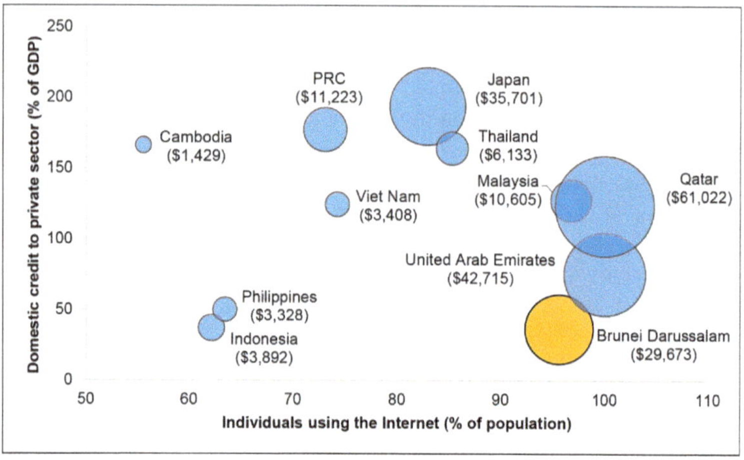

Fig. 3.1 Internet penetration, financial depth, and income levels (2021). Bubble size indicates GDP per capita. *Source* World Development Indicators, World Bank (various years)

Brunei Darussalam's high internet penetration rate of 95% positions it favorably compared to its regional peers, providing a solid foundation for expanding digital financial services. However, the country's financial depth, measured by domestic credit to the private sector as a percentage of GDP (35.71%), remains relatively low compared to countries with similar or even lower internet penetration rates. This highlights a significant gap between the availability of digital connectivity and the development of financial products and services capable of leveraging this infrastructure to drive greater financial inclusion.

Figure 3.1 also emphasizes that while internet access is a key enabler of digital financial services, it alone does not guarantee financial depth or inclusion. Factors such as regulatory frameworks, financial literacy, and the availability of digital financial products are equally crucial in translating digital access into meaningful financial inclusion. For Brunei Darussalam, bridging the gap between its high internet penetration rate and the underdeveloped financial sector will be vital to achieving a more inclusive digital economy.

Figure 3.2 offers a comparative overview of financial access relative to income levels (real GDP per capita in parentheses), focusing on various countries, including Brunei Darussalam. The data highlights the availability of financial services, such as access to bank branches and ATMs, and illustrates how this access correlates with income levels across different countries.

Brunei Darussalam's financial access indicators show a moderate level of infrastructure development, with 17.6 bank branches and 73.96 ATMs per 100,000 adults. These indicators are comparable to those of the countries in the sample. Generally speaking, there appears to be a correlation between higher numbers of bank branches and a greater presence of ATMs per 100,000 adults. However, the relationship between financial access and income levels is not always straightforward.

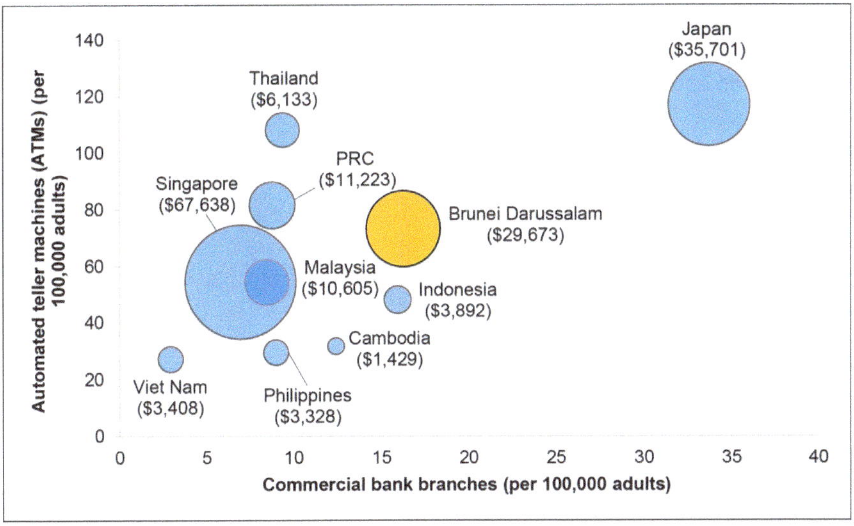

Fig. 3.2 Financial access and income levels (2021). Bubble size indicates GDP per capita. *Source* World Development Indicators, World Bank (various years)

For instance, Japan, with its relatively high income levels, also has a greater number of ATMs and physical bank branches. In contrast, Singapore, which has double the income level of Japan, has fewer ATMs and bank branches.

The data highlights Brunei Darussalam's unique position as a resource-rich, small-state economy, where the banking infrastructure has traditionally been adequate to meet the needs of its population; however, this reliance on physical banking infrastructure may present challenges as the demand for digital financial solutions continues to grow. This underscores the importance of aligning traditional banking access with broader efforts to promote digital inclusion and ensure that the country's financial sector evolves to meet the demands of a digital economy.

In the context of financial inclusion, the figures indicate that even economies with higher income levels still face challenges in translating income into financial accessibility, highlighting the need to focus not only on infrastructure but also on financial literacy, regulatory reform, and diversifying financial products to ensure that services are accessible to all segments of the population. To fully leverage the benefits of financial inclusion, Brunei Darussalam must bridge the gap between income levels and access to advanced financial services, particularly in rural and underserved areas. By strengthening both the financial and technological ecosystems, Brunei Darussalam can enhance its financial inclusion landscape, offering more comprehensive digital financial services to its citizens.

The findings from Figs. 3.1 and 3.2 highlight a clear disconnect between Brunei Darussalam's robust digital infrastructure and its relatively underdeveloped financial depth and access. Despite having one of the highest internet penetration rates in the region (95%), Brunei Darussalam's financial access indicators suggest a continued reliance on physical banking infrastructure. This indicates that while the country has established a strong foundation for digital financial services, there are still significant gaps in effectively utilizing this digital infrastructure to enhance financial inclusion.

Additionally, while Brunei Darussalam's banking infrastructure, as reflected in the number of bank branches and ATMs, is relatively well developed, the limited range of financial products, such as credit and capital market services, hampers broader financial inclusion. To close this gap, Brunei Darussalam will need to focus on developing more sophisticated financial products and enhancing financial literacy, especially in underserved areas. This will be key to ensuring that the country's digital advancements translate into genuine financial inclusion for all segments of society.

3.4.2 Futures Scenario

Figure 3.3 presents a 2x2 matrix that explores the relationship between financial inclusion and technology adoption, outlining four distinct future scenarios for Brunei Darussalam. The matrix is divided into two axes: one representing financial inclusion (high and low) and the other representing technology adoption (high and low). Each quadrant illustrates a different potential outcome for Brunei Darussalam's financial ecosystem, depending on how these two factors develop over time.

In the ideal scenario, where both financial inclusion and technological adoption are high, Brunei Darussalam would transition into a full Digital Financial Inclusion model. This vision involves the widespread adoption of digital financial services, such as mobile banking and eWallets, reaching even the most underserved populations. The synergy between advanced technology and broad financial inclusion would ensure seamless, efficient banking experiences for both urban and rural communities,

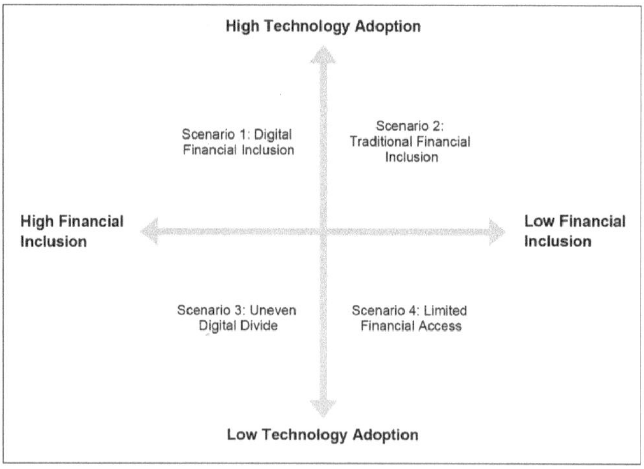

Fig. 3.3 2 × 2 Matrix: financial inclusion vs technology adoption. *Source* Authors' compilation

minimizing barriers to accessing financial services. In this scenario, FinTech innovations would be pivotal, with the banking sector fully embracing digital solutions to meet the diverse needs of Brunei Darussalam's population.

In the scenario where financial inclusion is high but technology adoption remains low, Brunei Darussalam would experience a more traditional form of financial inclusion. In this scenario, while access to financial services would be widespread, the reliance on traditional banking channels—such as physical branches and paper-based processes—would limit the efficiency and reach of the banking sector. Although financial access would improve, the lack of technological integration would hinder the overall modernization of the financial system, preventing Brunei Darussalam from fully capitalizing on the advantages of digital transformation. This scenario would result in a slower, less dynamic financial ecosystem.

A more concerning scenario arises when technology adoption is high but financial inclusion remains low, creating an uneven digital divide. In this case, advanced financial technologies are available, but they fail to reach large segments of the population due to barriers such as low digital literacy, inadequate infrastructure in rural areas, and socioeconomic challenges. This results in a situation where only a tech-savvy minority can access and benefit from these innovations, while others are left behind, widening the gap between different demographic groups and potentially exacerbating existing inequalities.

The least favorable outcome occurs when both financial inclusion and technology adoption are low, leading to a limited financial access scenario. In this case, Brunei Darussalam's financial sector remains largely stagnant, relying on traditional banking methods with limited innovation and restricted access to financial services. Without significant advancements in either technology or inclusion, the country's ability to serve underserved populations remains constrained, hindering overall economic growth and financial stability.

The 2x2 matrix underscores the critical role that both technology and inclusive financial strategies play in shaping Brunei Darussalam's financial future. For Brunei Darussalam to achieve meaningful financial inclusion, efforts must be focused not only on expanding access to financial services but also on ensuring that technological advancements are effectively integrated and accessible to all segments of the population.

3.4.3 Descriptive Analysis

Figure 3.4 presents a historical snapshot of the growth of ATMs and bank branches in Brunei Darussalam, highlighting the evolution of physical financial infrastructure. This figure brings to light a key trade-off that Brunei Darussalam must navigate as it seeks to enhance financial inclusion through both traditional and digital means. While the initial steady increase in the number of ATMs and bank branches prior to 2010 demonstrates the country's commitment to expanding physical access to financial services, there seems to be a declining trend in recent years. This raises the

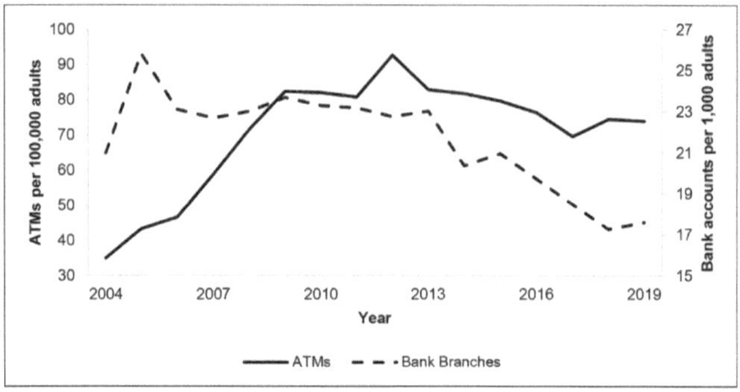

Fig. 3.4 Evolution of ATMs and bank branches in Brunei Darussalam. *Source* World Development Indicators, World Bank

question of sustainability in the face of digital financial adoption as the country must ensure that all users can utilize digital financial services in the long run; otherwise, there is a strong risk of falling into the scenario of an uneven digital divide.

The trade-off centers on the allocation of resources between maintaining and expanding physical banking infrastructure versus investing in digital financial technologies. On the one hand, the continued expansion of ATMs and bank branches serves to improve accessibility, particularly for populations in rural areas or those who may not be digitally literate. On the other hand, however, with the rise of digital financial services, such as mobile banking and eWallets, there is a potential overlap where physical infrastructure may become less critical over time, especially for urban and tech-savvy populations. As digital solutions become more prevalent, the need for access to physical banking could decline, raising the question of whether ongoing investments in traditional infrastructure are the most efficient use of resources.

This trade-off becomes even more pronounced when considering the relatively high cost of maintaining physical banking infrastructure compared to the lower-cost scalability of digital platforms. Brunei Darussalam must weigh the benefits of providing tangible, location-based services through ATMs and bank branches against the growing demand for digital financial solutions, which can be accessed remotely by a broader population. Focusing too heavily on either strategy may leave certain segments of the population underserved: A rapid shift to digital services could alienate those without access to technology, while overinvestment in physical infrastructure could limit the country's ability to fully embrace digital financial inclusion.

Figure 3.5 exhibits the overall value of digital transactions by digital commerce, remittances, and mobile POS payments, including projections by Statista (2024). On a positive note, the decline in physical bank infrastructure may be potentially compensated by Brunei Darussalam's digital transaction landscape, which has experienced a notable transformation, particularly during the post-COVID-19 era. The total digital transaction value has shown a significant upward trajectory, highlighting the broader adoption of digital commerce.

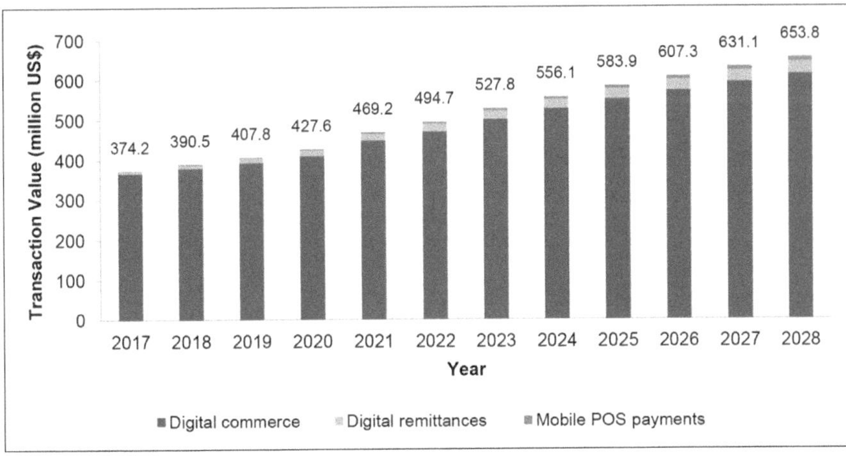

Fig. 3.5 Digital transaction value by segment. *Source* Statista Research Department, Statista (2024)

It can also be seen that from 2020 to 2023, digital transactions grew steadily, which can be attributed to the catalyzing effect of the pandemic on digital payment solutions and the adoption of contactless commerce. This also provides some evidence of the shift in consumer preferences and habits towards the digital landscape, which coincides with the increased availability of digital payment options. This implies that digital financial payment tools are becoming more embedded in everyday financial activities at the macro level.

However, Fig. 3.6 highlights a contrasting narrative at the micro level, where the average transaction value per user demonstrates a declining trend despite the overall growth in user numbers and the total transaction value. In fact, it can be seen that digital commerce is decreasing steadily over time and is projected to continue this declining trend, with the COVID-19 pandemic meaning that the year from 2020 to 2021 was the only period in which the average value per user was consistent. In addition, average digital remittances per user were rising prior to the pandemic, and this is expected to decline and level off after 2025. On a positive note, mobile POS payment systems are rising steadily, which may be attributed to the nature of the financial products in Brunei Darussalam, which is focused on mobile-based applications.

Nonetheless, the overall decline in digital commerce and remittances per user suggests there is variability in user engagement, which implies that some individuals are conducting fewer or lower-value transactions. This trend points to an uneven utilization of digital financial services among users, indicating that while digital payment platforms may be reaching more people, their actual usage patterns vary significantly. This raises the question of the depth of engagement and whether all segments of the population are benefitting equally from the digital transition and the reduction in physical financial presence.

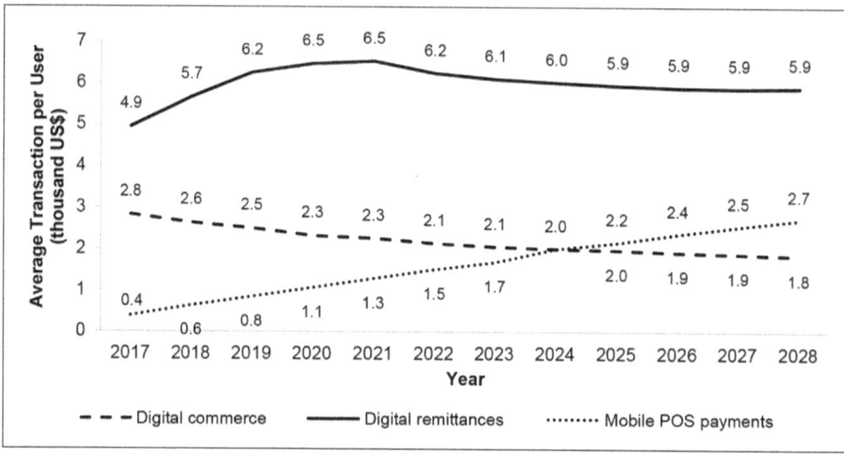

Fig. 3.6 Average digital transaction value by segment. *Source* Statista Research Department, Statista (2024)

This issue is concerning as the technological infrastructure in Brunei Darussalam has advanced significantly. Figure 3.7 presents the previous and projected 4G network coverage in Brunei Darussalam, while Fig. 3.8 shows the previous and projected number of secure internet servers in the country. The general trend shows that technological infrastructure has improved and this positive tendency is projected to continue; however, the declining average digital transaction value per user, shown in Fig. 3.6, stands in stark contrast to this improvement.

In fact, Fig. 3.7 implies that the whole of Brunei Darussalam has virtually full 4G network coverage and this was complemented by an average speed in 2024 of

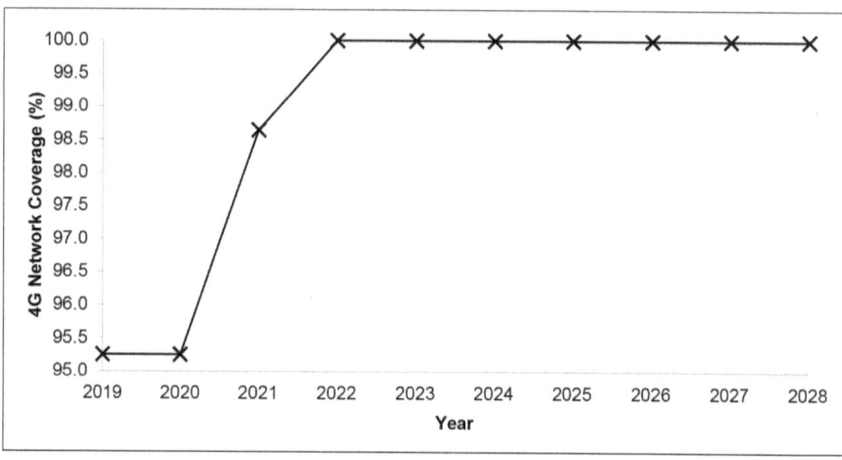

Fig. 3.7 4G network coverage. *Source* Statista Research Department, Statista (2024)

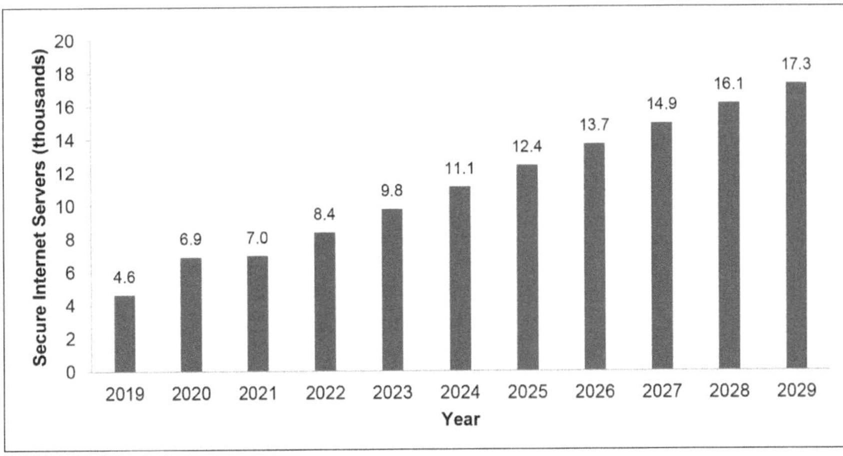

Fig. 3.8 Secure internet servers. *Source* Statista Research Department, Statista (2024)

36 Mbps, which ensures faster and more reliable internet access for both households and businesses alike. In parallel, Fig. 3.8 demonstrates a steady rise in the number of secure internet servers; this emphasizes Brunei Darussalam's efforts to strengthen its digital security framework, with a view to ensuring safe online financial activities. The growth in secure internet infrastructure aligns with broader efforts to encourage digital adoption by mitigating security concerns among users.

However, these infrastructure advancements contrast sharply with the micro-level trend of declining average digital transaction values. Despite improved connectivity and security, the lower transaction value per user indicates disparities in the extent to which individuals and businesses are leveraging these technological improvements, and this discrepancy suggests that while the digital ecosystem has become more robust, the actual usage patterns may not fully reflect the potential offered by these advancements in Brunei Darussalam's technological infrastructure.

Figure 3.9 sheds light on a potential factor contributing to the declining average digital transaction value per user, even amidst significant infrastructure advancements. The data reveal a downward trend in spending on ICT equipment, particularly in the post-COVID-19 period. After peaking in 2022, expenditure on ICT equipment has declined and is expected to level off. This reduction in spending of nearly 50% from 2022 to 2023 suggests a shift in consumer habits and preferences, with less emphasis on upgrading or acquiring digital devices and equipment.

Furthermore, this decline in spending may reflect a normalization of consumption patterns following the pandemic-driven surge in digital adoption. During the pandemic, there was a heightened need for ICT equipment to support remote work, online education, and digital commerce. However, as these demands have stabilized, investment in new equipment appears to have diminished, potentially limiting the ability of some users to fully leverage the enhanced infrastructure even as digital financial products continue to develop in Brunei Darussalam. While the reduced

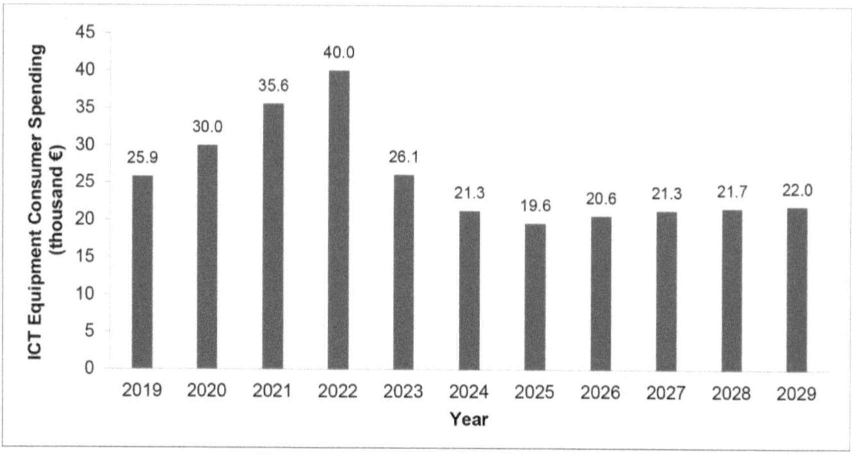

Fig. 3.9 ICT equipment consumer spending. *Source* Statista Research Department, Statista (2024)

spending could also indicate financial constraints or a saturation of device ownership among certain segments of the population, it could potentially imply and contribute to the uneven adoption and usage patterns of digital financial services.

Figure 3.10 provides further insight into the declining average transaction value per user by highlighting disparities in internet access among households in Brunei Darussalam. The data show that while urban areas maintain nearly universal internet connectivity, rural areas, particularly in districts such as Temburong, have significantly lower access levels. Overall, in 2023, internet penetration in households was generally below 70% and this gap was potentially larger in rural areas, suggesting that a substantial proportion of the population continues to face barriers in accessing digital financial platforms.

The lack of universal internet access in households may explain why, despite advancements in infrastructure, many users have reverted to physical transactions post-COVID. During the pandemic, internet use surged as consumers adapted to remote work and e-commerce; however, the unequal distribution of internet access likely limited the ability of rural populations to sustain digital engagement as physical services reopened. This disparity may also highlight the broader challenge of ensuring that technological improvements translate into equitable access across all demographic and geographic segments.

The stagnation in the projected household internet access creates an environment where digital financial services can potentially remain underutilized in certain areas, contributing to the observed decline in transaction values. For households that are unable to rely consistently on digital connectivity, physical banking and cash-based transactions become more viable alternatives, further illustrating the uneven digital adoption across Brunei Darussalam.

Finally, Fig. 3.11 illustrates the state of banking usage in Brunei Darussalam, revealing that bank account penetration is relatively low at around 65.7% as of 2024.

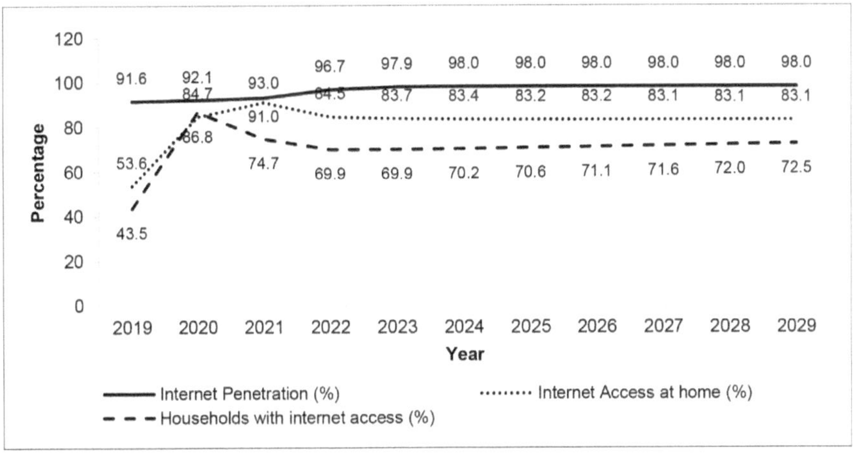

Fig. 3.10 Internet penetration breakdown. *Source* Statista Research Department, Statista (2024)

Even more concerning is the fact that online banking penetration is lower at 35.9% while debit card penetration is at 51.1%. This gap highlights a persistent reliance on traditional banking methods among a substantial proportion of the population, which restricts the full potential of digital financial services. While the overall trend for online banking penetration is projected to increase, the adoption rate is relatively low compared to other countries in Southeast Asia, implying that there is a limited subset of users who are deeply integrated into the digital financial ecosystem.

This becomes a bigger concern as the reliance of most FinTech products on bank accounts and associated debit or credit cards for functionality compounds this issue (see Table 3.4). In Brunei Darussalam, most digital payment services, such as mobile

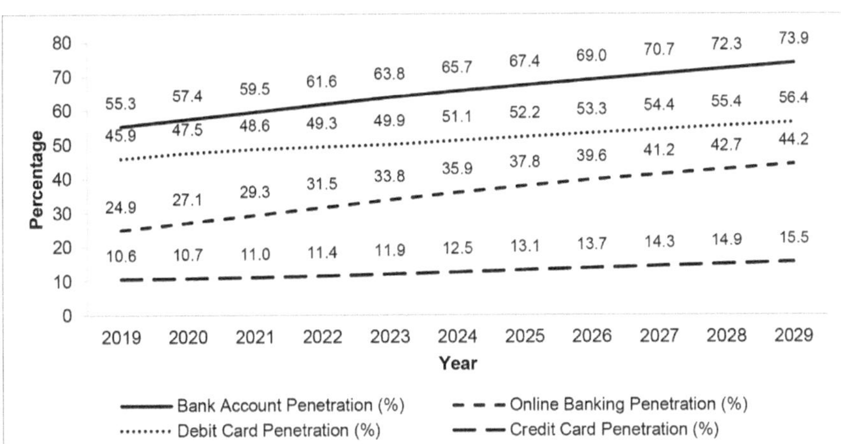

Fig. 3.11 Banking usage breakdown. *Source* Statista Research Department, Statista (2024)

wallets and QR code-based payment platforms, require users to link their accounts to existing banking infrastructure. This creates an inherent barrier for individuals without access to bank cards, who remain a notable proportion of the population, particularly in rural and lower-income segments. As a result, these individuals are effectively excluded from the benefits of digital financial innovations, reinforcing the disparity in access and utilization.

There is also a large population group that remains unbanked, and the digital divide is particularly pronounced in this group, as they are entirely excluded from participating in FinTech platforms that necessitate a formal banking relationship. This exclusion not only limits their ability to transact digitally but also restricts their access to the broader benefits of financial inclusion, such as savings products, credit facilities, and remittances services.

The overreliance on bank-linked digital platforms in Brunei Darussalam further exacerbates these challenges. Unlike other markets where mobile money services or alternative financial products offer nonbank-linked solutions, Brunei Darussalam's digital financial landscape remains tightly coupled to its traditional banking sector. This dependency restricts the scalability of FinTech solutions, as their reach is inherently bounded by the penetration of bank accounts and cards, which are unequally distributed across the population. This highlights a critical limitation in the adoption of digital financial services in Brunei Darussalam, where structural dependencies on traditional banking hinder the potential for broader inclusion.

3.4.3.1 A Digital Landscape with Limited Adoption

A growing digital landscape with limited adoption paints a complex picture of Brunei Darussalam's financial ecosystem, as advancements in digital infrastructure and payment platforms remain counterbalanced by uneven access and engagement. The observed decline in the average digital transaction value per user, despite the overall growth in transaction numbers, underscores the financial environment in Brunei Darussalam. As the country transitions towards digital financial services, it must manage the trade-off between maintaining physical banking infrastructure and scaling up digital platforms, ensuring that all segments of society benefit equally from these changes.

Brunei Darussalam's position within the "uneven digital divide" quadrant of Fig. 3.3 reflects its current standing, where technology adoption is high but financial inclusion remains moderate. While digital payment systems and platforms like mobile banking and QR-based payment services have gained traction, their reach is often limited to urban and tech-savvy populations. Barriers such as low financial literacy, limited access to banking infrastructure in rural areas, and disparities in access to technology further exacerbate these challenges, leaving large portions of the population unable to participate fully in the digital financial ecosystem.

Despite Brunei Darussalam's strong digital infrastructure—evident in widespread 4G coverage, increasing broadband speeds, and a robust network of secure servers—digital transaction engagement remains fragmented. We show that variability in transaction values, declining spending on ICT equipment, and limited internet penetration in certain areas reveal significant gaps in digital accessibility. These issues highlight the need for foundational changes to ensure that the nation's digital transformation does not leave certain populations behind.

Additionally, we find a systemic limitation tied to banking usage in Brunei Darussalam. With bank account penetration at just 65.7%, and online banking usage and debit card ownership even lower, the reliance on bank-linked digital platforms creates barriers to widespread adoption. FinTech solutions in Brunei Darussalam, which are heavily reliant on existing banking infrastructure, inherently exclude individuals without formal banking relationships, thereby further deepening the divide. This overdependence on traditional banking limits the scalability and inclusivity of digital solutions, leaving significant portions of the population—particularly the unbanked and rural residents—without access to digital financial innovations.

Ultimately, while Brunei Darussalam's digital landscape continues to evolve, its limited adoption underscores the importance of addressing structural challenges. The gaps in financial literacy, internet access, and banking penetration reveal a segmented financial ecosystem, where technological advancements and digital platforms serve only a subset of the population. To achieve a more inclusive digital financial system, Brunei Darussalam must overcome these barriers and foster a more equitable distribution of digital opportunities. Thus, a balanced approach is required, and Brunei Darussalam will need to assess which populations still rely heavily on physical banking and provide for their needs, while simultaneously scaling up digital financial platforms to meet the growing demand for technological solutions.

3.4.4 Drivers of Change

To transition Brunei Darussalam towards Scenario 1—where both financial inclusion and technological adoption are high—several key drivers of change must be addressed. These drivers revolve around enhancing infrastructure, improving financial literacy, regulatory innovation, and fostering public-private partnerships. A summary of these drivers is provided in Table 3.5.

3.4.4.1 Enhanced Digital Infrastructure

Enhanced digital infrastructure is a critical driver for advancing Brunei Darussalam's digital financial ecosystem, with significant progress already evident in network coverage, internet speeds, and security. As shown in Fig. 3.7, Brunei Darussalam boasts near-universal 4G coverage, complemented by rising broadband speeds enabling seamless access to digital financial services. Additionally, the number of

Table 3.5 Drivers of change

Driver of change	Description
Enhanced digital infrastructure	Expand mobile and broadband connectivity, especially in rural and underserved areas, to ensure wider access to digital financial services
Improved financial literacy	Increase education and awareness on using digital financial products, targeting less tech-savvy populations to boost adoption
Regulatory support and innovation	Create a favorable regulatory environment that encourages FinTech innovation while ensuring consumer protection and lowering costs
Public-private sector collaboration	Foster collaboration between government, banks, FinTechs, and telecom providers to develop integrated, user-friendly digital solutions
Building trust in digital financial systems	Implement strong cybersecurity and data protection measures to build trust and ensure the safety and reliability of digital transactions

Source Authors' compilation

secure internet servers has grown steadily over time (Fig. 3.8), ensuring safer environments for online transactions and fostering user trust. However, disparities in household internet penetration, potentially in remote regions like Temburong, reveal gaps that limit the accessibility of these advancements. These areas are also where physical banking infrastructure is potentially limited.

3.4.4.2 Improved Financial Literacy

Improved financial literacy is another key driver of change in advancing digital financial inclusion in Brunei Darussalam. While the nation has made significant progress in building its digital infrastructure, its effectiveness is constrained by varying levels of understanding and adoption among the population. Figure 3.6, for instance, highlights a decline in the average transaction value per user, suggesting uneven utilization of digital financial services. This trend may be partially attributed to limited awareness or understanding of how to effectively use digital platforms, particularly among rural populations or less tech-savvy individuals (Sait et al. 2024).

Furthermore, Fig. 3.11 shows that a low percentage of bank account holders actively engage in online banking, indicating a significant gap between access and actual usage. This disparity points to the importance of financial education programs that not only promote digital tools but also build confidence and trust in using them. Such initiatives are crucial for bridging knowledge gaps and empowering individuals to transition from traditional banking methods to digital platforms.

3.4.4.3 Regulatory Support and Innovation

Third, regulatory support and innovation are critical drivers. The government and the Brunei Darussalam Central Bank must continue to create a favorable regulatory environment that encourages innovation in the financial sector while ensuring consumer protection. Expanding initiatives like the FinTech Regulatory Sandbox, which allows new digital financial products to be tested in a controlled environment, can help foster innovation. In addition, regulatory reforms that reduce the costs of digital transactions and remittances will be crucial for driving widespread use of digital payment systems.

Despite these advancements, regulatory gaps remain a challenge. Figure 3.11 and Table 3.4 reveal the overreliance of FinTech products on bank accounts and cards, which excludes unbanked populations from accessing digital financial services. To address this, regulatory frameworks must focus on fostering inclusive financial solutions, such as enabling nonbank-linked digital wallets and reducing transaction costs for underserved communities.

3.4.4.4 Public-Private Sector Collaboration

Fourth, collaboration between the public and private sectors is necessary to build a sustainable digital financial ecosystem. Government-driven initiatives like the Digital Economy Masterplan, which is aimed at creating a Smart Nation, will need to be complemented by private sector innovation. Banks, FinTech firms, and telecom providers must work together to develop integrated, user-friendly digital financial solutions that cater to the needs of different population segments, including MSMEs. In addition, disparities in digital engagement, as shown by the declining average transaction value per user in Fig. 3.6, point to areas where collaboration can be strengthened. For instance, partnerships can focus on extending internet connectivity to underserved households (Fig. 3.10) or developing more inclusive financial tools for the unbanked population (Fig. 3.11).

3.4.4.5 Building Trust in Digital Financial Systems

Finally, building trust in digital financial systems is vital for widespread adoption. As Fig. 3.8 demonstrates, Brunei Darussalam has invested significantly in enhancing digital security infrastructure, with the number of secure internet servers increasing over the last few years. These advancements are critical for addressing concerns around data protection and transaction safety, particularly as digital payment platforms become more prevalent. However, the declining average transaction value per user (Fig. 3.6) suggests that trust and confidence in using digital financial services may still be lacking among certain segments of the population, especially during the post-COVID-19 era.

This issue is compounded by low online banking penetration rates, as highlighted in Fig. 3.11, where only 35.9% of account holders actively use online banking services. Ensuring the reliability and security of digital platforms through robust cybersecurity measures and transparent practices is key to overcoming these barriers. Additionally, public awareness campaigns and consumer education initiatives can help alleviate concerns over fraud and misuse, thus fostering greater confidence in digital financial systems.

By addressing these drivers, Brunei Darussalam can move towards a future where financial inclusion and technology adoption are both high, ensuring that digital financial services are accessible, trusted, and beneficial for all segments of society.

3.5 Conclusion and Recommendations

Brunei Darussalam has made considerable progress in developing its digital infrastructure, particularly through the expansion of mobile and internet connectivity, positioning itself as a leader in these areas within the ASEAN region. However, financial inclusion remains moderate, with a significant gap between technological capabilities, financial depth, banking usage, and digital transactions. As such, Brunei Darussalam experiences an uneven digital divide in relation to digital financial inclusion. There are several recommendations for Brunei Darussalam and other economies facing the same scenario:

1. **Strengthen Digital Infrastructure**
   a. Expand *reliable internet connectivity*, particularly in rural and underserved households.
   b. Address *disparities in households' internet penetration* to promote equitable access to digital financial services.
2. **Enhance Financial Literacy**
   a. Develop *national targeted financial literacy programs* to empower individuals to use digital tools more confidently.
   b. Integrate *digital financial education* into school curriculums and community outreach programs to build long-term awareness and confidence.
3. **Create an Adaptive Regulatory Framework**
   a. Encourage *private-led nonbank financial solutions* to extend services to unbanked populations.
   b. Strengthen *regulations* on cybersecurity, fraud prevention, and data privacy.
4. **Foster Public-Private Collaborations**
   a. Promote *partnerships* between government, financial institutions, and tech companies to drive FinTech adoption.

  b. Provide *incentives* for financial service providers to extend digital products to underserved markets.

5. **Address Data Gaps and Support Research**
  a. *Improve data collection* by collaborating with financial institutions and regulatory bodies to gather insights into FinTech usage, adoption rates, and consumer satisfaction.
  b. *Facilitate access to anonymized financial literacy* data to better understand barriers to digital financial inclusion.
  c. *Support targeted research* into the socioeconomic factors affecting technology adoption, informing future policy design.

However, this study is not without limitations. While it focuses on the broader financial landscape, it does not fully explore the specific socioeconomic barriers that might impede technology adoption in Brunei Darussalam. Our findings suggest that digital financial inclusion is closely tied to increasing financial transactions on digital channels, which is primarily focused on financial depth. However, the study overlooks the crucial role of financial literacy among the population, which could serve as a significant barrier to the usage and acceptance of FinTech products. Addressing this gap would require further research into the socioeconomic factors that influence digital adoption and the development of targeted educational initiatives to enhance financial literacy.

Moreover, there is a lack of data on the market penetration rates of specific FinTech products, as well as their usage frequency and user satisfaction. To the best of our knowledge, the study by Sait et al. (2024) is the only one that briefly addresses this area. Therefore, future research could further explore consumer sentiment towards FinTech products in Brunei Darussalam, offering valuable insights into user preferences, challenges, and expectations. Additionally, comparative studies examining similar economies that are experiencing an uneven digital divide could provide a deeper understanding of whether digital financial access alone is sufficient to foster digital financial inclusion. Future research should also identify which barriers—such as digital literacy, infrastructure limitations, or socioeconomic factors—are most significant in hindering the broader adoption of digital financial services in Brunei Darussalam and other similar markets.

References

AMRO. 2023. *AMRO annual consultation report Brunei Darussalam—2023*. Singapore: ASEAN+3 Macroeconomic Research Office (AMRO).

Arine, M. A., H. A. Zain, and N. H. Rashid. 2020. Advancing towards a cashless society: The acceptance of eWallet in Brunei Darussalam. In *Financial technology and disruptive innovation in ASEAN*, edited by M. Anshari, M. Almunawar, and M. Masri, 203–215. Hershey, PA: IGI Global Scientific Publishing. https://doi.org/10.4018/978-1-5225-9183-2.ch011.

Beck, T., A. Demirgüç-Kunt, and P. Honohan. 2009. Access to financial services: Measurement, impact, and policies. *World Bank Research Observer* 24 (1): 119–145. https://doi.org/10.1093/wbro/lkn008.

Bhattacharyay, B., and M. Bhattacharyay. 2022. Financial sector development in Brunei Darussalam: Depth, access, and efficiency: A comparative analysis. CESifo Working Papers 9960. https://doi.org/10.2139/ssrn.4235475.

Brunei Darussalam Central Bank. 2016. Financial sector blueprint (2016–2025). Available from https://www.bdcb.gov.bn/financial-sector-development/financial-sector-blueprint. [Accessed 08 Oct 2025].

Brunei Darussalam Central Bank. 2019. *Digital payment roadmap for Brunei Darussalam 2019–2025*. Bandar Seri Begawan: Brunei Darussalam Central Bank.

Brunei Darussalam Central Bank. 2020. *The state of FinTech in Brunei Darussalam year 2020*. Bandar Seri Begawan: Brunei Darussalam Central Bank.

Brunei Darussalam Central Bank. 2023. *2023 Annual report*. Bandar Seri Begawan: Brunei Darussalam Central Bank.

Centre for Strategic and Policy Studies. 2024. Brunei economic outlook. Available from http://www.csps.org.bn/publications/economic-outlook/. [Accessed 08 Oct 2025].

Demirgüç-Kunt, A., and L. Klapper. 2013. Measuring financial inclusion: Explaining variation in use of financial services across and within countries. *Brookings Papers on Economic Activity* 340 (SPRING 2013): 279–321. https://doi.org/10.1353/eca.2013.0002.

Department of Economic Planning and Statistics. 2024. *Population estimates 2024*. Bandar Seri Begawan: Ministry of Finance and Economy.

Dev, M. S. 2006. Financial inclusion issues and challenges. *Economic and Political Weekly* 41 (41): 4310–4313. https://www.jstor.org/stable/4418799.

Digital Brunei. n.d. Initiatives. Digital Brunei. Available from https://digitalbrunei.bn/initiatives/.

Haini, H., and P. Wei Loon. 2022. Information communication technologies, globalisation and growth: Evidence from the ASEAN economies. *Economic Papers: A Journal of Applied Economics and Policy* 41 (1): 34–53. https://doi.org/10.1111/1759-3441.12332.

Hawkins, P. 2006. *Financial access and financial stability*. London: BIS and HM Treasury.

International Monetary Fund. 2023. Brunei Darussalam: selected issues. IMF Country Report No. 23/347. https://doi.org/10.5089/9781513596173.002.

Iqbal, B. A., and S. Sami. 2017. Role of banks in financial inclusion in India. *Contaduria y Administracion* 62 (2): 644–656. https://doi.org/10.1016/j.cya.2017.01.007.

Johnson, S., and S. Arnold. 2012. Inclusive financial markets: Is transformation under way in Kenya? *Development Policy Review* 30 (6): 719–748. https://doi.org/10.1111/j.1467-7679.2012.00596.x.

José, M., and R. García. 2016. Can financial inclusion and financial stability go hand in hand? *Economic Issues* 21 (2): 81–103.

Kapoor, A. 2014. Financial inclusion and the future of the Indian economy. *Futures* 56 (2014): 35–42.

Mader, P. 2018. Contesting financial inclusion. *Development and Change* 49 (2): 461–483. https://doi.org/10.1111/dech.12368.

Mahadeva, M. 2011. Poverty of access to financial services and its alleviation: Some lessons to India from the United Kingdom. *Journal of Asian Public Policy* 4 (2): 187–200. https://doi.org/10.1080/17516234.2011.595911.

Morgan, P. J., and V. Pontines. 2014. Financial stability and financial inclusion. ADBI Working Paper No. 488, 75. Tokyo, Japan: Asian Development Bank Institute.

Ozili, P. K. 2020. Theories of financial inclusion. *Uncertainty and Challenges in Contemporary Economic Behaviour* 89–115. https://doi.org/10.1108/978-1-80043-095-220201008.

Ozili, P. K. 2021. Financial inclusion research around the world: A review. *Forum for Social Economics* 50 (4): 457–479. https://doi.org/10.1080/07360932.2020.1715238.

Pg Hj Md Salleh, P. M. H. A., and R. Baha. 2020. Retirement concerns and financial literacy in Brunei. *International Journal of Sociology and Social Policy* 40 (3–4): 342–365. https://doi.org/10.1108/IJSSP-09-2019-0193.

Sait, M. A., M. A. Ali, M. N. Almunawar, and H. M. Haji Masri. 2024. Understanding factors to digital wallet discontinuance intention among past users: An exploratory study. *Journal of Science and Technology Policy Management.* https://doi.org/10.1108/JSTPM-01-2024-0005.

Sarma, M., and J. Pais. 2011. Financial inclusion and development. *Journal of International Development* 23:613–628. https://doi.org/10.1002/jid.1698.

Statista. 2024. FinTech—Brunei Darussalam. Statista Research Department. Available from https://www.statista.com/outlook/dmo/fintech/brunei-darussalam.

The Star. 2024, July 15. Brunei Sultan announces plans to set up digital payment hub. *The Star.* Available from https://www.thestar.com.my/aseanplus/aseanplus-news/2024/07/15/brunei-sultan-announces-plans-set-up-digital-payment-hub.

World Bank. 2022, September 13. Financial inclusion overview. Available from https://www.worldbank.org/en/topic/financialinclusion/overview. [Accessed 15 Sept 2025].

World Bank. various years. World development indicators. Available from http://databank.worldbank.org/data/reports.aspx?source=world-development-indicators. [Accessed 20 Sept 2025].

Yap, T. I., and A. D. Borhan. 2021. Implications of the digital economy on policy-making. *Journal of Business and Economic Analysis* 4 (2): 157–176. https://doi.org/10.1142/s2737566821500092.

Chapter 4
Financial Inclusion, Fintech, and Banking Stability in Asia and Pacific Economies

Niraj Koirala

Abstract This paper examines the interplay between financial inclusion and FinTech in shaping banking stability, with a focus on Asia Pacific Economies. Using an unbalanced panel from 21 countries from 2000 to 2021, we find that financial inclusion enhances banking stability in the region. However, we find that FinTech adoption affects banking stability adversely perhaps due to regulatory gaps which might be associated with possible rapid expansion of credits. Furthermore, we find that FinTech is likely to moderate the stabilizing effects of financial inclusion, potentially over-leveraging and borrower repayment risks. In addition to these main variables, the paper also finds that variables like regulatory practices, foreign ownership in the banking sector, and monetary policy also play significant roles in influencing banking sector stability in the region. Finally, we find that operational efficiency and risk management emerge as critical channels through which financial inclusion and FinTech impact stability. These findings highlight the empirical relevance of FinTech adoption for policy makers in Asia Pacific while formulating plans to enhance banking sector stability.

JEL Classification Codes E44 · G28

Keywords Financial access · FinTech · Banking stability · Asia Pacific

4.1 Introduction

FinTech and financial inclusion have emerged as transformative forces in the financial sector, offering new avenues for improving financial stability, especially in emerging economies. Financial inclusion expands access to financial services, enabling households and businesses to participate in the formal financial system, and this has been shown to diversify bank portfolios, reduce credit concentration risks, and foster

N. Koirala (✉)
California State University, Los Angeles, CA, USA

R. Gulati et al. (eds.), *Emerging Challenges in Banking in Asia and the Pacific*, Economics, Law, and Institutions in Asia Pacific,
https://doi.org/10.1007/978-981-92-2144-8_4

resilience during economic downturns (Demirgüç-Kunt and Klapper 2013). At the same time, FinTech innovations are revolutionizing how these services are delivered, improving efficiency and accessibility, and through technologies like mobile banking, peer-to-peer lending, and digital payments (Carbo-Valverde et al. 2021). However, as these forces reshape financial ecosystems, their combined impact on financial stability remains a topic of active debate.

Recent studies have highlighted both the opportunities and challenges presented by FinTech and financial inclusion. While financial inclusion enhances financial stability by fostering operational efficiency and reducing risks through greater borrower diversity (Beck et al. 2007), its effectiveness depends heavily on robust risk management practices. Similarly, FinTech offers tools for better credit assessment and monitoring (Ozili 2018), thus influencing banking stability positively (see, for example, Yudaruddin et al. 2023). However, FinTech has also been described as a double-edged sword that can lead to unintended consequences such as rapid credit expansion, and over-leveraging, ultimately affecting banking stability in the absence of adequate regulatory frameworks (Buchak et al. 2018; Nguyen and Dang 2022; Chinoda and Kapingura 2024).

Notwithstanding the above-mentioned advances in the literature on the topic, significant gaps remain. While the existing literature, as mentioned above, explores the effect of financial inclusion and FinTech on banking stability, the primary focus has been on developed Western economies, and fewer studies have investigated the combined effects in the context of economies in the Asia-Pacific region. Although there have been some recent advancements in the context of the Asia-Pacific (see, for example, Loo 2019; ADB 2023; Basnayake et al. 2024; Vuković et al. 2024), these papers focus too much on financial inclusion and the scope of FinTech rather than on financial stability in the region. In addition, these papers also give little attention to the channel through which FinTech and financial inclusion influence financial stability. Although the region is home to some of the fastest-growing FinTech markets globally, with economies like the People's Republic of China (PRC), India, and Indonesia leading the way in terms of mobile payments and digital banking, these economies are also vulnerable to external shocks, making financial sector stability a major concern. This paper attempts to allay this worry by focusing on how FinTech-driven financial inclusion affects financial stability in the region. Moreover, the paper aims to fill the gap in the literature by investigating the channels through which FinTech affects the role of financial inclusion in promoting financial stability. Using panel data from emerging economies in Asia, we focus on key banking indicators such as the Z-score to analyze the relationship.

This paper makes significant contributions to the literature on financial inclusion, FinTech, and financial stability. First, it examines the synergies between FinTech and financial inclusion, offering insights into how these forces interact to influence financial stability. While prior studies have analyzed their individual effects, this paper uniquely focuses on their combined impact, highlighting the complementary relationship between financial inclusion and FinTech through operational efficiency and risk management channels. Second, by exploring these two channels—operational efficiency (proxied by the cost-to-income ratio) and risk management (proxied by the nonperforming loan ratio)—the paper enables a detailed understanding of the mechanisms through which FinTech and financial inclusion affect banking stability. Third, the study contributes to regional-specific research by focusing on emerging economies in Asia, where rapid FinTech adoption and significant financial inclusion efforts coexist with diverse financial development levels. This regional focus offers insights that are not only relevant to Asia but also to other emerging markets facing similar challenges. Finally, the findings of this paper carry practical policy implications, emphasizing the need for balanced strategies that harness the synergies between FinTech and financial inclusion while mitigating risks. By highlighting the importance of robust regulatory frameworks, the paper provides actionable recommendations for policymakers aiming to enhance financial stability in an era of rapid technological advancements.

The paper presents the following major findings. First, it reports that there is a positive relationship between financial inclusion and banking stability. This suggests that financial inclusion improves stability, perhaps by increasing the customer base, which diversifies credit portfolios and enhances funding stability through greater access to retail deposits. Second, we find that FinTech is likely to decrease financial stability in Asia and the Pacific. This could be due to a lack of strong regulatory practices for overseeing rapidly expanding FinTech operations or the potential risks associated with the rapid increase in credit issuance without adequate risk assessment.

Third, FinTech is likely to put negative pressure on the positive effects of financial inclusion on banking stability. This may be because the rapid adoption of FinTech, while enhancing credit accessibility, can weaken borrower repayment discipline and increase overleveraging, which reduces the stabilizing benefits of financial inclusion.

Fourth, apart from FinTech and financial inclusion, the paper finds that variables such as foreign bank assets (positively), capitalization (positively), and monetary policy rates (negatively) are also likely to influence banking stability. Foreign bank assets contribute positively to stability by diversifying risk exposure and introducing higher regulatory standards, and higher bank capitalization provides a buffer against potential losses, thereby improving resilience. Conversely, higher monetary policy rates affect stability negatively by increasing borrowing costs, reducing loan demand, and potentially increasing default rates.

Fifth, we use an instrumental variable (IV) method, utilizing proxies such as ICT penetration and literacy rates for financial inclusion, to address endogeneity concerns. The findings from the IV method reaffirm the robustness of the benchmark findings.

Lastly, the paper identifies two key channels—operational efficiency and risk management—through which FinTech and financial inclusion affect the banking sector. Financial inclusion improves operational efficiency by reducing costs and increasing service outreach, while FinTech strengthens risk management by enhancing credit assessment and monitoring. However, the interaction between these channels also highlights potential trade-offs, as FinTech is likely to introduce inefficiencies in the short term.

The paper proceeds as follows: In Sect. 4.2, we explain data and methodology; Sect. 4.3 reports the results; and Sect. 4.4 concludes the paper with a discussion.

4.2 Data and Methodology

4.2.1 Data and Variables

This subsection explains the data and variables used in the analysis. We collect variables related to the banking sector and macroeconomy for 21 economies from the Asia-Pacific region, namely: Hong Kong, China; the PRC; Japan; the Republic of Korea; Singapore; Malaysia; Mongolia; Viet Nam; Thailand; Brunei Darussalam; Bangladesh; India; Fiji; Nepal; Bhutan; Maldives; the Lao PDR; the Philippines; Cambodia; Myanmar; and Timor-Leste. The variables, which are explained below, are collected on an annual basis and are available from 2000 to 2021. However, some economies do not have complete data for that time frame, which effectively makes our data an unbalanced panel. First, we use the Z-score as a measure of bank stability, which is a popular practice in the literature (see, for example, Laevan and Levine 2009; Ahamed and Mallick 2019). The Z-score is defined as the inverse of the probability of bank failure; therefore, a higher value of Z-score represents less bankruptcy exposure, indicating more stability. The data for the Z-score is collected from the World Bank International Financial Development Database.

One of the main predictors is financial inclusion. Although a formal definition of financial inclusion is yet to be agreed upon, various proxies and methods have been used previously. One of the common approaches used to calculate proxies is principal component analysis (PCA). Following Wang and Luo (2022), we use information from the IMF Financial Access Survey (FAS). Previous studies have shown that financial inclusion indices can be calculated by using financial proxies in two dimensions: financial access and usage (see, for example, Sarma 2015; Wang and Luo 2022). For the former dimension, we use several indices, including the number of banks per 1000 km^2, the number of banks per 100,000 adults, the number of ATMs per 1000 km^2, and the number of ATMs per 100,000 adults. Following Wang and Luo (2022), we use the total outstanding loans from commercial banks and the total outstanding deposits to commercial banks both as a percentage of GDP.

Another important predictor is financial technology (FinTech). Just like financial access, there is no definite answer to what signifies FinTech; however, FinTech has been broadly defined as the integration of technology into financial services to facilitate efficiency and accessibility. In the literature, various attempts have been made to study the effect of FinTech on the financial sector using different proxies, including online lending and mobile payment, among others (see, for example, Bofondi and Gobbi 2017; Haddad and Hornuf 2019). Although these papers use those proxies individually, an integrated FinTech index is rarely constructed in the literature; however, we construct a FinTech index using principal component analysis (PCA). To do so, we use several variables from the Financial Access Survey (FAS): the number of registered mobile money account agents per 100,000 adults; the number of registered mobile money accounts; the value of mobile and internet banking transactions as a part of GDP; and the number of mobile money transactions as a percentage of GDP. As PCA maximizes variance, it provides a greater weight on larger variances; therefore, each variable needs to be standardized before conducting PCA. The estimated factors and their eigenvalues are reported in Table 4.1 below.

The combined PCA table reveals insights into the underlying structure of two distinct sets of indicators: the financial access indicator and the FinTech indicator. Each section of the table summarizes the variance explained by each principal component, offering a clearer understanding of the primary dimension of the data.

For the financial access indicator, the first component (Comp1) has the highest eigenvalue, capturing 40.58% of the total variance, while the second component (Comp2) explains an additional 29.94%. Together, these two components account for 70.52% of the cumulative variance, indicating that they capture most of the information within the financial access indicators. This substantial cumulative variance suggests that the underlying data structure is strongly influenced by a few key factors, potentially related to the accessibility and usage of financial services. The remaining components contribute less variance, with Comp3 adding only 16.27%, thus confirming that the first two components are sufficient to encapsulate most of the variation in this dataset.

For the FinTech indicator, Comp1 also emerges as the dominant component, explaining nearly half of the variance at 49.57%. Comp2 adds a further 15.95%, making the first two components together responsible for 65.52% of the variance.

Table 4.1 Principal component analysis (PCA) summary for financial access and FinTech indicators

Component	Eigenvalue	Difference	Proportion (%)	Cumulative (%)
Financial access indicator PCA analysis				
Comp1	2.8404	0.7448	40.58	40.58
Comp2	2.0956	0.9564	29.94	70.51
Comp3	1.1392	0.5002	16.27	86.79
Comp4	0.6389	0.3838	9.13	95.92
Comp5	0.2551	0.2356	3.64	99.56
Comp6	0.0196	0.0084	0.28	99.84
Comp7	0.0112	–	0.16	100.00
FinTech PCA analysis				
Comp1	3.9656	2.6897	49.57	49.57
Comp2	1.2759	0.2178	15.95	65.52
Comp3	1.0581	0.2510	13.23	78.75
Comp4	0.8072	0.3431	10.09	88.84
Comp5	0.4641	0.1578	5.80	94.64
Comp6	0.3063	0.2262	3.83	98.47
Comp7	0.0801	0.0375	1.00	99.47
Comp8	0.0426	–	0.53	100.00

This high degree of variance explained by the first two components implies that a major underlying trend—likely linked to technology adoption and usage—connects most FinTech indicators. As in the financial access section, subsequent components account for increasingly smaller portions of variance, underscoring that the first two principal components effectively capture the core patterns within the FinTech data.

Other independent variables include GDP growth, monetary policy, foreign and government assets, market structure variable, and crisis dummy, among others. We use the growth rate in the real GDP as a proxy of the business cycle as the previous literature suggests that bank stability is influenced by the state of the economy, as variables like profits, credit volume, and quality are seriously impacted during recessions (see, for example, Albertazzi and Gambacorta 2009). The data for GDP growth rates are from the World Bank Development Indicators (WBDI). As the literature suggests that monetary policy affects banking stability (see, for example, Valencia 2014), the paper uses monetary policy as an independent variable. For that purpose, the annual lending rate from the World Bank Development is used. Following previous studies on banking stability, ownership variables are also used as foreign ownership in the banking sector is accused of aggravating the adverse situations faced by domestic banking sectors (see, for example, De Haas and Horen 2012). For that purpose, we use foreign bank assets and government bank assets as part of GDP. Both of these data are collected from the World Bank Financial Database. We also use the market structure variable, as it has been considered an important factor in the risk-taking decisions of banks. We use the Herfindahl–Hirschman index (HHI) from the World Bank Database as a proxy of market structure, with higher values representing strong market-influencing power. Additionally, we employ deposit insurance as another predictor as a source of moral hazard causing a rise in bank risks (see, for example, Wang and Luo, 2022). For collecting data on deposit insurance, we use the World Bank Deposit Insurance database constructed by Demirgüç-Kunt et al. (2005). Lastly, according to Barth et al. (2004, 2008, 2013), bank regulations play an important role in the stability and profitability of the banking sector; therefore, we construct three variables, namely: entry requirements, supervision, and market discipline. Once these variables are created, we construct the regulations indicator by adding them linearly. Thus created regulation variable is between 0 and 1, with higher values representing stronger regulations. Variables needed for the regulation index construction are collected from the Bank Regulation and Supervision Survey hosted on the World Bank website.

Table 4.2 reports the descriptive statistics of the main variables of interest in this paper. The table provides insights into key financial variables, illustrating significant diversity across economies in terms of stability, capitalization, ownership, and regulatory conditions. Bank stability, measured by the log of Z-score (lzscore), averages 2.65 but has a moderate spread, indicating that while most economies have relatively stable banking sectors, some experience notable instability. Capitalization, or the level of equity relative to assets, averages 45.53% but varies widely, with some economies having fully capitalized and others holding minimal equity, highlighting the diverse approaches to financial safety and risk management.

Table 4.2 Asia and Pacific economies financial inclusion summary with adjusted rankings

Economy	FI index	FinTech index	Adjusted FI Compl rank	Adjusted FinTech index rank
Hong Kong, China	6.897960	4.2848	1	2
Japan	2.416799	5.2322	2	1
Korea, Rep of	2.602427	4.9887	3	3
PRC	1.647900	1.2728	4	7
Singapore	2.001727	1.99009	5	6
Malaysia	1.043427	1.2322	6	8
Mongolia	0.798297	0.6789	7	9
Viet Nam	0.481211	0.68234	8	10
Thailand	0.599492	0.65790	9	11
Brunei Darussalam	0.137024	0.2322	10	12
Bangladesh	−0.955337	3.764458	11	5
India	−0.498593	−0.0324	12	14
Fiji	−0.273392	−0.970000	13	21
Nepal	−0.314611	−0.169576	14	15
Bhutan	−0.274225	−0.2727	15	17
Maldives	−0.644400	−0.2323	16	16
Lao PDR	−0.909111	0.2021	17	13
Philippines	−0.988214	−0.417711	18	18
Cambodia	−0.514785	−0.747275	19	19
Myanmar	−1.533231	−0.900635	20	20
Timor-Leste	−1.335620	−1.45679	21	22

Ownership structure also shows considerable variation. Foreign bank assets average around 22.87%, with some banks reporting substantial foreign ownership and others none. Government-owned assets have a mean of 18.04%, suggesting moderate government involvement overall, though a significant range shows that some banks rely heavily on government backing while others are fully privatized. GDP growth averages 4.27% but ranges broadly from negative to high values, reflecting stark differences in lending practices across economies. The lending rate, which averages 12.47%, also shows a large range, suggesting differing credit costs influenced by local economic and regulatory factors. Regulatory constraints are relatively consistent, with an average regulatory stringency of 0.515 on a 0–1 scale, indicating a moderately restrictive environment across banks. Lastly, the market structure variable has an average of 0.164, indicating a relatively small market influence. Table A1 in the Appendix reports the correlation between the variables mentioned in this subsection.

4.2.2 Empirical Framework

We first estimate the determinants of banking stability as follows:

$$Z - score_{i,t} = d + \theta X_{i,t} + f_i + \varepsilon_{i,t}, \tag{4.1}$$

where Z-score is the banking sector-specific Z-score for the economy i in year t. $X_{i,t}$ includes a vector of control variables such as bank ownerships, monetary policy variables, and macroeconomic variables. We then introduce financial inclusion (FI) in the model as follows (Table 4.3):

$$Z - score_{i,t} = d + \gamma FI_{i,t} + \theta X_{i,t} + f_i + \varepsilon_{i,t}, \tag{4.2}$$

where $FI_{i,t}$ is the financial inclusion index calculated using PCA above for economy i in year t. Now, we introduce the FinTech variable both as an independent variable and an interaction term in Eq. (4.2) as follows:

$$Z - score_{i,t} = d + \gamma FI_{i,t} + \zeta FinTech_{i,t} + \omega FI_{i,t} * FinTech_{i,t} + \theta X_{i,t} + f_i + \varepsilon_{i,t}, \tag{4.3}$$

where coefficient ζ captures the independent impact of FinTech on the dependent variable. The coefficient ω shows the joint effects of financial inclusion and FinTech. In subsequent sections and subsections, we estimate Eqs. (4.1)–(4.3) using panel fixed effects and instrumental variable methods.

4.3 Results

4.3.1 Determinants of Financial Stability

In this section, we first calculate the determinants of financial stability, which is done by estimating Eq. (4.2) without financial inclusion and FinTech variables. Table 4.4 reports the results. In Model I, only ownership and capitalization variables are controlled, while in Model II, banking regulation-related variables are also controlled. The table offers insights into how different bank characteristics and contextual factors influence bank stability. First, government bank assets appear to have no significant impact on stability across both models. This suggests that government ownership, in this context, neither stabilizes nor destabilizes banks, in line with the mixed findings in the literature. For instance, studies like that of La Porta et al. (2002) argue that government ownership may introduce inefficiencies, potentially destabilizing banks due to political interference, but our results do not confirm any effect in either direction.

Table 4.3 Summary statistics of main variables

Variable	Count	Mean	Std. dev.	Min	25%	50%	75%	Max
lzscore	886	2.650	0.755	−3.912	2.311	2.809	3.098	4.194
Capitalization	2108	45.532	108.991	0.000	10.000	23.158	55.524	1777.540
Foreign bank assets	2294	22.870	23.800	0.000	2.083	15.333	40.167	92.000
Gov. bank assets	868	18.038	22.997	0.000	0.000	1.300	37.067	72.260
GDP growth rate	2707	4.271	7.739	−102.255	1.770	4.772	7.268	60.432
Monetary policy	1199	12.471	7.968	0.994	7.468	10.917	15.489	96.100
Regulations	2294	0.515	0.181	0.000	0.448	0.534	0.621	1.000
Deposit insurance	3410	0.204	0.403	0.000	0.000	0.000	0.000	1.000
HHI index	402	0.164	0.162	0.040	0.071	0.010	0.190	0.880

Table 4.3 reports the summary statistics of the main variables used in the paper. The variable lzscore in the table refers to the log of Zscore of the banking sector. Data for the variables Zscore, capitalization, foreign bank assets, and government bank assets are collected from the World Bank Global Financial Development Database. Data on GDP growth rates and monetary policy rates are obtained from the World Development Indicators (WDI). Regulations is an index number constructed based on Barth et al. (2004, 2008, 2013). Deposit Insurance is a dummy variable assigned based on the World Bank Deposit Insurance Database. Lastly, the HHI index, a proxy of market structure, is obtained from the World Integrated Trade Solution (WITS) of the World Bank

Foreign bank assets, however, show a significant positive effect on stability in Model 2, indicating that banks with greater foreign ownership tend to be more stable. This is consistent with Claessens and Horen (2014), who found that foreign banks often bring better risk management practices and access to diversified funding, contributing positively to stability in emerging markets. The finding suggests that foreign bank involvement might be beneficial for stability in settings with developing regulatory frameworks.

Capitalization exhibits a complex relationship with stability. In Model 1, higher capitalization is associated with slightly lower stability, though the effect is only marginally significant. In Model 2, however, capitalization becomes positively significant, suggesting that well-capitalized banks are indeed more resilient, especially when controlling for other stability-related factors. This supports findings by Berger and Bouwman (2013), who argue that higher capital buffers enhance bank resilience, particularly during economic downturns. The difference in results between models may reflect how the impact of capitalization on stability varies in accordance with the surrounding economic and regulatory context.

The role of financial inclusion also reveals an interesting pattern. In Model 1, financial inclusion is positively associated with stability, suggesting that a broader deposit base might reduce funding volatility and improve soundness, in line with

Table 4.4 Fixed-effects regression results for bank stability

Variable	Model 1	Model 2
Gov bank assets	0.0064 (0.0305)	−0.0036 (0.0213)
Foreign bank assets	0.0093 (0.0109)	0.0173** (0.0088)
Capitalization	−0.0002* (0.0001)	0.0018** (0.0006)
Financial access	0.0844*** (0.0247)	0.0097 (0.0696)
Deposit insurance dummy	–	0.1397 (0.1185)
Crisis dummy	–	−0.2448 (0.1732)
Regulations	–	−0.1423 (0.1246)
Lending rate	–	−0.0475*** (0.0134)
HHI index	–	−0.112(0.095)
Constant	2.3290*** (0.5751)	2.9229*** (0.6107)
Year effects	Yes	Yes
R-squared	0.28	0.29
N	19	19
Groups	190	190
F-state	3.69***	8.35***

Note Standard errors are in parentheses. ***, **, and * indicate significance at the 1%, 5%, and 10% levels, respectively

Ahamed and Mallick (2019). However, this effect becomes insignificant in Model 2, suggesting that the benefits of financial inclusion in terms of stability may diminish in the presence of additional stability factors or regulations.

The deposit insurance dummy variable, while positive, is not statistically significant, suggesting that the presence of deposit insurance has no clear impact on stability in this context. This is in line with Barth et al. (2004), who found that deposit insurance can have ambiguous effects, as it may either reassure depositors or incentivize banks to take on more risk. Similarly, the crisis variable has a negative but insignificant effect, implying that economic crises may generally reduce stability, although this effect isn't robust enough to confirm a strong trend, which is somewhat consistent with the findings of Laeven and Valencia's (2013) on increased financial vulnerability during downturns.

The regulations variable is also negative and insignificant in Model 2, indicating that stricter regulatory environments may not necessarily promote stability. This is in line with Barth et al. (2004), who found that stringent regulation sometimes increases risk by imposing additional costs and limiting operational flexibility.

The lending rate shows a significant negative effect on stability in Model 2, suggesting that higher interest rates may destabilize banks. This aligns with the "monetary risk-taking channel" proposed by Borio and Zhu (2012), which argues that higher lending rates may lead banks to take on riskier assets, thereby increasing vulnerability.

Lastly, the findings indicate that market structure proxied by HHI has insignificant negative impacts on banking stability in the Asia and Pacific region. This suggests that less competitive banking environments in the region might correlate with increased systemic risk, possibly due to decreased pressure to achieve risk management efficiency. Previous studies suggest that highly concentrated markets may lead to "too-big-to-fail" dynamics, where larger institutions take on greater risks, anticipating potential government bailouts during financial distress (see, for example, Boyd and De Nicoló 2005).

4.3.2 FinTech, Financial Access, and Financial Stability

In this subsection, we attempt to quantify the role of financial technology in enhancing financial access. To do so, we estimate Eq. (4.3). Table 4.5 reports the results.

Table 4.5 offers insights into how bank characteristics, financial inclusion, financial technology, and the interactions between them affect bank stability, measured by Z-Score. When comparing these results with the financial access-only model, it is evident that introducing financial technology variables and their interactions between them alters the effects of traditional financial access factors on stability. Additionally, the decrease in sample size in models that include financial technology

Table 4.5 Financial technology, financial inclusion, and banking stability

Variable	Model without interaction	Model with interaction
Government bank assets	−0.0111 (0.0263)	−0.0109 (0.0279)
Foreign bank assets	−0.0052 (0.0118)	−0.0083 (0.0203)
Capitalization	0.0014* (0.0008)	0.0014 (0.0008)
Financial access	0.0401 (0.2901)	0.0548 (0.3161)
Regulations	−0.4653 (0.8960)	−0.6689 (1.4130)
GDP growth	−0.0400** (0.0201)	−0.0364 (0.0283)
Lending rate	−0.1849*** (0.0370)	−0.1898*** (0.0467)
HHI index	−0.10 (0.085)	−0.19 (0.115)
FinTech index	−0.0501 (0.0442)	−0.0910 (0.2156)
Financial access × FinTech	–	−0.0515 (0.2650)
Year effects	Yes	Yes
Constant	5.9007*** (0.8255)	6.0257*** (1.0848)
R-squared	0.98	0.99
N	94	94
Groups	12	12

Note Standard errors are in parentheses. ***, **, and * indicate significance at the 1%, 5%, and 10% levels, respectively may contribute to some of the ambiguity in these results, as a smaller sample may reduce statistical power.

For example, the coefficients for government and foreign bank assets are negative but not statistically significant, indicating that neither government ownership nor foreign involvement has a clear influence on stability in this model. This contrasts with the findings of Claessens and Horen (2014), which suggest that foreign banks often contribute to stability by introducing better risk management practices. The inclusion of financial technology and interaction terms may moderate the stability benefits typically associated with foreign bank ownership.

Capitalization, which is generally viewed as an indicator of resilience, shows a positive association with stability in the first model, supporting literature suggesting that well-capitalized banks are better able to withstand economic shocks (Berger and Bouwman 2013). However, the significance of this effect decreases in the model with interaction terms, suggesting that financial technology factors may reduce the need for high capitalization levels to stabilize banks.

Financial access, which previously exhibited a positive effect on stability in the financial access-only model, is insignificant here—a change that implies that while inclusion can provide a more diversified deposit base and reduce the reliance on volatile funding, its benefits in terms of stability may diminish when accounting for factors such as financial technology and lending rates. Ahamed and Mallick (2019) suggest that financial inclusion strengthens bank soundness, but our results imply that its impact on stability may depend on the broader economic and technological context.

The lending rate displays a consistently negative and significant impact on stability across both models, indicating that higher rates are associated with increased instability. This finding aligns with Borio and Zhu's (2012) "monetary risk-taking channel," suggesting that higher lending rates incentivize banks to adopt riskier lending practices to maintain profitability, which reduces stability.

The robust significance of lending rates underscores their central role in shaping bank risk profiles, regardless of other variables. The market concentration variable proxied by HHI continues to exhibit negative but insignificant impacts on banking stability as in the benchmark model.

The financial technology variables, represented by the FinTech Index and the interaction terms, are both negative but not statistically significant. This suggests that while financial technology and access combined may not directly enhance stability, they could introduce complexities in risk management. The negative sign on the interaction terms hints that the interaction of FinTech with financial access might slightly destabilize banks if not adequately managed. Philippon (2016) points out that rapid FinTech expansion can introduce new forms of credit risk, and although our results do not confirm this effect, they suggest that the relationship between technology, access, and stability is complex and might require regulatory oversight to ensure that these innovations do not inadvertently increase risk.

Comparing these results with the financial access-only model reveals critical differences. In the simpler model, factors such as foreign bank assets and financial access contribute significantly to stability, supporting the view that broadening access reduces risk. However, in this expanded model, where financial technology and lending conditions are included, these effects diminish. This suggests that stability in Asian markets is influenced not only by financial access but also by how financial technology interacts with traditional banking practices. Additionally, the smaller sample size in this expanded model might partly explain the decreased significance of some variables, as a limited sample can reduce the ability to detect effects reliably.

4.3.3 *Robustness Analysis on Financial Inclusion, FinTech, and Banking Stability*

In this subsection, we study the impacts of financial inclusion and FinTech on bank stability in the Asia and Pacific economies using an alternative proxy of banking stability. In addition, we also use alternative econometric specifications. Despite the difference in approach and proxies, we obtain the same findings that financial inclusion might enhance banking stability while FinTech might reduce such a positive influence.

4.3.3.1 Alternative Measures of Banking Stability

In this subsection, we use alternative measures of bank performance and stability. We employ the standard deviation of the ratio of private credit of deposit money banks to GDP, henceforth SD_{FD}, as a measure of banking stability, while the relative volatility is calculated using a five-year time window. The use of SD_{FD} is a logical choice as an indicator of banking stability as it captures the volatility of credit expansion, which is one of the major reasons behind financial instability. A smooth banking system has a lower value of SD_{FD}, while a higher value represents financial distress. The use of SD_{FD} is standard in literature—for instance, Fernandez et al. (2016) employ SD_{FD} as a proxy of banking stability and find that it is related to higher economic volatility in an economy with less market concentration. Table 4.6 reports the results with the new dependent variable. The table suggests that financial inclusion has negative but insignificant impacts on SD_{FD}. The insignificance could be due to a change in sample size in the new framework; however, the insignificance could also be telling a story that financial inclusion alone cannot negate the risks in the banking sector but might depend upon regulatory measures as well. FinTech and the interaction term appear to have positive impacts on SD_{FD}, suggesting that FinTech-driven financial inclusion might amplify banking instability due to rapid credit expansion or regulatory gaps. This finding in the context of Asia and the Pacific is in line with the general understanding that FinTech, while increasing financial access, might bring a credit boom in the short run while dampening the traditional risk management practices in the

Table 4.6 The relative standard deviation of the ratio of private credit of deposit money banks to GDP as an alternative measure of banking stability

Dependent variable	SD_{FD}
Financial Inclusion (FI)	−0.0017 (0.06)
FI × FinTech	0.12*** (0.038)
FinTech index	0.094*** (0.03)
Year effects	Yes
Economy effects	Yes
R-squared	0.99
Observations	71
Number of economies	15
F-statistic	36.93**

Note Robust standard errors are in parentheses. p-values: * $p < 0.1$, ** $p < 0.05$, *** $p < 0.01$

banking industries. Overall, these findings are in line with the baseline results indicating that financial inclusion might have a positive influence on banking stability while FinTech might undermine it.

4.3.3.2 IV Method

Previous analyses suggest that financial access might increase banking stability, while FinTech puts negative pressure on it. However, it could be that the results in Table 4.5 might be suffering from an endogeneity problem, as shocks hitting the dependent variable and independent variables like FinTech and financial access might be the same. To verify the findings in the benchmark model and address possible endogeneity problems, we use an instrumental variable (IV) method. One of the assumptions of the instrumental variable is that it should not influence the dependent variable without affecting the variables being instrumented; in other words, possible instrumental variables should only affect banking stability through financial access and FinTech. Based on the literature in the field, we choose ICT goods import as a percentage of total goods imports and the ratio of female literacy in the secondary level to the male literacy in the same level as possible instruments. We choose ICT goods import as a ratio of GDP as a possible instrument because a higher proportion of ICT imports signifies a higher level of economic growth and financial development. In addition, higher ICT imports indicate a better information infrastructure that leads to a reduction in the transaction cost, paving the way for better financial inclusivity (see, for example, Pradhan et al. 2016; Ahamed and Mallick 2019). In addition, the choice of the ratio of women's enrollment in secondary level to that of men as another instrument is backed by theoretical and empirical relevance to financial inclusion. A higher ratio of female to male enrollment suggests reduced gender inequalities in educational outcomes, leading to better financial literacy and inclusivity (see, for example, Klapper et al. 2015; Grohmann et al. 2018). The new empirical framework is:

$$FI_{it} = \pi_0 ICT_{it} + \pi_2 LiteracyRate_{it} + \mu_i + \nu_{it} \quad (4.4)$$

$$\begin{aligned} FinTech_{it} \times FI_{it} = {} & \alpha_0 + \alpha_1 (FinTech_{it} \times ICT_{it}) \\ & + \alpha_2 (FinTech_{it} \times LiteracyRate_{it}) \\ & + \alpha_3 FinTech_{it} + \mu_i + \xi_{it} \end{aligned} \quad (4.5)$$

$$lzscore_{it} = beta_0 + \beta_1 FinTech_{it} + \beta_2 \hat{FI}_{it} + \beta_3 \widehat{FinTech_{it} \times FI_{it}} + \gamma X'_{it} + \mu_i + \varepsilon_{it} \quad (4.6)$$

The coefficients in Eqs. 4.4 and 4.5 represent the determinants of financial inclusion (FI_{it}) and the interaction term ($FinTech_{it} \times FI_{it}$). In the equation for financial inclusion, π_0 is the constant term, π_1 captures the effect of ICT on financial inclusion, π_2 represents the effect of the literacy rate, and π_3 measures the effect of FinTech on financial inclusion. The control variables, denoted by $\mathbf{X}_{it}$, have the coefficients δ, which reflect their individual impacts on financial inclusion. The fixed effects, μ_i, account for unobserved heterogeneity across individuals or panels, while v_{it} is the idiosyncratic error term.

For the interaction term ($FinTech_{it} \times FI_{it}$), the constant term is α_0, α_1 captures the effect of the interaction between FinTech and ICT, and α_2 represents the effect of the interaction between FinTech and the literacy rate. The direct effect of FinTech on the interaction term is measured by α_3, while the coefficients θ indicate the effects of control variables on the interaction term. Fixed effects, μ_i, and the error term, ξ_{it}, also play similar roles to those in the financial inclusion equation.

In the second-stage equation, β_0 is the constant term, while β_1 represents the direct effect of FinTech on banking sector stability, measured by the Z-Score. The coefficient β_2 indicates the corrected effect of financial inclusion on the Z-Score after accounting for endogeneity, and β_3 captures the interaction effect, showing how the impact of financial inclusion on the Z-Score changes with the level of FinTech. The coefficients of the control variables, γ, measure their effects on banking sector stability, while fixed effects (μ_i) and the error term (ϵ_{it}) account for individual-specific factors and random noise, respectively. Table 4.7 reports the estimation results.

From the table, we see that financial inclusion is positively associated with bank stability, and FinTech puts negative pressure on the positive effects of financial inclusion on bank stability. These findings are similar to what we found in the benchmark model. With regard to the econometric suitability of the instruments, diagnostic tests like the underidentification LM test, the weak identification F test, and the overidentification Hansen J test suggest that our instruments are valid. The first-stage regression coefficients reported in the table support our prior belief that ICT infrastructure and women's literacy rate increase financial inclusiveness. Furthermore, the F-statistics of the first equation suggest that the first model is statistically valid.

Table 4.7 First-stage and second-stage results

Variables	FI	Z-score
ICT	0.016* (0.049)	
Literacy rate	0.082* (0.07)	
FI		0.82* (1.23)
FI × FinTech		−0.02* (0.3) −0.02* (0.3)
Economy effects	Yes	Yes
Year effects	Yes	Yes
Observations	204	175
Groups	21	21
R-squared	0.93	
Centered R-squared		0.05
LM statistic (P-value)		7.14 (0.05)
Stock-yogo (F-statistic)		9.76
Hansen J statistic		0.51 (0.5)
F-statistic	2012.5***	

Note The dependent variable in the first stage is financial inclusion (FI), while in the second stage it is the Z-score, a measure of banking sector stability. ICT represents the import of information and communication technology, and literacy rate refers to the ratio of female to male secondary enrollment. The interaction term *FI* × FinTech captures the combined effect of financial inclusion and FinTech. Economy and year effects are included in all regressions. Standard errors are in parentheses. *, **, and *** denote significance at the 10%, 5%, and 1% levels, respectively

4.3.3.3 Financial Inclusion, FinTech, and Banking Stability Using an Alternative Instrument

In the previous section, we attempted to study the impacts of financial access and FinTech on banking stability in the Asia and Pacific region using ICT infrastructures and women's literacy rate as instruments. In this subsection, we use the legal origin of economies as another instrument of financial access. The legal origin of an economy is widely used in the literature as a proxy for financial inclusion—for example, Demir et al. (2019) study the effect of FinTech and financial inclusion on inequality using a quantile regression framework, employing the legal framework as an instrument of financial inclusion. In addition, Lacalle-Calderon et al. (2019), using the legal origin of economies as an instrument of financial inclusion, study the impact of microfinance on inequality. The use of legal origin as an instrument for financial inclusion is logical, given the fact that legal origin shapes financial regulations, contract enforcement, and property rights, thus impacting the inclusivity of the financial system. In addition, it

Table 4.8 First-stage and second-stage results

Variables	FI	Z-score
British common law	1.16*** (0.17)	
ICT	0.08*** (0.004)	
FI		0.16 (0.80)
FI × FinTech		−0.13* (0.07) −0.02* (0.056)
Economy effects	Yes	Yes
Year effects	Yes	Yes
Observations	208	175
Groups	21	21
R-squared	0.37	
Wald χ^2		939.52***
Hansen J statistic		0.28 (0.59)
F-statistic	24,996.5***	

The dependent variable in the first stage is financial inclusion (FI), while in the second stage it is the Z-score, a measure of banking sector stability. ICT represents the import of information and communication technology, and literacy rate refers to the ratio of female to male secondary enrollment. The interaction term *FI* × FinTech captures the combined effect of financial inclusion and FinTech. Economy and year effects are included in all regressions. Standard errors are in parentheses. *, **, and *** denote significance at the 10%, 5%, and 1% levels, respectively

is shown in the literature that economies following the British Common Law perform better in contract enforcement and property rights, which are precursors to innovation (see Beck et al. 2003). Table 4.8 reports the results of the new IV estimations, wherein the use of a new instrument gives the same result as the previous one. Specifically, we see that financial inclusion appears to have positive impacts on banking stability in an economy while FinTech is likely to exert a negative and significant impact on it. This finding confirms once again the contrasting impacts of financial access and FinTech on the banking industry in Asia and the Pacific.

4.3.4 Study of Channels Through Which FinTech and Financial Inclusion Affect Bank Stability in Asia

Previous analyses suggest that financial inclusion might enhance banking stability while FinTech might exert negative pressure on banking sector stability. In this subsection, we examine the channel through which such outcomes might be possible.

To do so, we regress financial inclusion, FinTech, and the interactions between them on the operational efficiency channel and risk management channel. In line with the literature (see, for example, Wang and Luo 2022), we use the cost-to-income ratio as a proxy of operational management efficiency. We proxy risk management with the NPL ratio, with both of these variables being collected from the World Bank International Financial Database.

Theoretically, financial inclusion should improve banking stability by broadening the customer base through reducing per-unit transaction costs and reliance on volatile revenue streams (see, for example, Beck et al. 2007). However, the role of FinTech's is dual-edged, as while digital innovations might improve service delivery, adopting them could introduce short-term inefficiencies, such as integration costs and cyber-security risks, by adversely impacting banking stability (see, for example, Buchak et al. 2018). Risk management, on the other hand, benefits significantly from financial inclusion by diversifying credit portfolios and fostering responsible borrowing behavior, reducing nonperforming loans (NPLs) and hence stabilizing the banking sector (see, for instance, Demirgüç-Kunt and Klapper 2013). FinTech might further strengthen this effect by enabling better credit risk assessment and consistent monitoring. At the same time, however, it might pose a serious threat to bank stability through rapid expansion of credit and lax screening of borrowers. In light of these possibilities, in this section we study the implications of financial inclusion and FinTech for bank stability through these channels (Table 4.9).

Table 4.9 Channels through which financial inclusion and FinTech influence financial stability

Dependent variable: Z-score	Operational efficiency (cost/income ratio)	Risk management (NPL ratio)
Financial inclusion (FI)	1.76* (0.88)	−7.12** (3.52)
FinTech index	−1.43** (0.70)	4.3** (1.80)
FI × FinTech	−1.41 (0.72)	2.98* (1.78)
Year effects	Yes	Yes
Economy effects	Yes	Yes
R-squared	0.69	0.86
Observations	199	141
Number of economies	11	10
Wald χ^2	362.87***	605.43***

The dependent variable is the Z-score, a measure of banking sector stability. The operational efficiency channel is proxied by the cost-to-income ratio, and the risk management channel by the nonperforming loan (NPL) ratio. Standard errors are in parentheses. Year and economy effects are included in all regressions. *, **, and *** denote significance at the 10%, 5%, and 1% levels, respectively

The results align with and extend the existing literature on the relationship between financial inclusion, FinTech, and financial stability through distinct channels. For the operational efficiency channel, the positive coefficient of 1.76* ($p < 0.10$) for financial inclusion suggests that greater financial inclusion enhances stability by reducing transaction costs and increasing economies of scale. This finding resonates with Beck et al. (2007), who argue that financial inclusion expands access to banking services, improving operational performance by lowering overhead costs per customer. However, the significant negative coefficient for the FinTech index (−1.43**, $p < 0.05$) points to potential operational inefficiencies associated with the adoption of FinTech. This aligns with Buchak et al. (2018), who note that while FinTech improves access to services, initial implementation costs and integration challenges can temporarily reduce operational efficiency. The interaction term (−1.41) for financial inclusion and FinTech is insignificant, suggesting that FinTech does not significantly modify the effect of financial inclusion on operational efficiency, in line with Philippon (2016), who highlights the gradual impact of technological advances on banking operations.

For the risk management channel, the significant negative effect of financial inclusion (−7.12**, $p < 0.05$) indicates that it improves credit risk management by diversifying borrowers and fostering repayment discipline, a notion supported by Demirgüç-Kunt and Klapper (2013). FinTech, with its significant positive coefficient of 4.3** ($p < 0.05$), improves stability by enhancing risk assessment and credit monitoring capabilities. This is consistent with the findings of Ozili (2018), who emphasizes the role of FinTech in improving loan quality through better data analytics and automation. Moreover, the positive and significant interaction term (2.98*, $p < 0.10$) suggests that FinTech increases the risk-reducing effects of financial inclusion, in line with Carbo-Valverde et al. (2021), who find that FinTech enables better-targeted financial services and monitoring tools, thereby strengthening the benefits of financial inclusion in managing systemic risks.

The model's goodness-of-fit statistics reinforce these conclusions. The R^2 values (0.69 for operational efficiency and 0.86 for risk management) indicate strong explanatory power, while the significant Wald χ^2 statistics (362.87*** and 605.43***) confirm the robustness of the models.

4.4 Conclusions and Discussion

This study examines the role of financial technology (FinTech) in enhancing financial inclusion and its impact on banking stability in emerging markets across Asia. The findings reveal a complex relationship in which financial inclusion positively influences banking stability by diversifying depositor bases and mitigating funding risks. This is in line with prior research that finds that broader financial access reduces volatility and improves operational efficiency. However, the impact of FinTech is more nuanced, as while FinTech facilitates financial inclusion and enhances credit monitoring through innovations like mobile banking and digital payments, it also introduces risks to banking stability stemming from initial implementation inefficiencies, regulatory gaps, and potential cybersecurity vulnerabilities. From the policy perspective, the dual impact of FinTech suggests a need for strong regulatory oversight and responsible FinTech integration in the financial system. In addition, the dual impacts of FinTech suggest that policymakers in East Asia should promote FinTech sandboxes to assess innovations before it is fully implemented.

The analysis also highlights two critical channels through which these dynamics operate, namely operational efficiency and risk management. Financial inclusion improves stability by reducing transaction costs and diversifying credit portfolios. FinTech, on the other hand, while improving credit monitoring, may initially reduce operational efficiency due to integration challenges. These insights emphasize the dual-edged nature of FinTech in emerging markets, offering opportunities for inclusion while introducing systemic risks.

We identify three main directions for future research. First, a detailed understanding of the relationship between financial inclusion and FinTech at the bank level is needed. Second, future studies should focus on constructing a more comprehensive FinTech index by including a broader set of variables in finance and technology industries. The current version of the paper has relied primarily on mobile accounts as a proxy of FinTech, partly due to dimensionality issues arising from adding new variables, so addressing this limitation would add value to the topic. Lastly, future research should examine the role of institutions in shaping the overall impact of FinTech and financial inclusion on the banking industry.

Appendix

Cross-Correlation Matrix with Significance Levels

The Table A1 reports the pairwise correlation between variables considered in this paper. *s represents the level of significance.

Table A1 Cross-correlation matrix with significance levels

Variables	Lending rate	Z score	Capitalization	Foreign bank assets	Government assets	Financial inclusion	FinTech index	Regulations	GDP growth	Deposit insurance
Lending rate	1.00									
Z score	−0.21**	1.00								
Capitalization	−0.15*	0.14*	1.00							
Foreign bank assets	0.11	0.22**	0.18**	1.00						
Government bank assets	−0.07	−0.06	0.05	0.06	1.00					
Financial inclusion index	0.05	0.25***	−0.02	0.19**	−0.05	1.00				
FinTech index	−0.03	−0.18**	−0.05	0.07	−0.01	0.27***	1.00			
Regulations	−0.22**	−0.24***	0.02	0.15*	−0.08	0.21**	0.18**	1.00		
GDP growth	0.12	0.18**	0.07	0.11	−0.02	0.23***	0.15*	0.06	1.00	
Deposit insurance	0.08	−0.05	0.01	0.03	0.05	0.06	−0.03	0.02	0.04	1.00

References

Ahamed, M. M., and S. K. Mallick. 2019. Is financial inclusion good for bank stability? International evidence. *Journal of Economic Behavior & Organization* 157:403–427.

Albertazzi, U., and L. Gambacorta. 2009. Bank profitability and the business cycle. *Journal of Financial Stability* 5 (4): 393–409.

Asian Development Bank. 2023. *Financial digitalization and its implications for ASEAN+3 regional financial stability*. Manila: Asian Development Bank.

Barth, J. R., G. Caprio, and R. Levine. 2004. Bank regulation and supervision: What works best? *Journal of Financial Intermediation* 13 (2): 205–248.

Barth, J. R., G. Caprio, and R. Levine. 2008. Bank regulations are changing: For better or worse? World Bank Policy Research Working Paper 4646, The World Bank, Washington, DC.

Barth, J. R., C. Lin, Y. Ma, J. Seade, and F. M. Song. 2013. Do bank regulation supervision and monitoring enhance or impede bank efficiency? *Journal of Banking and Finance* 37 (8): 2879–2892.

Basnayake, D., A. Naranpanawa, S. Selvanatha, and J. S. Bandara. 2024. Financial inclusion through digitalization and economic growth in Asia-Pacific countries. *International Review of Financial Analysis* 96:103596.

Beck, T., A. Demirgüç-Kunt, and R. Levine. 2003. Law and finance: Why does legal origin matter? *Journal of Comparative Economics* 31:653–675.

Beck, T., A. Demirgüç-Kunt, and R. Levine. 2007. Finance, inequality, and the poor. *Journal of Economic Growth* 12 (1): 27–49.

Berger, A. N., and C. H. S. Bouwman. 2013. How does capital affect bank performance during financial crises? *Journal of Financial Economics* 109 (1): 146–176.

Bofondi, M., and G. Gobbi. 2017. The big promise of FinTech. *European Economy: Banks, Regulations, and the Real Sector* 2:107–119. https://european-economy.eu/2017-2/thebig-promise-of-fintech/.

Borio, C., and H. Zhu. 2012. Capital regulation, risk-taking and monetary policy: A missing link in the transmission channel? *Journal of Financial Stability* 8 (4): 236–251.

Boyd, J. H., and G. De Nicoló, 2005. The theory of bank risk taking and competition revisited. *The Journal of Finance* 60 (3): 1329–1343.

Buchak, G., G. Matvos, T. Piskorski, and A. Seru. 2018. FinTech, regulatory arbitrage, and the rise of shadow banks. *Journal of Financial Economics* 130 (3): 453–483.

Carbo-Valverde, S., P. Cuadros-Solas, and F. Rodríguez-Fernández. 2021. FinTech and banking: An evolving relationship. In *Disruptive technology in banking and finance. Palgrave studies in financial services technology*, ed. T. King, F. S. S. Lopes, A. Srivastav, and J. Williams, 161–194. Cham: Palgrave Macmillan.

Chinoda, T., and F. M. Kapingura. 2024. Fintech-based financial inclusion and banks' risk-taking: The role of regulation in sub-Saharan Africa. *Journal of Economic and Administrative Sciences* 2054:6238.

Claessens, S., and N. V. Horen. 2014. Foreign banks: Trends and impact. *Journal of Money, Credit, and Banking* 46 (1): 295–326.

De Haas, R., and V. N. Horen. 2012. International shock transmission after the Lehman Brothers collapse: Evidence from syndicated lending. *American Economic Review* 102 (3): 231–237.

Demir, A., V. Pesque-Cela, Y. Altunbas, and V. Murinde. 2019. Fintech, financial inclusion and income inequality: A quantile regression approach. *The European Journal of Finance* 28 (1): 86–107.

Demirgüç-Kunt, A., and L. Klapper. 2013. Measuring financial inclusion: Explaining variation in use of financial services across and within countries. *Brookings Papers on Economic Activity* 2013 (1): 279–321.

Demirgüç-Kunt, A., B. Karacaovali, and L. Laevan. 2005. Deposit insurance around the world: A comprehensive database. Policy Research Working Paper Series 3628, The World Bank, Washington, DC.

Fernandez, A. I., F. Gonzalez, and N. Suarez. 2016. Banking stability, competition, and economic volatility. *Journal of Financial Stability* 22:101–120.

Grohmann, A., T. Kluhs, and L. Menkhoff. 2018. Does financial literacy improve financial inclusion? Cross country evidence. *World Development* 111:84–96.

Haddad, C., and L. Hornuf. 2019. The emergence of the global Fintech market: Economic and technological determinants. *Small Business Economics* 53 (1): 81–105.

Klapper, L., L. Lusardi, and P. V. Oudheusden. 2015. *Financial literacy around the world.* Washington, DC: Standard & Poor's Ratings Services Global Financial Literacy Survey.

La Porta, R., F. Lopez-de-Silanes, and A. Shleifer. 2002. Government ownership of banks. *Journal of Finance* 57 (1): 265–301.

Lacalle-Calderon, M., J. M. Larru, S. R. Garrido, and M. Perez-Trujillo. 2019. Micro-finance and income inequality: A new macrolevel evidence. *Review of Development Economics* 23 (2): 860–876.

Laevan, L., and R. Levine. 2009. Bank governance, regulation, and risk taking. *Journal of Financial Economics* 93 (2): 259–275.

Laevan, L., and F. Valencia. 2013. Systemic banking crises database. *IMF Economic Review* 61 (2): 225–270.

Loo, M. K. L. 2019. Enhancing financial inclusion in ASEAN: Identifying the best growth markets for Fintech. *Journal of Risk and Financial Management* 12 (181): 1–21. https://doi.org/10.3390/jrfm12040181.

Nguyen, Q. K., and V. C. Dang. 2022. The effect of FinTech development on financial stability in an emerging market: The role of market discipline. *Research in Globalization* 5:100105.

Ozili, P. K. 2018. Impact of digital finance on financial inclusion and stability. *Borsa Istanbul Review* 18 (4): 329–340.

Philippon, T. 2016. The FinTech opportunity. NBER Working Paper No. 22476, National Bureau of Economic Research, Cambridge, MA.

Pradhan, R., M. B. Arvin, and J. H. Hall. 2016. Economic growth, development of telecommunications infrastructure, and financial development in Asia, 1991–2012. *The Quarterly Review of Economics and Finance* 59:25–38.

Sarma, M. 2015. Measuring financial inclusion. *Economic Bulletin* 35 (1): 604–611.

Valencia, F. 2014. Monetary policy, bank leverage, and financial stability. *Journal of Economic Dynamics and Control* 47 (C): 20–38.

Vuković, D. B., M. K. Hassan, B. Kwakye, A. Febtinugraini, and M. Shakib. 2024. Does FinTech matter for financial inclusion and financial stability in BRICS markets? *Emerging Markets Review* 61:101164.

Wang, R., and H. Luo. 2022. How does financial inclusion affect banking stability in emerging economies? *Emerging Markets Review* 51:100876.

Yudaruddin, R., et al. 2023. Financial technology and bank stability in an emerging market economy. *Heliyon* 9 (5): e16183.

Chapter 5
Financial Inclusion and Policy Shocks: An Application of Topic Modeling on Central Banks' SDG-Driven Policy Predilection for Asia and Pacific Economies

Avik Ghosh

Abstract Financial Inclusion (FI) plays a determining role in achieving inclusive and sustainable macroeconomic policy outcomes, one of the fundamental premises of the Sustainable Development Goals (SDGs). Further, the countries' central banks formulate related policies and contribute as enablers to the transmission pathway from inclusive policymaking to sustainable and equitable economic growth. Country-specific studies, mostly restricted to a specific financial inclusion scheme/initiative, examined the role of financial inclusion in shaping SDG deliverables, with a particular focus only on poverty alleviation and equitable income generation. Also, no empirical exploration has yet been performed to ascertain the role of central banks' policy biases/priorities in expediting the attainment of sustainable macroeconomic targets. By deploying a fixed-effect panel regression strategy and an instrumental variable technique on fifteen major Asia-Pacific economies for 31 years, this study negates the solitary role of FI factors in influencing the changing spectrum of SDG targets. This research further explores Millennium Development Goals (MDGs), SDGs, the Asian financial crisis of 1997, and the global financial crisis of 2008 as policy shocks/interventions and observes their positive contribution in shaping the results of sustainable economic development targets. Further, this study uniquely deploys a Natural Language Processing (NLP) technique on Central Bank's annual reports, monetary policy statements, and press releases for the fifteen countries from 2000-2022 and analyzed 1815 documents through Topic Modeling. This paper concludes that central banks' policy inclination toward sustainable macroeconomic development has increased over the years and substantially improved with the emergence of policy shocks. With the country clustering/grouping observed in this exploration, it is evident that central banks of the Asia Pacific countries have a unidirectional, however heterogeneous, intent to contribute to the broader national objectives of attaining SDGs.

A. Ghosh (✉)
Reserve Bank of India, Kanpur, India

R. Gulati et al. (eds.), *Emerging Challenges in Banking in Asia and the Pacific*, Economics, Law, and Institutions in Asia Pacific,
https://doi.org/10.1007/978-981-92-2144-8_5

Keywords Financial inclusion · Sustainable development goals · Policy shocks · Instrumental variable strategy · Topic modeling

5.1 Introduction

Sustainable development primarily involves responsible management of economic, social, and environmental resources with a view to creating an inclusive and promising future world (Ginting 2020)—a holistic approach balancing economic growth, environmental protection, and social equity (LaBelle 2000). Financial inclusion (FI) and sustainable development are intrinsically linked, as access to financial services enables individuals and communities to participate in, and contribute to, sustainable progress (Ozili 2022). However, the transmission channel and the magnitude of the relationship between these two crucial concepts remain areas of active research and debate. Policy shocks or interventions significantly accelerate sustainable economic development by including underserved populations in the financial ecosystem (Ötker-Robe and Podpiera 2013). Positive externalities like the Millennium Development Goals (MDGs) and Sustainable Development Goals (SDGs) have provided momentum to the integration of financial inclusion and sustainable development (Al-Roubaie and Sarea 2019). Despite its negative impact on the global economy, the global financial crisis (GFC) demonstrated inclusive development in the long run (Deléchat et al. 2020), and although the more extensive Asian economies were less impacted by the GFC, the Asian financial crisis (AFC) in 1997 affected the macroeconomic balance and growth trajectory of Asian economies generally (Goldstein 1998; Das 2011; Nawrot 2020). However, economies in the Asia and the Pacific region demonstrated significant resilience to these external diseconomies, resulting in an inclusive and holistic economic development (Bird and Milne 2004). This study aims to connect FI factors with macroeconomic SDGs in light of policy shocks.

Governments play a pivotal role in shaping the overall intent regarding sustainability of any nation (Van Niekerk 2020). Similarly, central banks are instrumental in shaping economic policies that include inclusivity and equitable coverage of policy measures (Swain and Yang-Wallentin 2019; Arner et al. 2020). The central banks predominantly control the transmission channel, driving FI initiatives to maturity as regards equitable policy outcomes (Alexander and Karametaxas 2021). The policy priorities and biases of the central banks toward sustainability play a decisive role in using policy shocks as enablers to improve macroeconomic determinants (Stephens and Sokol 2023). Economies in the Asia and Pacific region have exhibited strong resilience to adverse economic policy shocks, mainly attributed to their effective policy responses and robust macroeconomic fundamentals observed by the central banks (Bird and Milne 2004; IMF 2022). Further, these nations have displayed inclusive economic growth with improved financial inclusion factors (Biswas and Ahamed 2023). However, no empirical exploration has yet been performed to ascertain the role of central banks' policy priorities in expediting the attainment of sustainable macroeconomic targets.

The scope of this research encompasses a few broad domains, namely financial inclusion, SDG indicators, policy interventions, and equitable economic policymaking. I start this empirical examination by addressing the question: Can financial inclusion factors alone improve SDGs pertaining to inclusive economic development? If not, do external policy shocks/interventions play a decisive role in fulfilling such SDG targets? Incidentally, economies' central banks formulate FI policies and set actionable objectives that are reflected in their policy papers/documents (Ferrari and Landi 2023), and efficient implementation of these policies entails favorable financial inclusiveness and equitable economic development (Deléchat et al. 2020). To elaborate on the role of central banks in inclusive policymaking and to supplement the first two questions from policy perspectives, I examine the comparative policy bias of central banks in light of major policy shocks. Do these policy shocks influence the inclusive policy bias of central banks? If so, this may cause a shift in SDG achievements. In answering these questions, this study interlinks the role of major policy interventions on FI targets through the inclusive policymaking of central banks for the Asia and Pacific economies.

5.1.1 Research Contribution

Economy-specific studies have examined the role of financial inclusion in shaping SDG deliverables, with a particular focus on poverty alleviation and equitable income generation (Azimi 2022). These studies are restricted to a specific financial inclusion scheme/initiative or explore the relationship in subordinated administrative arrangements like those for a district or state (Lal 2018; Omar and Inaba 2020). Moving a step forward, by analyzing various FI and SDG variables of 15 major Asia and the Pacific economies over a period of 31 years, this study concludes that FI alone cannot improve the targeted SDG indicators. By deploying a fixed-effect panel regression strategy as well as an instrumental variable technique, the study negates the solitary role of FI factors in improving the changing spectrum of SDG targets related to unprejudiced income generation, all-inclusive economic growth, and employment generation. Second, this research investigates the pivotal role of policy shocks and strategic intervention by international agencies/fora in shaping the transformation path of FI factors towards desired SDG results. This study tests the contribution of FI factors to SDG indicators in light of two global policy interventions (positive externalities), viz., the Millennium Development Goals (MDGs) in 2000 and the SDGs in 2015. It also incorporates two major policy shocks (negative externalities), namely the Asian financial crisis in 1997 and the global financial crisis of 2008, to test the hypothesis. By deploying rigorous instrumental variable techniques and a dynamic panel strategy to address the possible endogeneity of the FI variables, I uniquely examine the decisive role played by policy shocks and interventions in this context. I also check the causality treatment effects (average treatment effect on the treated) of all four shocks/interventions on the SDG deliverables through FI initiatives.

Third, taking my cue from the role of policy intervention in shaping SDG dynamics, I examine the capacity of policymakers to formulate SDG-friendly regulations/guidelines. Researchers have explored the policy behavior/orientation of lawmakers through natural language processing (NLP) of national policy documents such as budgets, policy papers, and ministerial reports; however, the crucial role of economies' apex banks in framing economic policies in light of the SDGs is yet to be explored using a structured NLP approach. To do this, I deploy an NLP technique on central banks' annual reports, monetary policy statements, and press releases for the 15 economies from 2000 to 2022. A total of 1815 documents have been analyzed through topic modeling. The novelty of this study lies in the multilevel classification of the topics into the desired SDGs through pretrained classification models and calculating their contributory weights through the term frequency-inverse document frequency (TF-IDF) tool. Further, I determine that the shift of policy bias towards SDGs, driven by intermediate policy shocks, contributes enormously to the SDG deliverables. The exploratory analysis through topic modeling has uniquely contributed to the SDG orientation of policymakers in leapfrogging policy shocks through an equitable policy drive. The economy groupings obtained based on their apex banks' policy cogency towards SDGs is a ready reckoner for international policymakers in strategizing their priorities. With the ever-increasing global focus on achieving SDGs, this study explores the occurrence of policy shocks and the possibility of economic policy-level tweaking by central banks to transform such shocks from "crisis to resilience" in the macroeconomic space of the Asia and Pacific economies.

5.2 Brief Literature Review

Standard growth models, such as the Solow (1956) model, highlight factors like physical and human capital accumulation and technological progress as drivers of economic growth. These models assume that resources are allocated efficiently across the population, but this assumption often overlooks the role of access to financial services in ensuring equitable growth. Financial inclusion addresses this gap by integrating underserved populations into the formal financial system (Kuada 2019), thereby enabling inclusive economic growth. Financial inclusion and a sustainable economy are interlinked through common objectives and mutually reinforcing mechanisms (Ozili 2022). Researchers have explored the nexus between financial inclusion (FI) and various inclusive macroeconomic determinants, and FI has been found to improve equitable income generation through enhanced formal banking facilities at the grassroots level (Pham and Thi Phuong 2020), while also reducing income inequality and poverty (Sood 2013). Moreover, FI enables poor households to save, invest, and manage risks efficiently, thus increasing their resilience to economic shocks. The rise in formal banking penetration in rural and backward areas positively impacts economic growth and common financial well-being (Sood 2013). FI is also decisive in improving household consumption patterns, asset holding, and overall socioeconomic development (Naceur et al. 2020), and researchers have determined a positive relationship between FI and expenditure-driven inclusive growth worldwide, especially in developing nations. FI creates avenues for generating employment by providing equitable formal banking facilities to the underserved and poor (Demirgüç-Kunt et al. 2019). An increase in the number of depositors in the formal banking channel indicates greater participation in economic activities and acts as an enabler to facilitate equitable economic growth (Mukherjee and Sood 2020). Moreover, financial inclusion promotes savings, providing a financial cushion that supports consumption smoothing and resilience against economic shocks (Honohan 2008). From an institutional perspective, inclusive financial systems enhance governance by formalizing economic transactions, reducing corruption, and increasing tax revenues (Acemoglu and Robinson 2012). They also empower marginalized groups, especially women, by giving them control over financial resources, in line with social equity goals (Aghion and Bolton 1997; Allen et al. 2016). The impact of financial inclusion on shaping economic growth dynamics has been studied in economies in Sub-Saharan Africa, Asia's developing economies, the Middle East and North Africa, and Central Asian nations (Azimi 2022). Additionally, developed nations like the United States and countries in the European Union have exhibited positive results in terms of FI in demonstrating inclusive income generation, employment opportunities, and equitable economic development through an improved real economic spectrum[1] (Safdar et al. 2020; Thathsarani et al. 2021). Similar analyses have been performed for Asia and Pacific economies, and quantitatively relatable results have been obtained (Erlando et al. 2020; Ratnawati 2020). Empirical evidence links financial inclusion to poverty alleviation, income equality, and job creation, reinforcing its critical role in inclusive growth (Banerjee and Duflo 2011; UNDP 2022). Global initiatives like the Sustainable Development Goals (SDGs) also emphasize financial inclusion as a tool for fostering equitable growth and reducing inequalities (World Bank 2020); however, researchers have pointed out that FI factors sometimes inhibit equitable growth for various systemic reasons, including inferior infrastructure, poor service continuity, ineffective monitoring, and political rent-seeking (Ajide et al. 2020). To empirically examine these dichotomous claims, I formulate the first hypothesis:

$\mathbf{H1_0}$: Financial inclusion factors alone cannot improve sustainable and equitable macroeconomic development. An alternate hypothesis is $H1_1$: Financial inclusion factors alone can improve sustainable and equitable macroeconomic development.

Policy shocks and interventions emerge as significant externalities and affect the all-embracing growth perspectives (Gruss et al. 2019). External economies and diseconomies, as forms of international policy shocks, have reshaped nations' prevailing macroeconomic scenarios (Kuada 2019) and also distracted the growth trajectory (Rangan and Lekha 2020). Developed and emerging economies have witnessed similar disruption from policy shocks—unfavorable growth and inequitable income

[1] A real economy is the part of an economy that produces and sells goods and services. It includes activities such as manufacturing, agriculture, and services that meet the demands of consumers and businesses within a particular geographic area (Rim et al. 2020).

generation (Poverty and Shared Prosperity 2022: Correcting Course 2021). However, studies have also observed such policy shocks as enablers to make the inclusive sectoral policy transmission channel more efficient and sustainable (van der Ploeg and Venables 2022). For member countries of the Organisation for Economic Co-operation and Development (OECD), policy shocks such as the 2008 GFC reduced economic development and associated macroeconomic factors, whereas Asian countries absorbed it with a comparatively lower impact. Positive externalities like the MDGs and SDGs, targeted towards attaining an inclusive and equitable growth transition, have a heterogeneous impact on the global economy (Ament 2020). Researchers have observed that emerging economies struggled initially to meet MDGs; however, they were frontrunners in achieving SDGs, especially in the macroeconomic space (Alcamo et al. 2020). It has also been found that developed economies, with existing and robust sustainable economic premises and a conducive equality spectrum, started as trailblazers but lost track in many instances (Van Niekerk 2020). However, a structured study on the causal role of policy shocks in shaping the financial inclusion transmission channel toward inclusive economic growth is yet to be conducted. Asia and Pacific economies with a mix of advanced economies (six OECD nations) and emerging economies make it an even more exciting exploration. To contribute to the prevailing research gap, I define the second hypothesis:

$H2_0$: Policy shocks influence the financial inclusion-driven transmission channel toward equitable economic growth. An alternate hypothesis is $H2_1$: Policy shocks do not influence the financial inclusion-driven transmission channel toward equitable economic growth.

When determining the growing role of financial inclusion in securing SDGs, the role of economies' central banks in formulating conducive economic policies cannot be ignored. Apex banks contribute to monetary policymaking and inflation control and play a pivotal role in inclusive banking, resulting in income generation, equitable employment opportunities, and household consumption-driven real economic growth (Rojas-Suárez 2016). With the emergence of sustainability targets and a greater focus on the green economy, central banks are consistently shifting their focus toward inclusive capital formation, equitable economic growth, and poverty alleviation (Sustainable Banking Network Report 2019). The policy documents of central banks reflect their policy priorities, inclination, and goal orientation (Ferrari and Landi 2023), and researchers have explored central banks' policy priorities by focusing on green financial initiatives and issuing green financial instruments (D'Orazio and Popoyan 2022). However, while the outcomes of policy initiatives have been widely analyzed, the policy biases have not. Developed economies have been keen on formulating favorable inclusive banking policies and have displayed sustainable shifts in policy priorities; however, emerging nations' central banks have witnessed shifts in such priorities over the last two decades (Dikau and Volz 2021). Studies have also found that policy shocks and externalities influence the policy-making of central banks—either by demonstrating an impulse toward focusing on sustainability or by rerouting their macroprudential policy framework (Deléchat et al.

2020). The policy orientation of central banks impacts inclusive economic development through improved FI deliverables; further, the plausible dependency of such equitable development on major policy shocks casts doubt on its overriding influence on central banks' policy bias. Researchers have not yet explored the role of such external policy shocks in central banks' policy inclination, which perpetually affects inclusive economic development. Moreover, no studies have been performed to ascertain the role of central banks' policy sentiments/biases through NLP techniques and structure text analysis. This study aims to delve deeper into the policy priorities of central banks across economies from the Asia and Pacific region, examining their inclination toward sustainability objectives defined through SDGs. With this in mind, we formulate our third hypothesis:

$H3_0$: External policy shocks affect central banks' sustainable but heterogeneous policy formulation, which focuses on equality. An alternate hypothesis is $H3_1$: External policy shocks do not affect central banks' sustainable policy formulation.

5.3 Data and Variables

I use the World Bank Data Repository for this study. The three segments of World Bank data used for this research are the World Development Indicators, the Global Financial Inclusion Database, and the goals and targets of the Sustainable Development Goals (SDGs). I consider 15 Asia and Pacific economies for this study based on their economic size.[2] First, I identify the dependent and independent variables for this study, choosing two major financial inclusion (FI) factors as predictors: the number of commercial bank branches (Beck et al. 2007) and depositors with commercial banks (Nkuna et al. 2018). When determining the macroeconomic determinants of sustainable development, I consider per capita national income (Brown et al. 2013), household consumption expenditures (Brahma et al. 2022), and unemployment rates (Mikkelson 2013) as the key indicators. These cater to a broader economic growth perspective through income distribution, consumption-driven demand-side push, and employment generation. I also consider a range of control variables for this study design to address potential sources of omitted variable bias and confounding. As the outcome variables are macroeconomic determinants, I consider related indicators as controls: GDP growth, growth in gross capital formation, consumer price inflation, and the proportion of tax revenue (Chirwa and Odhiambo 2016; Lanzafame et al. 2016). These variables handle most of the economic development premises—both the supply side and the demand side. As this research deploys the instrumental

[2] The mean of nominal GDP size for the 30 years under consideration is the measure of the economic size. Based on the measure, the 15 economies identified are the People's Republic of China; Japan; India; the Republic of Korea; Australia; Indonesia; Thailand; Singapore; Bangladesh; the Philippines; Viet Nam; Malaysia; Hong Kong, China; Pakistan; and New Zealand. This study does not consider Taipei,China due to the paucity of time series data on multiple identified indicators.

variable technique, I decided on the instruments from the prevailing studies. The dependency of FI factors (independent variables) on various operational determinants (infrastructure, connectivity, institutional support, etc.) enables me to zero in on the instruments. Following Kolodinsky et al. (2004), Cámara and Tuesta (2014), and Cabeza-García et al. (2019), I consider the number of automated teller machines, borrowers from commercial banks, fixed broadband subscriptions, individuals using the Internet, and fixed telephone subscriptions as the instruments for the FI variables.

I deploy the four policy shocks as binary dummy variables that take a value of "0" up to the policy intervention and "1" after that. Table 5.1 summarizes all the variables, while Fig. 5.1 pictorially represents the mean of financial inclusion and sustainable economic growth variables over 31 years for the 15 economies. A strong heterogeneity is observed in both sets of variables; however, the policy shocks affect their movement significantly.

Figure 5.2 depicts economy-wise plotting of the mean of the major identified determinants. The economy-specific heterogeneity for all the variables across 15 economies makes this an interesting context. As this paper explores the impact of policy shocks (explicitly contributing to socioeconomic uncertainties) on the transmission channel toward sustainable macroeconomic development, I also plot the world uncertainty index[3] of the economies to ascertain plausible divergence (Fig. 5.3) in policy uncertainty. I find a similar uncertainty heterogeneity across Asia and the Pacific nations as observed in indicator-specific economy-level heterogeneity. These observations hint at a solid reason for finding a uniform impact of similar policy shocks on economies with heterogeneous predictors and outcome variables.

5.4 Empirical Strategy

Given the data structure with 15 economies (i) and 31 continuous years (t), I deploy panel regression strategies, starting with the fixed-effect (FE) technique as the base strategy, followed by an instrumental variable strategy to test the first hypothesis. When incorporating the policy shock variables in the study, I deploy an instrumental variable strategy and a dynamic panel strategy to test the second hypothesis. Lastly, the topic modeling NLP technique is used to test the third hypothesis.

---

[3] The world uncertainty index is a measure of global economic and financial uncertainty, calculated in line with the economic policy uncertainty index. It is measured by calculating the frequency of articles in leading newspapers that discuss economic policy uncertainty (https://www.policyuncertainty.com/wui_quarterly.html).

Table 5.1 Summary of variables

Variable	Description	Obs	Mean	Std. Dev.	Min	Max
Time	Period under study (1990–2020)	465	2005	8.954	1990	2020
GNIPC	GNI per capita (constant 2015 US$)	451	15,591.273	16,639.991	146.485	58,315.5
FCE	Households' final consumption expenditure (annual % growth)	460	4.361	3.754	−12.87	15.047
UNEMP	Unemployment, total (% of total labor force) (ILO estimate)	461	3.959	2.024	0.25	11.19
CBBR	Commercial bank branches (per 100,000 adults)	465	14.332	9.318	1.491	35.812
DEP	Depositors with commercial banks (per 1000 adults)	455	914.992	851.654	6.501	3191.32
GDPG	GDP growth (annual %)	465	4.656	3.514	−13.127	14.52
GCFG	Gross capital formation (annual % growth)	441	6.026	31.267	−164.509	435.616
INF	Inflation, consumer prices (annual %)	465	4.326	4.617	−4.009	58.451
TAX	Tax revenue (% of GDP)	465	14.247	6.064	4.415	31.986
ANS	Adjusted net savings (% of GNI)	465	15.597	8.672	−5.352	40.886
ATM	Automated teller machines (ATMs) (per 100,000 adults)	465	56.281	57.759	0.06	288.59
BOR	Borrowers from commercial banks (per 1000 adults)	451	351.83	317.028	0.625	1167.446
WUI	World uncertainty index	465	0.177	0.129	0	0.762
FBB	Fixed broadband subscriptions (per 100 people)	464	11.331	12.526	0.001	43.054
FTE	Fixed telephone subscriptions (per 100 people	464	21.998	20.238	0.328	61.4
INT	Individuals using the Internet (% of the population)	465	30.675	32.484	0	96.505
MDG	Millennium Development Goals (1 after 2000, 0 otherwise)	465	0.645	0.479	0	1

(continued)

Table 5.1 (continued)

Variable	Description	Obs	Mean	Std. Dev.	Min	Max
SDG	Sustainable Development Goals (1 after 2015, 0 otherwise)	465	0.161	0.368	0	1
AFC	Asian financial crisis (1 after 1997, 0 otherwise)	465	0.742	0.438	0	1
GFC	Global financial crisis (1 after 2008, 0 otherwise)	465	0.387	0.488	0	1

Source Author's own calculations

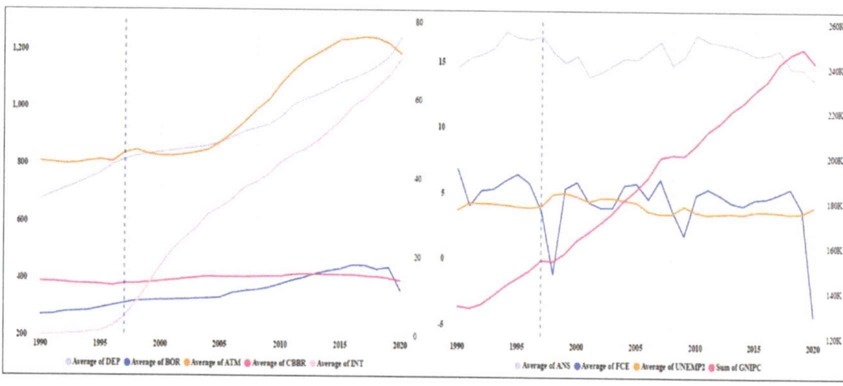

Fig. 5.1 Financial inclusion (L) and sustainable outcome (R) variables. DEP = depositors with commercial banks (per 1000 adults), BOR = borrowers from commercial banks (per 1000 adults), ATM = automated teller machines (ATMs) (per 100,000 adults), CBBR = commercial bank branches (per 100,000 adults), INT = individuals using the Internet (% of the population), ANS = adjusted net savings (% of GNI), FCE = households' final consumption expenditure (annual % growth), UNEMP2 = unemployment, total (% of total labor force as per ILO estimate), GNIPC = GNI per capita (constant 2015 US$). *Notes* 1. Dotted lines indicate the four policy shocks discussed in this paper. 2. The selection of financial inclusion factors and their reflection on sustainable growth are detailed in the data section. *Sources* World bank database from 1990 to 2020 and author's calculations

5.4.1 *Base Model: Fixed-Effect Panel Regression Strategy*

As this study has a period to number of countries (entities) ratio of $\frac{t}{i} > 2$, I primarily deploy a fixed-effect panel regression strategy to examine the role of FI factors alone in the inclusive sustainability policy goals of the macroeconomic determinants. Before the regression analysis, I conducted a panel-level unit root testing with a Fisher-type unit root/stationarity test for all the panel variables considered in this paper. I use the Augmented Dickey-Fuller regression with the lag effect of dependent variables when serial correlation is present:

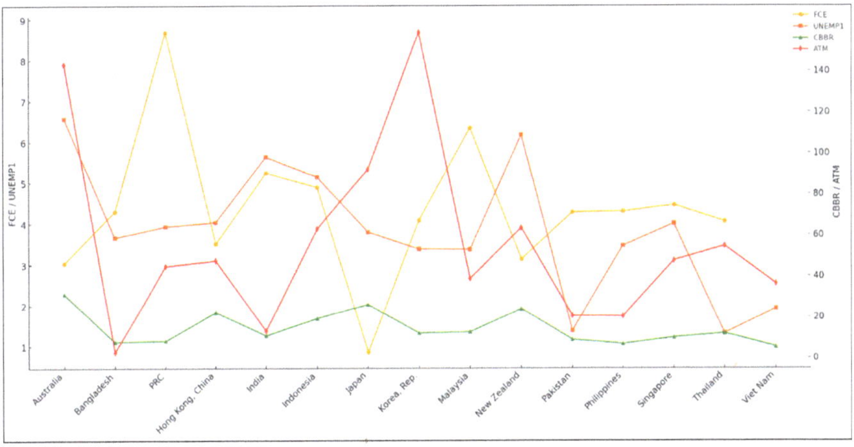

Fig. 5.2 Financial inclusion and sustainable outcome variables across economies. FCE = households' final consumption expenditure (annual % growth), UNEMP1 = unemployment, total (% of the total labor force as per ILO estimate), CBBR = commercial bank branches (per 100,000 adults), ATM = automated teller machines (ATMs) (per 100,000 adults). *Sources* World bank database from 1990 to 2020 and author's calculations

Fig. 5.3 Economy-Specific Uncertainty Heterogeneity. *Sources* World uncertainty index (WUI) and author's calculations

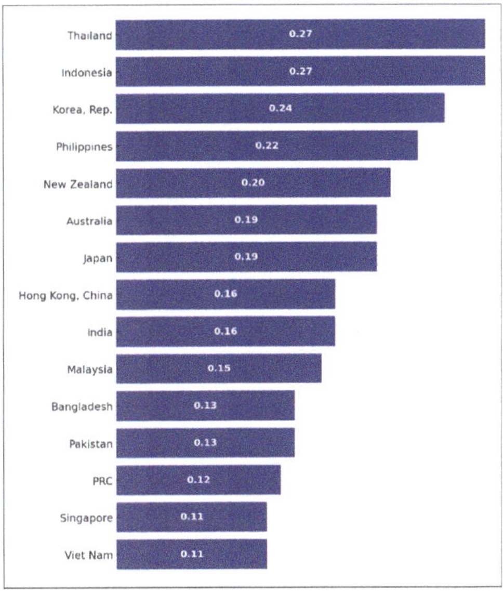

$$\Delta y_{it} = \varphi_i y_{i,t-1} + z'_{it}\lambda_i + \sum\nolimits_{j=1}^{p} \Delta y_{i,t-j} + \varepsilon_{it} \tag{5.1}$$

Here, i = 1,..., N represents 15 countries in the panel; t = 1,..., T_i indicates 31 years; p is the number of lags, and y_{it} is the outcome variable being tested for stationarity.

ε_{it} is a stationary error value. The z_{it} term indicates either a panel-specific mean or a panel-specific mean with a fixed time trend. I hypothesize the null hypothesis H_0: $\varphi_i = 0$ and an alternate hypothesis H_1: $\varphi_i < 0$ for all i. I assess the test results that establish the absence of unit roots and the stationarity of the variables. This study addresses the research questions pertaining to 15 countries over a period of 31 years. For such a study design, there are possibilities of both entity-specific and time-specific unobserved heterogeneity. The pooled OLS estimation technique assumes homogeneity among all observations, which may lead to biased estimates if unobserved factors, such as socioeconomic indicators, demographic factors, or policy biases, are correlated with the explanatory variables (Wooldridge 2010; Greene 2012). Fixed-effect models address this by controlling for these time-invariant unobservable factors through entity-specific intercepts and entity-invariant factors through time-specific intercepts. This two-way FE strategy ensures that any omitted variable bias arising from unobserved heterogeneity is minimized (Baltagi 2021). I then deploy a two-way fixed-effect regression strategy:

$$Y_{it} = \beta_1 X_{it} + \beta_2 W_{it} + \alpha_i + \mu_t + \varepsilon_{it} \tag{5.2}$$

Here, Y_{it} is the outcome variable, i.e., various inclusive economic growth indicators, namely per capita income, household consumption expenditure, and unemployment rate, of the ith country in the tth year. X_{it} is the predictor/independent variable. Here, I include two FI factors—the number of commercial bank branches and the number of depositors—as the predictors. W_{it} consists of all the control variables in this analysis, namely GDP growth rate, gross capital formation growth rate, consumer price inflation, and tax revenue as a percentage of GDP. α_i is the state fixed effect. μ_t is the time fixed effect. I ran the regression six times for the total combination of outcome and predictor variables. I use the Hausman test to compare the FE strategy with random effect (RE) for the selection of the optimum model. The Hausman test compares RE and FE estimators to check for correlation between entity-specific effects and explanatory variables. If differences are significant, FE is preferred, ensuring consistency in estimations (Hausman 1978; Greene 2012).

5.4.2 *Instrumental Variable (IV) Panel Regression Technique*

The predictors in Eq. 5.2 are the FI factors dependent on various operational determinants. I deploy a two-stage instrumental variable panel regression technique to obviate the plausible endogeneity of the primary independent variable and overcome the omitted variable bias (other than incorporating the control variables). Both the FI factors are instrumented by the number of automated teller machines (ATM), borrowers from commercial banks (BOR), fixed broadband subscriptions (FBB), individuals using the Internet (INT), and fixed telephone subscriptions (FTE). The first stage of the equation is:

$$X_{it} = \alpha_i + \delta_t + \delta_1 ATM_{it} + \delta_2 BOR_{it} + \delta_3 FBB_{it} + \delta_4 INT_{it} + \delta_5 FTE_{it} + \varepsilon_{it} \quad (5.3)$$

I then use the first-stage regression results in Eq. 5.2 to determine the relationship between the outcome and predictor variables when the plausible deciding factors/variables instrument the latter.

Further, incorporating policy shocks as externalities, I use the same two-stage instrumental variable strategy with the interaction of FI factors with the policy variables. While the first stage of the equation remains the same and the policy shock variable is exogenous, the second stage of the equation becomes:

$$Y_{it} = \beta_1 X_{it} + \beta_2 P_t + \beta_3 X_{it} * P_t + \beta_4 W_{it} + \alpha_i + \mu_t + \varepsilon_{it} \quad (5.4)$$

P_t is country-invariant policy shocks/interventions, and β_3 is the interaction coefficient. As β_3 indicates the causal impact of policy shocks, it is the coefficient of interest. I use the F-statistic (first-stage regression) to test whether the instruments are strongly correlated with the endogenous variables (Staiger and Stock 1997). Additionally, I conduct the Sargan test (for homoskedastic errors) (Sargan 1958) and the Hansen J-test (for robust errors) (Hansen 1982) to examine overidentifying restrictions in IV estimation. I also deploy the Durbin-Wu-Hausman test to investigate the endogeneity of the predictor variables (Hausman 1978).

To better understand the treatment effects of the policy interventions on the outcome variables through FI factors, I also deploy causal treatment calculations to arrive at the average treatment effect on the treated variables. Here, the three determinants of interest are: the potential-outcome mean (POM) $\alpha_t = E(y_t)$, the average treatment effect (ATE) $\beta_t = E(y_t - y_0)$, and the average treatment effect on the treated (ATET) $\theta_t = E\left(y_t - y_0 \mid t = \tilde{t}\right)$. The expected result of an outcome with a given treatment level $t \in \{0, 1, 2, \ldots, p\}$ is y_t.

5.4.3 *Dynamic Panel Regression Strategy*

I deploy a dynamic panel strategy to check the robustness of the instrumental variable estimator and to consider the plausible autocorrelation of the dependent variables. I check the correlation or covariance probability and Granger causality (Lopez and Weber 2017) at the panel level before using the dynamic panel strategy. The unbiased assessment of other model components is significantly affected when estimating the outcome variables with one or more delays, resulting in the need to examine the quantitative similarity of this strategy to earlier ones (Bond 2002). As a predictor in the dynamic model, the lagged dependent variables are correlated with the entity-specific fixed effect. A novel GMM (generalized method of moments) estimator for dynamic panel structures is proposed by Arellano and Bond (1991). Given the stationarity of the variables and following Arellano and Bond (1991), I regress:

$$Y_{i,t} - Y_{i,t-1} = \varphi \left(Y_{i,t-1} - Y_{i,t-2}\right) + \beta \left(X_{i,t,1} - X_{i,t-1,1}\right) + \eta_1 \left(X_{i,t,2} - X_{i,t-1,2}\right) + \cdots + \left(\varepsilon_{i,t} - \varepsilon_{i,t-1}\right) \quad (5.5)$$

Here, Y_{it} is the dependent/outcome variable of the ith country in the tth year. $X_{i,\,t}$ variables consist of the FI factors (primary independent variable) and the control variables. The FI variables are endogenous due to their dependence on digital and banking infrastructure support, viz., Internet connectivity, mobile networks, and banking penetration (Chatterjee 2020). I similarly deploy an instrument variable design with a two-stage least squares (2sls) technique (Arellano 2016). The first stage of the equation (with infrastructure and accessibility variables represented as $Z_1, Z_2, \ldots$) is:

$$X_{it} = \zeta_{1it} \left(Z_1\right)_{it} + \zeta_{2it} \left(Z_2\right)_{it} \ldots\ldots\ldots + \varepsilon_{it} \quad (5.6)$$

To test the policy shock hypothesis, following Elhorst (2010), I include the policyshock/intervention variables and use the interaction with the main regressor/predictor variable, i.e., FI factors. I regress:

$$Y_{i,t} - Y_{i,t-1} = \varphi \left(Y_{i,t-1} - Y_{i,t-2}\right) + \beta \left(X_{i,t,1} - X_{i,t-1,1}\right) + \theta * \dot{\mathrm{P}} * \left(X_{i,t,1} - X_{i,t-1,1}\right) + \eta_1 \left(X_{i,t,2} - X_{i,t-1,2}\right) + \cdots + \left(\varepsilon_{i,t} - \varepsilon_{i,t-1}\right) \quad (5.7)$$

Here, $\dot{\mathrm{P}}$ is the policy shock dummy. $\dot{\mathrm{P}}$ indicates policy shocks like MDGs, SDGs, AFC, and GFC. These variables take a value of "0" prior to the occurrence of such policy interventions and become "1" after the introduction of these policy shocks. For example, $\dot{\mathrm{P}}$ is 0 until 2000 for MDGs and is 1 for the remaining years. The interaction coefficient θ (and its comparability with β) is of primary importance in this study.

5.4.4 NLP and Topic Modeling

This study uses document repositories of central banks' annual reports, monetary policy documents, and speeches for unsupervised NLP-based topic modeling. After the text preprocessing of the central bank documents, BERTopic is used to develop unique topical themes, as it is more efficient than traditional topic models, i.e., the unigram model, latent semantic analysis, and latent Dirichlet allocation (Egger and Yu 2022). BERTopic is a neural topic model representing words as multidimensional vectors and capturing context information (Abuzayed and Al-Khalifa 2021) that produces detailed and more reliable attributes. Utilizing the unified manifold approximation and projection (UMAP) approach, the BERTopic model reduces the embedding depth of documents before grouping them. Dense clustering is produced

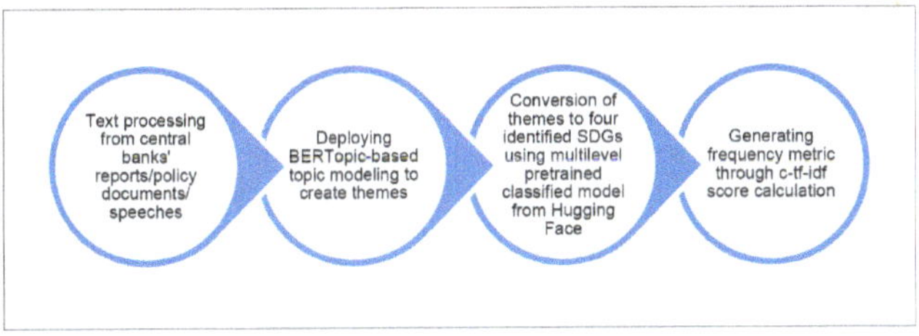

Fig. 5.4 Topic modeling steps for SDG frequency classification. *Sources* Author's illustration

using BERT embedding and cluster-based TF-IDF (Wang et al. 2023). I classify these thematic topics into four identified SDGs (8, 9, 10, and 13) engaging Hugging Face's pretrained SDG classifier model. These four SDGs are chosen based on the spectrum of central banks that influence the outcomes of the macroeconomic determinants, especially those affected by FI factors. I use the TF-IDF (term frequency-inverse document frequency) tool to measure the degree and consistency of central banks' policy focus (Grootendorst 2022) on SDGs, utilizing the following equations:

$$IDF_{t,D} = \log\left(\frac{N}{count\left(d\epsilon D : t\epsilon D\right)}\right); TFIDF_{t,d,D} = TF_{t,D} * IDF_{t,D} \quad (5.8)$$

Here, t is the term (word) for which this study wishes to determine commonality, and N is the sum of documents (d) in the repository (D). Figure 5.4 elaborates on the steps of the NLP techniques used for this analysis. The TFIDF score is a combination of total frequency (TF), which indicates how frequently one term appears in a document, and inverse document frequency (IDF), which penalizes the repetitive presence of common terms in the document repository. I deploy a principal component analysis (PCA) on the TFIDF scores of the four SDGs for the 15 countries across 23 years to reduce dimensionality and check the heterogeneity across countries through variance-based clustering.

5.5 Results

I present the results of this study in three sections. First, I discuss the relationship between FI factors and sectoral SDGs in the macroeconomic space. Next, I show the contribution of policy shocks/interventions to shaping the sectoral SDG outcome. And finally, I present the results of the topic modeling of the central banks' reports and policy documents to determine their sustainability stance for a resilient macroeconomic structure in light of policy shocks.

5.5.1 FI Factors and Sectoral SDGs

In the previous sections, I determined and discussed the rationale for choosing the FI factors and the sectoral sustainability indicators. I deploy Eq. 5.2 to ascertain the impact of FI indicators such as commercial bank branches and the number of depositors on the desired outcome variables: per capita gross national income, household consumption expenditure, and unemployment. Table 5.2 summarizes the results. Except for a significant reduction (at the 1% level) in unemployment due to an increased number of bank branches, the fixed-effect strategy fails to find any solid evidence of FI factors alone contributing to the inclusive development in the income-growth-employment space.

To test the robustness of the empirical strategy and the effectiveness of the applied model, I deploy an instrumental variable regression strategy to obviate the plausible endogeneity in the FI factors. I use Eq. 5.3 to incorporate the instruments to assess the first level for the FI determinants and apply it to Eq. 5.2 to arrive at the final results. Table 5.3 represents the results of the instrumental variable strategy. This study observes a significant rise in per capita income due to a higher number of bank branches and an increase in consumption expenditure (at the 1% significance level) due to a rise in the number of depositors in the formal banking channel. However, the other determinants do not significantly change because of the FI factors alone. As this study finds only 25% (3 out of 12) of the regression results to be significant, I fail to conclude that FI factors alone can improve sectoral inclusivity and growth.

5.5.2 Policy Shocks as Accelerating Force

Going forward, I consider four major economic interventions from the Asia and the Pacific region to ascertain their role in shaping FI factors toward sustainable economic outcomes. Starting with two global positive externalities or policy interventions, I find significant improvement in the sustainable economic growth factors backed by FI initiatives in congruence with the policy shocks. In deploying Eq. 5.4, Tables 5.4 and 5.5 represent the regression results for MDGs and SDGs, respectively. The interaction coefficients for both the FI factors with MDGs show an encouraging picture. With the emergence of the first-of-its-kind holistic and inclusive developmental framework at the global level, the increase in the number of bank branches improves per capita income and household consumption by 2.1% and 7.2%, respectively. There is a reduction in unemployment by 13.6% with MDG intervention. In the post-MDG era, per capita income and household consumption rose by 4.3% and 5.8%, with an increase in the number of depositors in the banking system. There is also a reduction in unemployment by 0.3%, and all the results are significant (at least at the 5% level). SDG intervention in 2015 displays quantitatively similar results. I observe a lower improvement value in the sectoral outcomes due to SDG intervention. For example, income and consumption rise by 1.1% and 2.4%, respectively, with bank

Table 5.2 Fixed-effect regression results—Financial inclusion and sustainable economic outcome

	Gross national income	Household consumption expenditure	Unemployment	Gross national income	Household consumption expenditure	Unemployment
Commercial bank branches (per 100,000 adults)	−0.001	0.048*	−0.121***			
	(0.00)	(0.02)	(0.02)			
Depositors with commercial banks (per 1000 adults)				0.001	0.002*	−0.002
				(0.00)	(0.00)	(0.00)
GDP growth	−0.028***	0.895***	−0.087**	−0.023	0.937***	−0.082
	(0.01)	(0.05)	(0.03)	(0.02)	(0.15)	(0.05)
Gross capital formation growth	−0.001	−0.001	−0.001	0.003	0.008	0.010
	(0.00)	(0.00)	(0.00)	(0.00)	(0.03)	(0.01)
Inflation, consumer prices	−0.030***	0.042	−0.019	−0.031**	−0.013	−0.039*
	(0.01)	(0.03)	(0.02)	(0.01)	(0.09)	(0.02)
Tax revenue (% of GDP)	−0.048***	−0.041	0.226***	−0.020	−0.107	−0.076
	(0.01)	(0.07)	(0.05)	(0.03)	(0.11)	(0.05)
Constant	9.104***	0.138	3.206***	8.554***	0.683	6.264***
	(0.17)	(0.86)	(0.64)	(0.57)	(0.79)	(1.22)
Estimation method	Fixed Effect	Fixed Effect	Fixed Effect	Fixed Effect	Fixed Effect	Fixed Effect

(continued)

Table 5.2 (continued)

	Gross national income	Household consumption expenditure	Unemployment	Gross national income	Household consumption expenditure	Unemployment
Hausman test	91.54***	51.01***	53.88***	13.88**	11.62**	40.98***
Modified Wald test for heteroskedasticity (χ-sq)	1127.10***	165.32***	493.17***	7506.31***	126.70***	613.35***
R-squared	0.185	0.613	0.178	0.282	0.621	0.152
Obs	278	278	277	217	217	216

* $p < 0.10$, ** $p < 0.05$, *** $p < 0.010$
Source Author's own calculations

Table 5.3 Instrumental variable regression—Financial inclusion and sustainable economic outcome

	Gross national income	Household consumption expenditure	Unemployment	Gross national income	Household consumption expenditure	Unemployment
Commercial bank branches (per 100,000 adults)	0.144***	0.069	−0.037			
	(0.02)	(0.05)	(0.03)			
Depositors with commercial banks (per 1000 adults)				−0.012	0.001***	0.000
				(0.01)	(0.00)	(0.00)
GDP growth	0.110***	0.964***	−0.023	−0.974	1.061***	−0.035
	(0.04)	(0.08)	(0.05)	(0.70)	(0.13)	(0.06)
Gross capital formation growth	−0.041***	0.011	0.013	0.167	−0.004	0.007
	(0.01)	(0.03)	(0.02)	(0.14)	(0.04)	(0.02)
Inflation, consumer prices	−0.108***	−0.056	−0.137***	0.148	−0.100*	−0.055*
	(0.02)	(0.05)	(0.03)	(0.21)	(0.06)	(0.03)
Tax revenue (% of GDP)	0.021	−0.021	0.129***	1.276	−0.121**	0.045
	(0.02)	(0.04)	(0.03)	(0.78)	(0.06)	(0.04)
Constant	6.648***	−0.320	2.958***	2.633	0.617	3.460***
	(0.32)	(0.69)	(0.45)	(3.46)	(0.71)	(0.42)

(continued)

Table 5.3 (continued)

	Gross national income	Household consumption expenditure	Unemployment	Gross national income	Household consumption expenditure	Unemployment
Estimation Method	Instrumental variable	Instrumental variable	Instrumental variable	Instrumental variable	Instrumental variable	Instrumental variable
Wu-Hausman F	121.848***	2.08134	1.06079	1.88712	5.84923**	1.93703
First-stage regression F	16.7063***	16.7063***	16.7226***	24.0701***	40.8356***	24.0701***
Adjusted R-squared	0.409	0.659	0.347		0.655	0.268
Obs	184	184	183	184	184	184

* $p < 0.10$, ** $p < 0.05$, *** $p < 0.010$
Source Author's own calculations

branches increasing. These values are 0.1% and 1.9% for an increase in depositors in the formal banking channel. This may be attributed to the maiden global inclusive economic growth drive by MDG and the significant progress that has occurred since 2000, leaving less scope for a higher sectoral improvement (Lomazzi et al. 2014; Fukuda-Parr 2016).

This study similarly determines the impact of two negative externalities as policy shocks, namely AFC 1997 and GFC 2008. By deploying Eq. 5.4, Tables 5.6 and 5.7 represent the regression results for the AFC and the GFC, respectively. From the interaction coefficients, it is evident that the AFC, in the long run, positively impacted the inclusive economic growth orientation of the Asia and the Pacific countries. Improved bank branch penetration after the AFC contributes to a 3.7% and 7.8% rise in income and household consumption, respectively. With more depositors after the AFC, this study observes a 4.1% and 2.3% rise in income and household consumption, respectively. The post-AFC period also sees a significant reduction in unemployment (12.3% and 3.7% for the FI factors, respectively). These outcomes indicate the policymakers' understanding of the desired path they wish to traverse—from growth to development and from development to inclusive and sustainable development. The improvement in per capita income, household expenses, and the employment scenario strengthens the claims of the researchers (George et al. 2012; Ali et al. 2023; Li and Wu 2023). However, the interaction coefficients for GFC and FI factors do not display a coherent and significant result. For both the FI factors, post-SDG improvement in shaping the sectoral outcomes does not depend much on the intervention. There may be a twofold reason for this. First, the impact of the GFC on Asia and the Pacific economies (mostly countries with significant economic sizes, such as the PRC and India, in this study) has been minimal compared with that on the rest of the world (Tang, Ding, and Chen 2021). Hence, the improvement witnessed post-AFC has not been significantly negated by the emergence of the GFC. Second, the data span of only 5 years after the SDGs dilutes its average treatment impact compared to 26 years beforehand.

To address the plausible lag effect of the dependent variables and to ascertain the robustness of the instrumental variable models deployed previously for the policy shocks, I use dynamic panel strategies for both MDG and AFC interventions. I deploy Eq. 5.7 to obtain the results with the difference GMM and system GMM techniques, with bank branches as the FI factor. I also check the effectiveness of the dynamic models by performing the Sargan, Hansen, AR (1), and AR (2) tests. Tables 5.8 and 5.9 summarize the regression results. I find quantitatively similar results obtained earlier for both difference and system GMM strategies with full instruments set.

As a part of the robustness check and plausible causality of the policy interventions in the sectoral sustainability goals through FI factors, I use the causality treatment effects strategy to calculate the average treatment effect on the treated. Here, income, household consumption, and unemployment are the distinct outcome variables predicted separately by bank branches and depositors. Policy shocks/interventions like MDGs, SDGs, the AFC, and the GFC act as treatments. The potential outcome means (POMean) and average treatment effect (ATE) of all the interventions are tabulated in Tables 5.10 and 5.11 for bank branches and depositors

Table 5.4 Regression results—Millennium development goals (mdg) as policy shock

	Gross national income	Household consumption expenditure	Unemployment	Gross national income	Household consumption expenditure	Unemployment
Commercial bank branches (CBBR)	0.028***	0.045*	−0.023**			
	(0.00)	(0.03)	(0.00)			
Depositors with commercial banks (DEP)				0.000***	0.002*	−0.000
				(0.00)	(0.00)	(0.00)
Millennium Development Goals (MDG)	0.436***	2.160*	−1.897***	0.605***	0.556	−0.285
	(0.08)	(1.17)	(0.25)	(0.04)	(0.61)	(0.26)
CBBR X MDG	0.021***	0.072**	−0.136***			
	(0.01)	(0.04)	(0.02)			
DEP X MDG				0.043***	0.058***	−0.003***
				(0.00)	(0.00)	(0.00)
GDP growth	−0.018***	0.845***	−0.052**	−0.013	0.944***	−0.052
	(0.01)	(0.05)	(0.02)	(0.01)	(0.08)	(0.03)
Gross capital formation growth	−0.001**	−0.002	0.001	0.000	0.006	0.010
	(0.00)	(0.00)	(0.00)	(0.00)	(0.02)	(0.01)
Inflation, consumer prices	−0.012***	0.039	0.005	−0.011**	0.001	0.006
	(0.00)	(0.03)	(0.01)	(0.01)	(0.05)	(0.02)
Tax revenue (% of GDP)	0.026**	0.055*	−0.066*	0.016*	−0.088	−0.065*
	(0.01)	(0.03)	(0.03)	(0.01)	(0.09)	(0.04)
Constant	7.833***	0.522	5.293***	7.676***	11.555	−100.493***

(continued)

Table 5.4 (continued)

	Gross national income	Household consumption expenditure	Unemployment	Gross national income	Household consumption expenditure	Unemployment
	(0.14)	(0.98)	(0.46)	(0.14)	(69.63)	(28.98)
Estimation method	Instrumental variable	Instrumental variable	Instrumental variable	Instrumental variable	Instrumental variable	Instrumental variable
Wu-Hausman F	119.898***	135.109***	109.001***	121.011***	88.733***	97.008***
First-stage regression F	31.6063***	26.1064***	29.0987***	41.6098***	19.3091***	41.1834***
Adjusted R-squared	0.608	0.673	0.361	0.638	0.623	0.412
Obs	278	278	277	217	217	216

* $p < 0.10$, ** $p < 0.05$, *** $p < 0.010$
Source Author's own calculations

Table 5.5 Regression results—Sustainable development goals (SDG) as policy shock

	Gross national income	Household consumption expenditure	Unemployment	Gross national income	Household consumption expenditure	Unemployment
Commercial bank branches (CBBR)	−0.006	0.043*	−0.081***			
	(0.00)	(0.02)	(0.01)			
Depositors with commercial banks (DEP)				0.000***	0.001	−0.002***
				(0.00)	(0.00)	(0.00)
Sustainable Development Goals (SDG)	0.664***	0.218	−1.927***	0.556***	4.248***	−1.162***
	(0.16)	(0.89)	(0.42)	(0.07)	(1.35)	(0.27)
CBBR X SDG	0.011*	0.024***	−0.138***			
	(0.01)	(0.06)	(0.03)			
DEP X SDG				0.001***	0.019***	−0.039***
				(0.00)	(0.00)	(0.00)
GDP growth	−0.014*	0.908***	−0.036	−0.013	0.797***	−0.057
	(0.01)	(0.05)	(0.02)	(0.01)	(0.10)	(0.04)
Gross capital formation growth	−0.001	−0.001	0.000	0.002	0.017	0.008
	(0.00)	(0.00)	(0.00)	(0.00)	(0.03)	(0.01)
Inflation, consumer prices	−0.020***	0.052*	−0.000	−0.023***	−0.010	−0.024
	(0.01)	(0.03)	(0.01)	(0.01)	(0.06)	(0.02)
Tax revenue (% of GDP)	−0.029**	−0.021	−0.045	−0.004	−0.070	−0.057
	(0.01)	(0.07)	(0.03)	(0.01)	(0.09)	(0.04)
Constant	8.683***	−0.272	5.737***	8.287***	2.648*	5.751***

(continued)

Table 5.5 (continued)

	Gross national income	Household consumption expenditure	Unemployment	Gross national income	Household consumption expenditure	Unemployment
	(0.16)	(0.91)	(0.43)	(0.15)	(1.59)	(0.56)
Estimation method	Instrumental variable	Instrumental variable	Instrumental variable	Instrumental variable	Instrumental variable	Instrumental variable
Wu-Hausman F	69.098***	119.962***	94.53***	107.246***	132.678***	81.814***
First-stage regression F	19.0981***	31.9087***	24.7711***	30.9323***	33.7688***	36.6053***
Adjusted R-squared	0.346	0.616	0.282	0.443	0.687	0.226
Obs	278	278	277	217	217	216

* $p < 0.10$, ** $p < 0.05$, *** $p < 0.010$
Source Author's own calculations

Table 5.6 Regression results—Asian financial crisis (AFC) as policy shock

	Gross national income	Household consumption expenditure	Unemployment	Gross national income	Household consumption expenditure	Unemployment
Commercial bank branches (CBBR)	0.035***	0.050*	−0.026*			
	(0.01)	(0.03)	(0.02)			
Depositors with commercial banks (DEP)				0.001***	0.001	−0.002
				(0.00)	(0.00)	(0.00)
Asian financial crisis (AFC)	0.247***	2.008*	−1.942***	0.594***	2.796**	−1.219***
	(0.09)	(1.19)	(0.27)	(0.06)	(1.36)	(0.21)
CBBR X AFC	0.037***	0.078**	−0.123***			
	(0.01)	(0.04)	(0.02)			
DEP X AFC				0.041***	0.023**	−0.037***
				(0.00)	(0.00)	(0.00)
GDP growth	−0.004	0.844***	−0.045**	−0.016*	0.874***	−0.053
	(0.01)	(0.05)	(0.02)	(0.01)	(0.08)	(0.03)
Gross capital formation growth	−0.001**	−0.002	0.001	0.004	−0.000	0.011
	(0.00)	(0.00)	(0.00)	(0.00)	(0.03)	(0.01)
Inflation, consumer prices	−0.021***	0.057*	0.032**	−0.004	−0.002	0.004
	(0.00)	(0.03)	(0.01)	(0.01)	(0.06)	(0.02)
Tax revenue (% of GDP)	0.028**	0.061*	−0.049	0.012	0.055	−0.094***
	(0.01)	(0.03)	(0.04)	(0.01)	(0.05)	(0.04)

(continued)

Table 5.6 (continued)

	Gross national income	Household consumption expenditure	Unemployment	Gross national income	Household consumption expenditure	Unemployment
Constant	7.800***	0.246	4.745***	7.585***	1.184	4.816***
	(0.16)	(1.01)	(0.49)	(0.17)	(1.29)	(0.58)
Estimation method	Instrumental variable	Instrumental variable	Instrumental variable	Instrumental variable	Instrumental variable	Instrumental variable
Wu-Hausman F	113.511***	89.003***	141.113***	78.308***	101.115***	119.532***
First-stage regression F	18.1198***	21.1177***	39.6889***	19.3323***	28.8371***	44.7601***
Adjusted R-squared	0.551	0.674	0.347	0.530	0.678	0.389
Obs	278	278	277	217	217	216

* $p < 0.10$, ** $p < 0.05$, *** $p < 0.010$
Source Author's own calculations

Table 5.7 Regression results—Global financial crisis (GFC) as policy shock

	Gross national income	Household consumption expenditure	Unemployment	Gross national income	Household consumption expenditure	Unemployment
Commercial bank branches (CBBR)	−0.026***	0.029	−0.086***			
	(0.00)	(0.02)	(0.01)			
Depositors with commercial banks(DEP)				−0.000	0.002*	−0.002***
				(0.00)	(0.00)	(0.00)
Global financial crisis (GFC)	1.297***	−2.246*	0.885	1.150***	−4.037***	1.362**
	(0.12)	(1.17)	(0.61)	(0.09)	(1.31)	(0.68)
CBBR X GFC	0.004	0.061*	−0.035*			
	(0.00)	(0.04)	(0.02)			
DEP X GFC				−0.001***	−0.002	−0.003**
				(0.00)	(0.00)	(0.00)
GDP growth	−0.011*	0.852***	−0.021	−0.011*	0.809***	−0.019
	(0.01)	(0.05)	(0.03)	(0.01)	(0.10)	(0.05)
Gross capital formation growth	−0.001	−0.002	−0.000	0.001	0.016	0.008
	(0.00)	(0.00)	(0.00)	(0.00)	(0.03)	(0.01)
Inflation, consumer prices	−0.003	0.043	0.012	−0.005	−0.007	−0.014
	(0.00)	(0.03)	(0.02)	(0.00)	(0.06)	(0.03)
Tax revenue (% of GDP)	0.052***	0.043	−0.012	0.048***	−0.095	−0.041
	(0.01)	(0.03)	(0.04)	(0.01)	(0.09)	(0.05)

(continued)

Table 5.7 (continued)

	Gross national income	Household consumption expenditure	Unemployment	Gross national income	Household consumption expenditure	Unemployment
Constant	7.007***	0.813	5.132***	7.298***	2.713*	5.649***
	(0.39)	(0.96)	(0.70)	(0.11)	(1.59)	(0.83)
Estimation method	Instrumental Variable	Instrumental Variable	Instrumental Variable	Instrumental Variable	Instrumental Variable	Instrumental Variable
Wu-Hausman F	5.8791**	75.0616***	39.7092***	11.113**	21.007***	141.887***
First-stage regression F	21.8521***	33.3745***	44.8971***	39.135***	16.09***	27.613***
Adjusted R-squared	0.823	0.674	0.279	0.863	0.688	0.277
Obs	278	278	277	217	217	216

* $p < 0.10$, ** $p < 0.05$, *** $p < 0.010$

Source Author's own calculations

Table 5.8 Regression results—GMM estimation with policy shock (MDG)

	Gross national income	Household consumption expenditure	Unemployment	Gross national income	Household consumption expenditure	Unemployment
CBBR X MDG	0.002**	0.064**	−0.113**	0.003**	0.079**	−0.110**
	(0.00)	−0.02	(0.05)	(0.00)	−0.02	−0.03
GDP growth	0.008***	0.936***	−0.010	0.006***	1.056***	0.032
	(0.00)	(0.10)	(0.05)	(0.00)	(0.18)	(0.23)
Gross capital formation growth	−0.001	−0.001	−0.010	−0.000***	−0.004*	0.001
	(0.00)	(0.00)	(0.02)	(0.00)	(0.00)	(0.00)
Inflation, consumer prices	−0.002	0.117**	−0.007	−0.001	0.160	0.046
	(0.00)	(0.05)	(0.11)	(0.00)	(0.09)	(0.12)
Tax revenue (% of GDP)	0.002	−0.053	0.015	0.005**	0.101	0.266
	(0.00)	(0.08)	(0.09)	(0.00)	(0.10)	(0.30)
y(t-1)	0.951***	0.125**	0.283*	0.953***	−0.165**	0.090*
	(0.02)	(0.27)	(0.25)	(0.02)	(0.20)	(0.57)
Constant				0.299*	−2.718	0.479
				(0.15)	(2.61)	(4.25)
Estimation method	Difference GMM	Difference GMM	Difference GMM	System GMM	System GMM	System GMM
Type of instrument	Full instrument	Full instrument	Full instrument	Full Instrument	Full instrument	Full instrument
No. of instruments	225	229	225	240	240	243
Sargan test (p-val.)	1.000	0.764	0.390	0.291	0.444	0.454

(continued)

Table 5.8 (continued)

	Gross national income	Household consumption expenditure	Unemployment	Gross national income	Household consumption expenditure	Unemployment
Hansen test (p-val.)	1.000	1.000	1.000	1.000	1.000	1.000
AR(1) test (p-val.)	0.414	0.220	0.537	0.319	0.140	0.831
AR(2) test (p-val.)	0.562	0.921	0.673	0.501	0.130	0.949
No. of observations	260	260	258	269	269	267

CBBR = commercial bank branches, MDGs = Millennium Development Goals, y(t-1) = first lag of the predictor variable, AR(1) and AR(2) = Arellano-Bond tests for first- and second-order autocorrelation

* $p < 0.10$, ** $p < 0.05$, *** $p < 0.010$

Source Author's own calculations

Table 5.9 Regression results—GMM estimation with policy shock (AFC)

	Gross national income	Household consumption expenditure	Unemployment	Gross national income	Household consumption expenditure	Unemployment
CBBR X AFC	0.002***	0.129*	−0.094**	0.003**	0.046**	−0.078**
	(0.00)	(0.08)	−0.02	(0.00)	−0.01	−0.03
GDP growth	0.009***	0.438	−0.124***	0.007***	0.894***	−0.117***
	(0.00)	(0.42)	(0.02)	(0.00)	(0.18)	(0.03)
Gross capital formation growth	−0.000	0.127	0.000	−0.000***	−0.003*	0.001
	(0.00)	(0.14)	(0.00)	(0.00)	(0.00)	(0.00)
Inflation, consumer prices	−0.003	0.243	−0.018*	−0.002	0.067	−0.010
	(0.00)	(0.34)	(0.01)	(0.00)	(0.09)	(0.01)
Tax revenue (% of GDP)	0.004	−0.169	0.038	0.005**	0.039	0.084
	(0.00)	(0.27)	(0.03)	(0.00)	(0.10)	(0.05)
y(t-1)	0.956***	0.301	0.380	0.952***	0.014	0.399
	(0.02)	(0.30)	(0.31)	(0.02)	(0.14)	(0.28)
Constant				0.309*	−1.125	2.828***
				(0.16)	(3.07)	(1.07)
Estimation method	Difference GMM	Difference GMM	Difference GMM	System GMM	System GMM	System GMM
Type of instrument	Full instrument	Full instrument	Full instrument	Full instrument	Full instrument	Full instrument
No. of instruments	225	225	229	240	240	243
Sargan test (p-val.)	1.000	0.832	0.419	0.311	0.436	0.449

(continued)

Table 5.9 (continued)

	Gross national income	Household consumption expenditure	Unemployment	Gross national income	Household consumption expenditure	Unemployment
Hansen test (p-val.)	1.000	1.000	1.000	1.000	1.000	1.000
AR(1) test (p-val.)	0.393	0.280	0.230	0.084	0.055	0.220
AR(2) test (p-val.)	0.785	0.330	0.662	0.590	0.475	0.815
No. of observations	260	260	258	269	269	267

CBBR = commercial bank branches, AFC = Asian financial crisis, AR(1) and AR(2) = Arellano-Bond tests for first- and second-order autocorrelation

* $p < 0.10$, ** $p < 0.05$, *** $p < 0.010$

Source Author's own calculations

Table 5.10 Causality treatment effects—Predicted by bank branches

Predicted by commercial bank branches	MDGs	SDGs	AFC	GFC
Gross national income				
Average treatment effect (ATE)	0.3672***	0.3982***	0.4223**	0.3278***
Potential outcome means (POMean)	8.4357***	8.6593***	8.3674***	8.5806***
Household consumption expenditure				
Average treatment effect (ATE)	0.5601**	0.7817	0.2512**	0.2578
Potential outcome means (POMean)	4.7142***	5.0468***	4.2987***	4.5108***
Unemployment				
Average treatment effect (ATE)	−0.5603***	−0.42279**	−0.17144**	−0.25513**
Potential outcome means (POMean)	4.3188***	4.0281***	4.0843***	3.9509***

Source Author's own calculations

as predictors, respectively. The results are quantitatively similar to those determined previously. With this, this study not only negates the role of FI initiatives alone in improving economic sustainability goals but also affirms the significant role of global policy interventions (both positive externalities and external diseconomies[4]) in facilitating the conversion of FI factors into sustainable and inclusive economic development.

5.5.3 *Central Banks' SDG Focus*

This study establishes policy shocks such as MDGs, SDGs, the AFC, and the GFC as enablers to achieve sustainable and inclusive economic growth through the FI channel. I study the role of central banks in conducive and inclusive policymaking to facilitate the attainment of SDGs. As detailed in the empirical strategy section, this topic Modeling study primarily segments the central bank policy documents of 21 years for the 15 countries into sustainability topics. Figure 5.5 depicts the economy-specific SDG topics, with substantial heterogeneity being observed in the number of topics, varying from 21 in Pakistan to 91 in Japan.

[4] When a policy disruption affects the whole industry and increases the cost or complexity of doing business, it may be considered an external diseconomy. Alterations in international/government policy, whether substantive, unforeseen, or a side effect, may significantly influence the economy, and these are also known as "external diseconomies" (Ellis and Fellner 1943; Wirl and Dockner 1995).

Table 5.11 Causality treatment effects–Predicted by depositors

Predicted by depositors	MDGs	SDGs	AFC	GFC
Gross national income				
Average treatment effect (ATE)	0.4461***	0.3971*	0.4335**	0.4027*
Potential outcome means (POMean)	8.1257***	8.3569***	8.0918***	8.2646***
Household consumption expenditure				
Average treatment effect (ATE)	0.5694**	0.6028	0.5568**	0.5922**
Potential outcome means (POMean)	4.6931***	4.9309***	4.6586***	4.8531***
Unemployment				
Average treatment effect (ATE)	−0.9323***	−0.4171*	−0.6007***	−0.7784***
Potential outcome means (POMean)	4.3337***	3.7822***	4.1868***	4.0071***

Source Author's own calculations

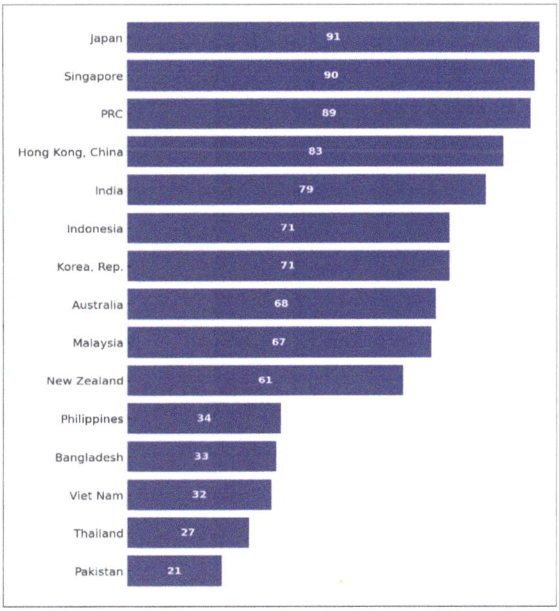

Fig. 5.5 Number of sustainability topics. *Notes* Number of themes/topics through topic modeling using BERTopic. A few generic themes or unrelated groups of words were removed when performing text cleaning. *Sources* Central banks' annual reports, monetary policy statements, and press releases for 15 countries from 2000 to 2022 and author's calculations. A total of 1815 documents have been analyzed in this research

This paper restricts this NLP study to four SDGs strongly interlinking with FI factors. It examines SDGs 8, 9, 10, and 13 by calculating year-wise tf-idf frequency scores for each goal for all 15 countries. As the period of this topic modeling is 2000–2022, GFC 2008 and SDG 2015 are the policy interventions during this period. Figure 5.6 represents the frequency scores of the four SDGs across years for the 15 countries, with a significant jump being evident in all the goals after 2008 and 2015. Goals 8 and 9 witness comparatively higher jumps after 2008, whereas Goals 10 and 13 see more remarkable growth after 2015. The core premises of the four goals justify my observation. Goal 8 focuses on economic growth, whereas

Goal 9 focuses on industry, innovation, and infrastructure. The 2008 GFC demanded structural economic stability, and central banks' policy focus displays a solid bias towards reshaping economic resilience to handle such a crisis. Goal 10 is aimed at reducing inequalities, and Goal 13 targets climate action. The emergence of SDGs in 2015 required a robust inclusivity bias and green orientation. The impulsive shifts in frequency scores for SDGs 10 and 13 reaffirm this.

Figure 5.7 demonstrates the economy-wise shift in central banks' focus on these four SDGs over the last 23 years. As mentioned earlier, SDGs 8 and 9 witnessed negligible growth between 2000 and 2008; however, they rose significantly afterwards. SDGs 10 and 13 saw insignificant growth from 2000 to 2008 and 2015; however, they jumped after that. This study empirically proves that policy shocks are game-changers in shaping inclusive and sustainable macroeconomic frameworks. Further, countries' apex banks, being the economic policy formulators, especially in the FI space, play a deciding role in achieving sustainability targets. The shift in the sustainable theme frequency scores affirms this.

This paper further evaluates the economy-specific heterogeneity amongst central banks towards sustainable policymaking. Figure 5.8 depicts the economy groupings based on the frequency scores of central banks' policy documents. Scores for all four SDGs display quantitatively similar results. Australia, Japan, the Republic of Korea,

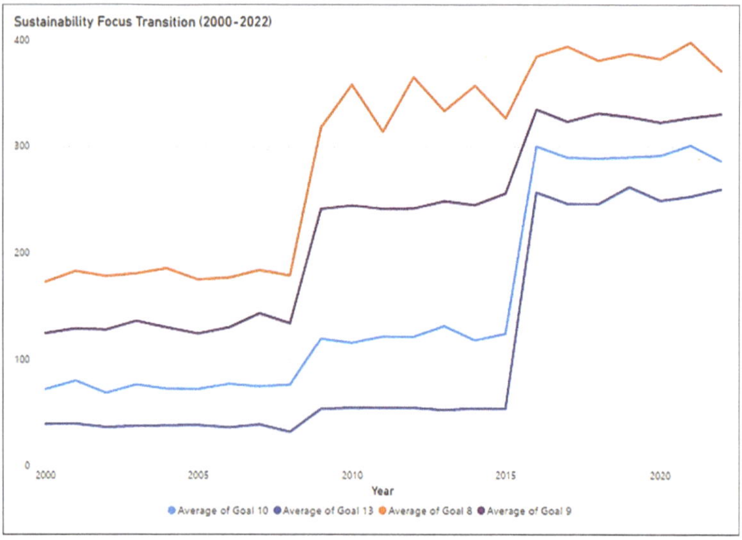

Fig. 5.6 Sustainability focus transition (2000–2020) through policy shocks. *Notes* 1.The frequency metric used in the chart is the c-tf-idf score. 2. The global financial crisis of 2008 and the implementation of Sustainable Development Goals in 2015 are major policy events during this period. 3. This paper restricts the sustainability goals to four (SDGs 8, 9, 10, and 13), considering their relevance to financial inclusion and policy shocks. *Sources* Central banks' annual reports, monetary policy statements, and press releases for 15 countries from 2000 to 2022, and the author's calculations. A total of 1815 documents have been analyzed in this research

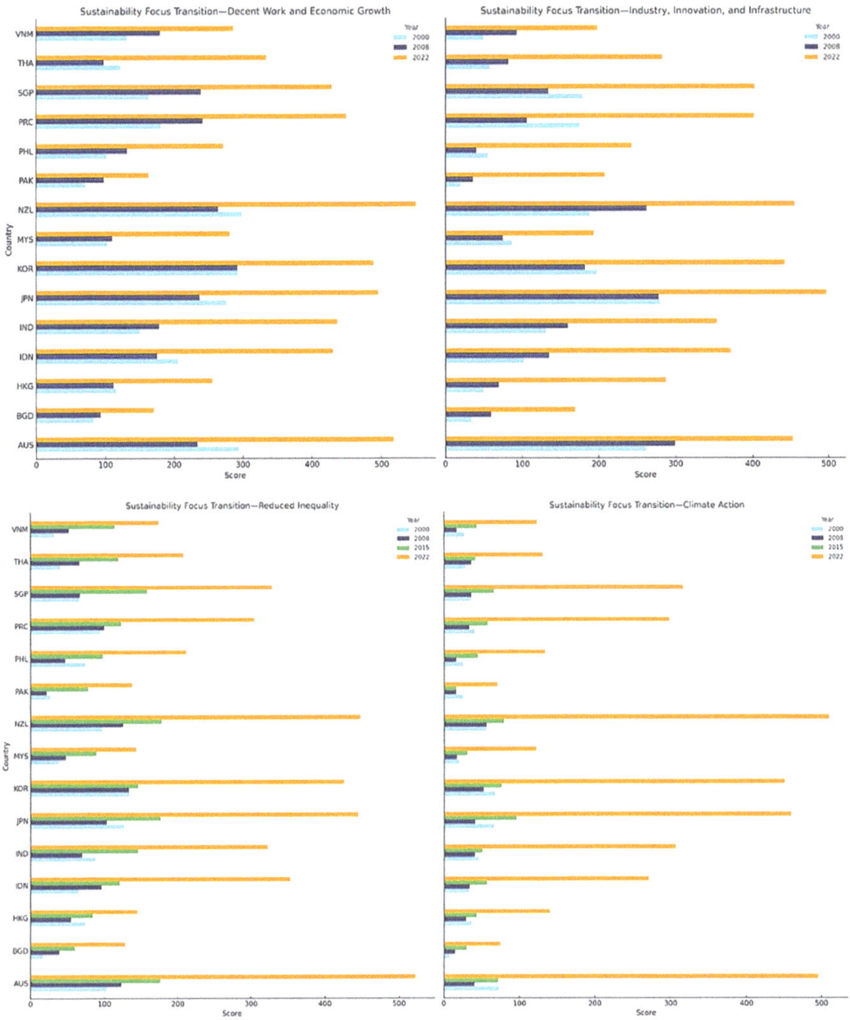

Fig. 5.7 Sustainability focus transition (2000–2022) of SDGs 8, 9, 10, and 13 through global shocks. *Notes* 1. The frequency metric used in the chart is the c-tf-idf score. 2. this paper restricts the sustainability goals to four (SDGs 8, 9, 10, and 13), considering their relevance to financial inclusion and policy shocks. *Sources* Central banks' annual reports, monetary policy statements, and press releases for 15 countries from 2000 to 2022, and the author's calculations. A total of 1815 documents have been analyzed in this research

and New Zealand are at the top of the spectrum in demonstrating sustainability focus, followed by India, the PRC, Singapore, and Indonesia. Pakistan and Bangladesh are at the bottom in terms of the frequency scores.

Interestingly, the top four countries are the only OECD countries among the 15 considered in this study, and they also top the overall sustainability performance

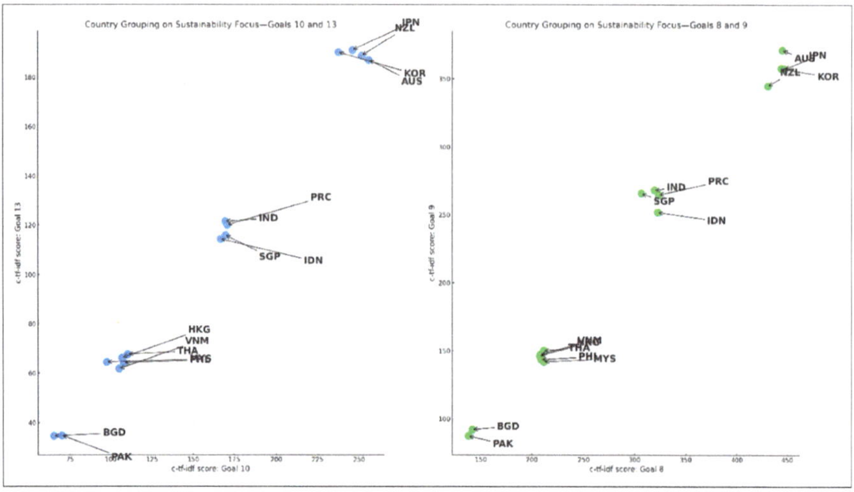

Fig. 5.8 Economy Groupings on c-tf-idf Frequency Score (SDGs 8, 9, 10, and 13). *Sources* Central banks' annual reports, monetary policy statements, and press releases for 15 countries from 2020 to 2022, and the author's calculations. A total of 1815 documents have been analyzed in this research

ranking. This emphasizes the policy priority of apex banks in broadly achieving SDGs. I deploy PCA for the four SDGs to ascertain the economy groupings through an empirical exploration, and the results are summarized in Table 5.12. The first two principal components cater to 97.55% of the total variance. Figure 5.9 represents the 2-D PCA plot (reduced from 4-D). The distribution clearly indicates that the central banks' policy focus toward Sustainability Goals varies across countries, and their variances differ from one economy group to another. The economy groupings in Fig. 5.9 replicate those in Fig. 5.8. I conclude that a robust economy-level heterogeneity in the policy orientation of the central banks facilitates SDGs.

Table 5.12 Results of principal component analysis (PCA)

Parameter	PC_1	PC_2	PC_3	PC_4
Eigenvalue	3.473	0.429	0.078	0.020
% of Variance	86.816	10.735	1.942	0.507
Cumulative (%)	86.816	97.551	99.493	100

PC_1, PC_2, PC_3, and PC_4 = first, second, third, and fourth primary components
Source Author's own calculations

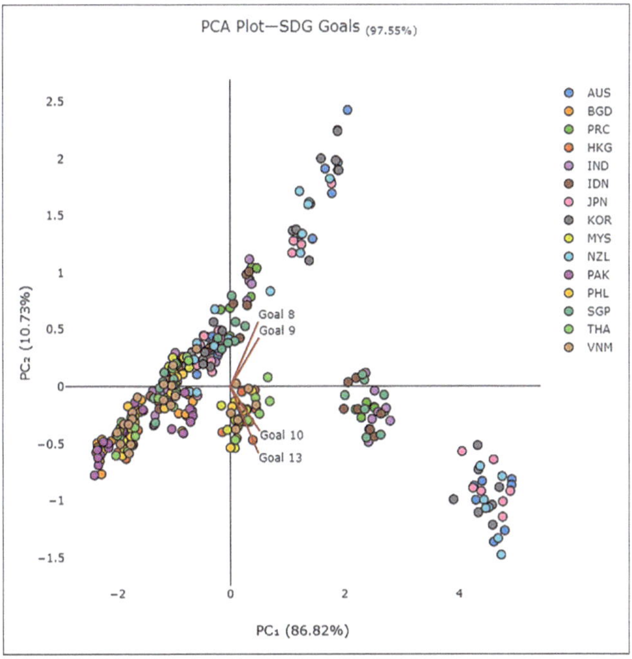

Fig. 5.9 Principal component analysis of four sustainability goals (SDGs 8, 9, 10, and 13). PC_1, PC_2 = first and second primary components. *Notes* Each economy is represented by one circle (23 circles for one economy) of a unique color for 2000–2022. *Sources* Author's own calculations

5.6 Discussion

This paper starts with a theoretical perspective of developmental public policy-making at the national level to attain equitable Sustainability Goals, mainly focusing on macroeconomic targets such as income generation, consumption, and employment. Financial inclusion (FI) initiatives have been pinpointed as major channels for improving such sectoral SDGs (Mishra et al. 2024). This study empirically depicts an indistinctive relation between FI factors and SDG variables. Why can FI factors alone not improve SDGs in the macroeconomic space? This may be attributed to the ineffective transmission mechanism, a lack of policy advocacy inequitable distribution of benefits, and prevailing high levels of inequality and poverty ("De Gruyter Handbook of Sustainable Development and Finance" 2022; Yap, Lee, and Liew 2023). To answer the question, this paper explores the occurrence of policy shocks or interventions during the period under study and observes significant improvement (with quantitatively similar results for multiple empirical designs) in SDG deliverables with an enhanced FI gambit. These interventions lead to expansionary policy preferences by addressing one or multiple policy barriers (Swinkels 2020; Cejudo and Trein 2022). MDGs and SDGs act as positive policy shocks in accommodating inclusive policy stances by policymakers; however, the AFC and the GFC, despite having strong negative externalities, steer the economic policy priorities toward equitable and sustainable growth (Försterling, Orth, and Gellert 2023). These adverse shocks also help targeted and substantive public policies to be more redistributive to develop higher systemic resilience (Healy and Bristow 2020; Arestis 2021).

This paper observes an increasing but heterogeneous intent among central banks in Asia and the Pacific to move towards sustainable economic goals. The increase in the SDG frequency score for all four identified SDGs over the last two decades shows the inclusive intent of the central banks in formulating regulatory guidelines and policies. The policy shocks through MDGs and SDGs help central banks to be more sustainability focused and inclined toward reducing inequality, as well as initiating suitable action to combat climate change and its impacts (Svartzman et al. 2020; Dinh et al. 2024). The increase in frequency scores for SDGs 10 and 13 since 2015 strengthens this fact. Further, the thriving trajectory of sustainable economic growth and both inclusive and sustainable industrialization after the AFC in 1997 and the GFC of 2008 highlights the reshaping of the macroeconomic structure of the countries (Biggeri et al. 2023; Feiferytė-Skirienė and Stasiškienė 2023). The focus of central banks on SDG 8 and SDG 9 themes after 2008 reiterates the past theoretical claims and pinpoints the equanimity of systemic sectoral resilience (Clemente et al. 2019; Durrani et al. 2020). Is there an economy-level heterogeneity amongst the apex banks in their sustainable policy focus? The answer is "yes." The significantly greater focus by the respective central banks on the SDG themes for high-income developed countries like Japan, the Republic of Korea, Australia, and New Zealand corroborates their higher ranking (with scores above 78%) in the latest Sustainable Development Report[5] (Park and Kim 2020; Ozili and Iorember 2023). Further, quantitatively similar unfavorable results for low-income nations like Bangladesh and Pakistan highlight the need for their apex banks to be more vigilant toward SDG-oriented policy formulation (Khairunnessa et al. 2021). The findings make it pertinent that policy shocks drive the attainment of SDGs for macroeconomic determinants through a robust policy framework of the central banks of Asia and the Pacific nations.

5.7 Conclusion

This study makes a novel attempt to bridge the prevailing research gaps in interlinking financial inclusion factors with macroeconomic sustainability in the emergence of global policy shocks. It also establishes the increasing role of central banks in determining the extent of inclusive macroeconomic development in Asia and the Pacific countries. The NLP-based topic modeling of the significantly sizeable central

[5] Economies are ranked by their all-encompassing progress towards attaining all 17 Sustainable Development Goals. The score can be seen as a percentage of attaining SDGs. A score of 100 indicates that all SDGs have been achieved. The details pertaining to the ranking can be found at https://dashboards.sdgindex.org/rankings.

bank document repository indicates a plausible contribution to policymaking through policy bias/priority analysis. It also prompts further research on the intricacies of heterogeneous central bank policymaking across countries targeting sustainable and inclusive macroeconomic goals. This study also highlights the need for a robust transmission channel to transform financial inclusivity measures into sustainable economic outcomes. Future studies may also perform NLP-based comparative analysis on sectoral policy papers and central banks' policy documents to determine the structural symmetry in institutional bias and priorities.

References

Abuzayed, A., and H. Al-Khalifa. 2021. BERT for Arabic topic modeling: An experimental study on BERTopic technique. *Procedia Computer Science* 189 (January): 191–194. https://doi.org/10.1016/j.procs.2021.05.096.

Acemoglu, D., and J. Robinson. 2012. *Why nations fail: The origins of power, prosperity, and poverty*. New York: Crown Business.

Aghion, P., and P. Bolton. 1997. A theory of trickle-down growth and development. *The Review of Economic Studies* 64 (2): 151. https://doi.org/10.2307/2971707.

Ajide, K., I. Raheem, O. Y. Alimi, and S. Asongu. 2020. The role of institutional infrastructures in financial inclusion–Growth relations: Evidence from SSA. *International Journal of Finance and Economics* 27 (1): 175–191. https://doi.org/10.2139/ssrn.3647533.

Alcamo, J., J. Thompson, A. Alexander, A. Antoniades, I. Delabre, J. Dolley, et al. 2020. Analysing interactions among the sustainable development goals: Findings and emerging issues from local and global studies. *Sustainability Science* 15 (6): 1561–1572. https://doi.org/10.1007/s11625-020-00875-x.

Alexander, K., and X. Karametaxas. 2021. *Digital transformation and financial inclusion*, 273–290. Routledge eBooks. https://doi.org/10.4324/9780429325670-15.

Ali, S. M., et al. 2023. Development goals towards sustainability. *Sustainability* 15 (12): 9443. https://doi.org/10.3390/su15129443.

Allen, F., A. Demirgüç-Kunt, L. Klapper, and M. S. Peria Martinez. 2016. Foundations of financial inclusion. *World Bank Economic Review* 30 (Supplement 1): S1–S17.

Al-Roubaie, A., and A. M. Sarea. 2019. Green investment and sustainable development: The case of Islamic finance. *Journal of Islamic Business and Management* 09 (01): https://doi.org/10.26501/jibm/2019.0901-002.

Ament, J. 2020. An ecological monetary theory. *Ecological Economics* 171 (May): 106421. https://doi.org/10.1016/j.ecolecon.2019.106421.

Arellano, M. 2016. Modelling optimal instrumental variables for dynamic panel data models. *Research in Economics* 70 (2): 238–261. https://doi.org/10.1016/j.rie.2015.11.003.

Arellano, M., and S. R. Bond. 1991. Some tests of specification for panel data: Monte Carlo evidence and an application to employment equations. *Review of Economic Studies* 58 (2): 277–297. https://doi.org/10.2307/2297968.

Arestis, P. 2021. Macro-economic and financial policies for sustainability and resilience. In *Economic policies for sustainability and resilience*, 1–44. Springer eBooks. https://doi.org/10.1007/978-3-030-84288-8_1.

Arner, D. W., R. P. Buckley, D. A. Zetzsche, and R. Veidt. 2020. Sustainability, fintech and financial inclusion. *European Business Organization Law Review* 21 (1): 7–35. https://doi.org/10.1007/s40804-020-00183-y.

Azimi, M. N. 2022. New insights into the impact of financial inclusion on economic growth: a global perspective. *PLoS One* 17 (11): e0277730. https://doi.org/10.1371/journal.pone.0277730.

Baltagi, B. H. 2021. *Econometric Analysis of Panel Data*. Springer Texts in Business and Economics. https://doi.org/10.1007/978-3-030-53953-5.

Banerjee, A. V., and E. Duflo. 2011. *Poor economics: A radical rethinking of the way to fight global poverty*. New York: PublicAffairs.

Beck, T., A. Demirgüç-Kunt, and M. S. Martinez Peria. 2007. Reaching Out: Access to and Use of banking services across countries. *Journal of Financial Economics* 85 (1): 234–266. https://doi.org/10.1016/j.jfineco.2006.07.002.

Biggeri, M., A. Ferrannini, S. Mehrotra, M. R. Di Tommaso, and P. Bianchi. 2023. Sustainable human development, capabilities and the new trajectories of industrial policy. In *The new challenges of industrial policy*, Edited by P. Bianchi and M. R. Di Tommaso, 106–131. Cheltenham, UK: Edward Elgar Publishing. https://doi.org/10.4337/9781800379091.00015.

Bird, G., and A. Milne. 2004. Miracle to meltdown: A pathology of the east Asian financial crisis. In *The New International Financial Architecture: A Functional Approach to Reform*, Edited by E. M. Truman, 74–91. London: Palgrave Macmillan UK. https://doi.org/10.1057/9780230599840_.6.

Biswas, G. K., and F. Ahamed. 2023. Financial inclusion and monetary policy: A study on the relationship between financial inclusion and effectiveness of monetary policy in developing countries. *arXiv (Cornell University)*, January. https://doi.org/10.48550/arxiv.2308.12542.

Bond, S. R. 2002. Dynamic panel data models: A guide to micro data methods and practice. *Portuguese Economic Journal* 1 (2): 141–162. https://doi.org/10.1007/s10258-002-0009-9.

Brahma, R., A. Chattopadhyay, D. Mukherjee, and T. Sadhukhan. 2022. *Analysis and estimation of consumer expenditure assuming uniform prices across FSUs: A step towards cost effectiveness*. Cornell University. https://doi.org/10.48550/arXiv.2208.

Brown, J. H., et al. 2013. Macroecology meets macroeconomics: Resource scarcity and global sustainability. *Ecological Engineering* 65 (August): 24–32. https://doi.org/10.1016/j.ecoleng.2013.07.071.

Cabeza-García, L., E. B. Del Brio, and M. Luz Oscanoa-Victorio. 2019. Female financial inclusion and its impacts on inclusive economic development. *Women S Studies International Forum* 77 (October): 102300. https://doi.org/10.1016/j.wsif.2019.102300.

Cadman, T., and T. Sarker, eds. 2022. *De Gruyter handbook of sustainable development and finance*. De Gruyter eBooks. https://doi.org/10.1515/9783110733488.

Cámara, N., and D. Tuesta. 2014. Measuring financial inclusion: A multidimensional index. *SSRN Electronic Journal*. January. doi:https://doi.org/10.2139/ssrn.2634616.

Cejudo, G. M., and P. Trein. 2022. Pathways to policy integration: A subsystem approach. *Policy Sciences* 56 (1): 9–27. https://doi.org/10.1007/s11077-022-09483-1.

Chatterjee, A. 2020. Financial inclusion, information and communication technology diffusion, and economic growth: A panel data analysis. *Information Technology for Development* 26 (3): 607–635. https://doi.org/10.1080/02681102.2020.1734770.

Chirwa, T. G., and N. M. Odhiambo. 2016. Macroeconomic determinants of economic growth: A review of international literature. *South East European Journal of Economics and Business* 11 (2): 33–47. https://doi.org/10.1515/jeb-2016-0009.

Clemente, G. P., R. Grassi, and C. Pederzoli. 2019. Networks and market-based measures of systemic risk: The European banking system in the aftermath of the financial crisis. *Journal of Economic Interaction and Coordination* 15 (1): 159–181. https://doi.org/10.1007/s11403-019-00247-4.

D'Orazio, P., and L. Popoyan. 2022. Realising central banks' climate ambitions through financial stability mandates. *Intereconomics* 57 (2): 103–111. https://doi.org/10.1007/s10272-022-1039-4.

Das, D. K. 2011. How did the Asian economy cope with the global financial crisis and recession? A revaluation and review. *Asia Pacific Business Review* 18 (1): 7–25. https://doi.org/10.1080/13602381.2011.601584.

Deléchat, C., L. Kiyasseh, M. MacDonald, and R. Xu. 2020. Drivers of financial access: The role of macroprudential policies. IMF Working Paper 2020 (074). doi:https://doi.org/10.5089/9781513545677.001.a001.

Demirgüç-Kunt, A., L. Klapper, D. Singer, S. Ansar, and J. Hess. 2019. The global FINDEX database 2017: Measuring financial inclusion and opportunities to expand access to and use of financial services. *The World Bank Economic Review* 34 (Supplement_1): S2–S8. https://doi.org/10.1093/wber/lhz013.

Dikau, S., and U. Volz. 2021. Central bank mandates, sustainability objectives and the promotion of green finance. *Ecological Economics* 184 (June): 107022. https://doi.org/10.1016/j.ecolecon.2021.107022.

Dinh, L. Q., T. T. K. Oanh, and N. T. H. Ha. 2024. Financial stability and sustainable development: Perspectives from fiscal and monetary policy. *International Journal of Finance & Economics*. https://doi.org/10.1002/ijfe.2981.

Durrani, A., M. Rosmin, and U. Volz. 2020. The role of central banks in scaling up sustainable finance—What do monetary authorities in the Asia-Pacific region think? *Journal of Sustainable Finance & Investment* 10 (2): 92–112. https://doi.org/10.1080/20430795.2020.1715095.

Egger, R., and J. Yu. 2022. A topic modeling comparison between LDA, NMF, Top2VEC, and BERTopic to Demystify Twitter Posts. *Frontiers in Sociology* 7 (May): https://doi.org/10.3389/fsoc.2022.886498.

Elhorst, J. P. 2010. Dynamic panels with Endogenous Interaction Effects when T Is Small. *Regional Science and Urban Economics* 40 (5): 272–282. https://doi.org/10.1016/j.regsciurbeco.2010.03.003.

Ellis, H. S., and W. Fellner. 1943. External economies and diseconomies. *The American Economic Review* 33 (3): 493–511. https://www.jstor.org/stable/1812987.

Erlando, A., F. D. Riyanto, and S. Masakazu. 2020. Financial inclusion, economic growth, and poverty alleviation: Evidence from Eastern Indonesia. *Heliyon* 6 (10): e05235. https://doi.org/10.1016/j.heliyon.2020.e05235.

Feiferytė-Skirienė, A., and Ž. Stasiškienė. 2023. Measuring economic crises impact transitioning to a circular economy. *Environment Development and Sustainability* 26 (7): 17849–17873. https://doi.org/10.1007/s10668-023-03367-x.

Ferrari, A., and V. N. Landi. 2023. Whatever it takes to save the planet? Central banks and unconventional green policy. *Macroeconomic Dynamics* 28 (February): 1–26. https://doi.org/10.1017/s1365100523000032.

Försterling, G., R. Orth, and B. Gellert. 2023. Transition to a circular economy in Europe through new business models: Barriers, drivers, and policy making. *Sustainability* 15 (10): 8212. https://doi.org/10.3390/su15108212.

Fukuda-Parr, S. 2016. From the millennium development goals to the sustainable development goals: Shifts in purpose, concept, and politics of global goal setting for development. *Gender and Development* 24 (1): 43–52. https://doi.org/10.1080/13552074.2016.1145895.

George, G., A. M. McGahan, and J. Prabhu. 2012. Innovation for inclusive growth: Towards a theoretical framework and a research agenda. *Journal of Management Studies* 49 (4): 661–683. https://doi.org/10.1111/j.1467-6486.2012.01048.x.

Ginting, P. 2020. Sustainable growth and development. *Sustainable Growth and Development*. https://doi.org/10.2991/aebmr.k.200606.082.

Goldstein, M. 1998. The Asian financial crisis: Causes, cures, and systematic implications, institute of international economics: Washington, DC., 77 pages, ISBN 0-88132-261-X. *Thunderbird International Business Review* 41 (6): 721–728. https://doi.org/10.1002/tie.4270410608.

Greene, W. H. 2012. *Econometric Analysis*. 7th ed. Upper Saddle River, NJ: Prentice Hall.

Grootendorst, M. 2022. BERTopic: Neural topic modeling with a class-based TF-IDF procedure. arXiv (Cornell University), January. https://doi.org/10.48550/arxiv.2203.05794.

Gruss, B., M. Nabar, and M. Poplawski-Ribeiro. 2019. Domestic amplifiers of external shocks: Growth accelerations and reversals in emerging market and developing economies. *SSRN Electronic Journal*. https://doi.org/10.2139/ssrn.3417721.

Hansen, L. P. 1982. Large sample properties of generalized method of moments estimators. *Econometrica* 50 (4): 1029. https://doi.org/10.2307/1912775.

Hausman, J. A. 1978. Specification tests in econometrics. *Econometrica* 46 (6): 1251. https://doi.org/10.2307/1913827.

Healy, A., and G. Bristow. 2020. Supranational policy and economic shocks: The role of the EU's structural funds in the economic resilience of regions. In *Economic Resilience in Regions and Organisations*, Edited by R. Capello and C. Lenzi. Cheltenham, UK: Edward Elgar Publishing. https://doi.org/10.4337/9781785360862.00023.

Honohan, P. 2008. Cross-country variation in household access to financial services. *Journal of Banking & Finance* 32 (11): 2493–2500. https://doi.org/10.1016/j.jbankfin.2008.05.004.

International Monetary Fund (IMF). 2022. *Regional economic outlook for Asia and the Pacific, October 2022: Asia sails into headwinds*. Washington, DC: IMF. https://www.imf.org/en/Publications/REO/APAC/Issues/2022/10/13/regional-economic-outlook-for-asia-and-pacific-october-2022.

Khairunnessa, F., D. A. Vazquez-Brust, and N. Yakovleva. 2021. A review of the recent developments of green banking in Bangladesh. *Sustainability* 13 (4): 1904. https://doi.org/10.3390/su13041904.

Kolodinsky, J. M., J. M. Hogarth, and M. A. Hilgert. 2004. The adoption of electronic banking technologies by US consumers. *International Journal of Bank Marketing* 22 (4): 238–259. https://doi.org/10.1108/02652320410542536.

Kuada, J. 2019. *Financial inclusion and the sustainable development goals*, 259–277. Elsevier eBooks. https://doi.org/10.1016/b978-0-12-814164-9.00012-8.

LaBelle, R. P. 2000. OCS resource management and sustainable development. *All Days*, June. https://doi.org/10.2118/61236-ms.

Lal, T. 2018. Measuring impact of financial inclusion on rural development through cooperatives. *International Journal of Social Economics* 46 (3): 352–376. https://doi.org/10.1108/ijse-02-2018-0057.

Lanzafame, M., J. Felipe, N. R. Sotocinal, and C. Bayudan-Dacuycuy. 2016. The pillars of potential growth and the role of policy: A panel data approach. *SSRN Electronic Journal*, January. doi:https://doi.org/10.2139/ssrn.2811550.

Li, N., and D. Wu. 2023. Nexus between natural resource and economic development: How green innovation and financial inclusion create sustainable growth in BRICS region? *Resources Policy* 85 (24): 103883. https://doi.org/10.1016/j.resourpol.2023.103883.

Lomazzi, M., B. Borisch, and U. Laaser. 2014. The millennium development goals: Experiences, achievements and what's next. *Global Health Action* 7 (1): https://doi.org/10.3402/gha.v7.23695.

Lopez, L., and S. Weber. 2017. Testing for granger causality in panel data. *The Stata Journal Promoting Communications on Statistics and Stata* 17 (4): 972–984. https://doi.org/10.1177/1536867x1801700412.

Mikkelson, G. M. 2013. Growth is the problem; Equality is the solution. *Sustainability* 5 (2): 432–439. https://doi.org/10.3390/su5020432.

Mishra, D., V. Kandpal, N. Agarwal, and B. Srivastava. 2024. Financial inclusion and its ripple effects on socio-economic development: A comprehensive review. *Journal of Risk and Financial Management* 17 (3): 105. https://doi.org/10.3390/jrfm17030105.

Mukherjee, S., and K. Sood. 2020. Triggers and barriers of financial inclusion: A country-wise analysis. *Asian Economic and Financial Review* 10 (9): 970–988. https://doi.org/10.18488/journal.aefr.2020.109.970.988.

Naceur, S. B., T. Beck, M. Belhaj, and A. Barajas. 2020. Financial inclusion: What have we learned so far? what do we have to learn? IMF Working Paper 2020 (157): 1. doi:https://doi.org/10.5089/9781513553009.001.

Nawrot, K. A. 2020. Does Confucianism promote cooperation and integration in East Asia? *International Communication of Chinese Culture* 7 (1): 1–30. https://doi.org/10.1007/s40636-020-00173-2.

Nkuna, O., A. F. Lapukeni, P. Kaude, and G. Kabango. 2018. The role of commercial banks on financial inclusion in Malawi. *Open Journal of Business and Management* 06 (04): 813–832. https://doi.org/10.4236/ojbm.2018.64061.

Omar, M. A., and K. Inaba. 2020. Does financial inclusion reduce poverty and income Inequality in developing countries? A panel data analysis. *Journal of Economic Structures* 9 (1): https://doi.org/10.1186/s40008-020-00214-4.

Ötker-Robe, I., and A. M. Podpiera. 2013. The social impact of financial crises: Evidence from the global financial crisis. World Bank Policy Research Working Paper. doi:https://doi.org/10.1596/1813-9450-6703.

Ozili, P. K. 2022. Financial inclusion and sustainable development: An empirical association. *Journal of Money and Business* 2 (2): 186–198. https://doi.org/10.1108/jmb-03-2022-0019.

Ozili, P. K., and P. T. Iorember. 2023. Financial stability and sustainable development. *International Journal of Finance & Economics*. https://doi.org/10.1002/ijfe.2803.

Park, H., and J. D. Kim. 2020. Transition towards green banking: Role of financial regulators and financial institutions. *Asian Journal of Sustainability and Social Responsibility* 5 (1): https://doi.org/10.1186/s41180-020-00034-3.

Pham, M. H., and L. D. Thi Phuong. 2020. The impact of financial inclusion on financial stability in Asian countries. *Journal of Asian Finance Economics and Business* 7 (6): 47–59. https://doi.org/10.13106/jafeb.2020.vol7.no6.047.

Rangan, D., and C. Lekha. 2020. COVID-19: Global diagnosis and future policy perspective. National Institute of Public Finance and Policy Working Paper No. 304. https://ideas.repec.org/p/npf/wpaper/20-304.html. Accessed on 25 September 2024.

Ratnawati, K. 2020. The impact of financial Inclusion on Economic Growth, Poverty, Income Inequality, and Financial Stability in Asia. *Journal of Asian Finance Economics and Business* 7 (10): 73–85. https://doi.org/10.13106/jafeb.2020.vol7.no10.073.

Rim, G.-N., S. N. Jang, C. J. An, S. H. Hwang, and S. H. Ri. 2020. State economic strength and some methodological issues on its assessment. *Social Indicators Research* 152 (2): 607–636. https://doi.org/10.1007/s11205-020-02459-9.

Rojas-Suárez, L. 2016. Financial inclusion in Latin America: Facts, obstacles and central banks' policy issues.https://doi.org/10.18235/0007016.

Safdar, M. N., T. Lin, and S. Amin. 2020. Cross-country income variations and inclusive financing. *Journal of Financial Economic Policy* 13 (3): 317–336. https://doi.org/10.1108/jfep-10-2019-0207.

Sargan, J. D. 1958. The estimation of economic relationships using instrumental variables. *Econometrica* 26 (3): 393. https://doi.org/10.2307/1907619.

Solow, R. M. 1956. A contribution to the theory of economic growth. *Quarterly Journal of Economics* 70 (1): 65–94. https://doi.org/10.2307/1884513.

Sood, N. 2013. India's approach towards financial inclusion. *SSRN Electronic Journa,* January. doi:https://doi.org/10.2139/ssrn.2290514.

Staiger, D., and J. H. Stock. 1997. Instrumental variables regression with weak instruments. *Econometrica* 65 (3): 557. https://doi.org/10.2307/2171753.

Stephens, J. C., and M. Sokol. 2023. Financial innovation for climate justice: Central banks and transformative 'creative disruption. *Climate and Development November* 16:1–12. https://doi.org/10.1080/17565529.2023.2268589.

Sustainable Banking Network Report. 2019. *Africa Research Bulletin Economic Financial and Technical Series* 56(9). doi:https://doi.org/10.1111/j.1467-6346.2019.09158.x.

Svartzman, R., P. Bolton, M. Despres, L. A. Pereira Da Silva, and F. Samama. 2020. Central banks, Financial stability and policy coordination in the age of climate uncertainty: A three-layered analytical and operational framework. *Climate Policy* 21 (4): 563–580. https://doi.org/10.1080/14693062.2020.1862743.

Swain, R. B., and F. Yang-Wallentin. 2019. Achieving sustainable development goals: Predicaments and strategies. *International Journal of Sustainable Development & World Ecology* 27 (2): 96–106. https://doi.org/10.1080/13504509.2019.1692316.

Swinkels, M. 2020. How ideas matter in public policy: A review of concepts, mechanisms, and methods. *International Review of Public Policy* 2 (3): 281–316. https://doi.org/10.4000/irpp.1343.

Tang, W., S. Ding, and H. Chen. 2021. Economic uncertainty and its spillover networks: Evidence from the Asia-Pacific countries. *Pacific-Basin Finance Journal* 67 (March): 101539. https://doi.org/10.1016/j.pacfin.2021.101539.

Thathsarani, U., J. Wei, and G. Samaraweera. 2021. Financial inclusion's role in economic growth and human capital in South Asia: An econometric approach. *Sustainability* 13 (8): 4303. https://doi.org/10.3390/su13084303.

United Nations Development Programme. 2022. *Annual Report 2022*. New York: UNDP. https://annualreport.undp.org/2022/index.html.

Van Der Ploeg, F., and A. J. Venables. 2022. Radical climate policies. CEPR Discussion Paper 17677. CEPR Press, Paris & London. Available at: https://cepr.org/publications/dp17677.

Van Niekerk, A. 2020. Inclusive economic sustainability: SDGs and global inequality. *Sustainability* 12 (13): 5427. https://doi.org/10.3390/su12135427.

Wang, Z., J. Chen, J. Chen, and H. Chen. 2023. Identifying interdisciplinary topics and their evolution based on BERTopic. *Scientometrics*. https://doi.org/10.1007/s11192-023-04776-5.

Wirl, F., and E. Dockner. 1995. Leviathan governments and carbon taxes: Costs and potential benefits. *European Economic Review* 39 (6): 1215–1236. https://doi.org/10.1016/0014-2921(94)00036-y.

Wooldridge, J. M. 2010. *Econometric analysis of cross section and panel data*. 2nd ed. Cambridge, MA: MIT Press.

World Bank. 2020. *Digital financial services*. Washington, DC: World Bank. https://pubdocs.worldbank.org/en/230281588169110691/Digital-Financial-Services.pdf.

World Bank. 2021. *Poverty and shared prosperity 2022: Correcting course*. Washington, DC: World Bank. https://doi.org/10.1596/978-1-4648-1893-6. Accessed on 25 September 2024.

Yap, S., H. S. Lee, and P. X. Liew. 2023. The role of financial inclusion in achieving finance-related sustainable development goals (SDGs): A cross-country analysis. *Economic Research-Ekonomska Istraživanja* 36 (3): https://doi.org/10.1080/1331677x.2023.2212028.

Chapter 6
Central Bank Digital Currency and the Multidimensional Bank Stability Index: Does Monetary Policy Play a Moderating Role?

Garima Gupta, Rachita Gulati, and Rishman Jot Kaur Chahal

Abstract Central Bank digital currency intends to boost financial inclusion and limit threats to bank stability put forward by private cryptocurrencies. Our study examines the impact of implementing CBDC on the bank stability of Asia-Pacific countries-China and India that initiated research on CBDC within the last 10 years (2013–2022). We construct a bank stability index by utilizing five dimensions, including capital adequacy, profitability, asset quality, liquidity, and efficiency, using a novel approach of "benefit-of-the-doubt." Utilizing the panel estimation techniques, we find a significant positive impact of CBDC adoption on bank stability and a moderating role of monetary policy. Also, we find that the effect is greater in India, a lower-middle-income country than in China, an upper-middle-income country. We conclude that during an accommodative monetary policy stance, CBDC adoption favors bank stability. We confirm our results with various robustness tests by introducing proxies for bank stability and other model specifications. Our findings underscore the potential of CBDC adoption when carefully managed alongside appropriate monetary policy, to enhance bank or overall financial stability.

Keywords Central bank digital currency · Bank stability index · Benefit-of-the-doubt · DEA · Monetary policy · Panel data models

G. Gupta · R. Gulati · R. J. K. Chahal (✉)
Department of Humanities and Social Sciences, Indian Institute of Technology Roorkee, Roorkee, Uttarakhand, India

R. Gulati
Asian Development Bank Institute, Tokyo, Japan

R. J. K. Chahal
Mehta Family School of DS and AI, Indian Institute of Technology Roorkee, Roorkee, Uttarakhand, India

R. Gulati et al. (eds.), *Emerging Challenges in Banking in Asia and the Pacific*, Economics, Law, and Institutions in Asia Pacific,
https://doi.org/10.1007/978-981-92-2144-8_6

6.1 Introduction

The last decade saw a wave of rapid advancements in the monetary system, while during the same period, economies underwent macro upheavals, for instance, the financial crisis of 2008–2009 and the COVID-19 pandemic, which necessitated such advancements. Hence, this decade can be viewed as a period of "creative destruction" (Chen and Siklos 2022). On the other hand, increased competition among financial players has also heightened the need for more adaptable monetary and fiscal policies to meet current demands and effectively tackle emerging challenges within the financial system (Dionysopoulos et al. 2023). For instance, recently, the increased demand for cryptocurrencies and the advent of new players such as stablecoins (e.g., Libra) have posed threats to monetary policy and financial stability (Opare and Kim 2020; Ricoy-Casas 2022). In an attempt to mitigate growing risks and safeguard the overall financial system, central banks around the globe have begun exploring central bank digital currencies (CBDCs); however, these are still nascent, and there remains uncertainty about their effects on financial stability. Therefore, a key concern with CBDC is that central banks are proposing something without a comprehensive understanding of the effects of issuing this currency might have on financial stability (M'bakob and Tchounga 2024). In light of this, the relationship between monetary policy and preserving financial stability has been the subject of recent discussion. However, the literature on CBDC is dominated by a variety of discussions, theoretical models, and speculation, and the conclusions drawn are inconclusive and require empirical support. In a cross-country analysis, Luu et al. (2023) made the first empirical attempt to evaluate the effects of CBDCs on financial stability, but did not address the role of monetary policy. Therefore, our study contributes to the empirical literature on CBDC and constitutes a first attempt to investigate the moderating role of monetary policy in shaping the impact of CBDC on financial stability, particularly in the context of emerging economies such as India and the PRC.

The payment system has changed drastically over the last thousand years, moving from basic bartering to sophisticated digital payment systems. After the barter system, which involved the exchange of goods for goods, the concept of commodity money was implemented around the seventeenth century, and gold remained a crucial commodity for a long time (Bordo 2005). In the 1970s, when the Bretton Woods system collapsed, the adoption of fiat money became common (Peneder 2022). Due to growing social demands and technological advancements, fiat money took the form of coins, paper currency, cheques, and plastic money (Auer et al. 2020). The outcomes of the global financial crisis, however, led to the emergence of a more complex electronic system, Bitcoin, commonly known as a cryptocurrency (Bibi 2023). The proliferation of cryptocurrencies and the emergence of new players, such as stablecoins (e.g., Libra), pose tangible threats to the efficacy of monetary policy and financial stability (Opare and Kim 2020; Ricoy-Casas 2022).

As previously mentioned, central banks are adopting CBDCs in response to the growing threats of private cryptocurrencies, with their primary objectives being to ensure price and financial stability. Auer et al. (2022) posit that the COVID-19 pandemic was a major reason behind the intensification of research into CBDCs. According to a poll, 86% of countries are testing CBDCs, while 14% have started pilot projects, and the rest are experimenting with the technology (Boar and Wehrli 2021). The Atlantic Council tracker[1] indicates that almost 130 countries (98% of the world's GDP) are investigating CBDCs. However, as of January 2024, only 11 nations have launched CBDCs; 21 countries are in the pilot stage, 33 in the development stage, 46 in the research stage, 16 are inactive, and 2 have canceled. The Central Bank of the Bahamas became the first to launch a CBDC in October 2020, aiming to expand financial inclusion in the country (Bharathan 2020). The central banks of Nigeria, Jamaica, and the Eastern Caribbean have also launched digital currencies in their respective countries. According to the Atlantic Council tracker, central bankers in key advanced economies such as the US, the UK, and the European Union are skeptical of CBDCs and are in the very early stages of adopting them. However, emerging economies like India and the PRC are optimistic and moving quickly to adopt CBDCs, and are further along the path towards launching them than developed economies.

Bech and Garratt (2017) outline four key properties of CBDCs: they are universally accessible, issued by a central bank, enable peer-to-peer exchanges, and exist in digital form. While these features offer considerable promise, their adoption is not without costs and challenges, spanning technological infrastructure, financial stability, and environmental sustainability. Additionally, concerns regarding privacy and data protection are increasingly controversial and a serious issue worldwide. The digital nature of CBDCs can enable granular surveillance of consumer data, and the extent to which anonymity is preserved depends heavily on the design choices made by central banks (Annunziata et al. 2025). However, the appropriate degree of anonymity is a political and social question (RBI 2022). In the Asian context, the People's Republic of China's e-CNY incorporates a "controllable/managed anonymity" approach in which small-value payments may be more private while larger-value or suspicious transactions are designed to be traceable, raising concerns about surveillance in a broader governance context (Marmefelt 2024). In India, the Reserve Bank of India notes that CBDC design must comply with AML/CFT requirements; therefore, full anonymity is unlikely, although the RBI has discussed a middle path that could allow limited anonymity for small-value transactions while maintaining compliance (RBI 2022). Further, Japan's approach to a digital yen reflects more cautious and privacy-conscious institutional structures. The literature has also proposed various privacy-enhancing technologies to mitigate privacy risks (Zhang 2024; Brand et al. 2025); however, the main concern persists that CBDC infrastructure, once established, may be modified over time in response to shifting political priorities, as highlighted by Freiman (2024). Thus, it is crucial to thoroughly consider the implications of CBDCs to prevent or minimize unintended consequences. Also, the significant and growing interest of countries in launching CBDCs motivates this study to empirically investigate the potential impacts of adopting a retail digital currency on financial stability.

---

[1] https://www.atlanticcouncil.org/cbdctracker/ Accessed on January 25, 2025.

There remains a high degree of uncertainty over the impact of CBDCs on financial stability, with the latter being defined as "a persistent state of robust functioning of various financial system components (markets, institutions, market infrastructure), endowing the system to face any endogenous or exogenous financial shock with minimal disruptive impact" (Financial Stability Report 2010). Boar and Wehrli (2021) emphasize that CBDCs should not be used for negotiating monetary or financial stability. Further, they state that CBDC-related concerns include the design choice, the financial system structure, and the extent of user adoption. However, the existing literature presents an unclear stance on the relationship between CBDC and bank stability. Some studies suggest that adopting CBDC may pose a threat to bank stability, while others contend that it could strengthen it. However, many findings remain inconclusive. Shen and Hou (2021) emphasize that interest-bearing CBDCs may hasten bank runs, thereby leading to financial instability. Similarly, Temperini et al. (2024) conclude that a CBDC might decrease bank deposits and, more importantly, loans, posing a threat to financial stability. On the other hand, Yang and Zhou (2022) argue that CBDC supports monetary policy goals and effectively manages the banking system without jeopardizing financial stability (Brunnermeier and Niepelt 2019). However, many studies suggest that the design of a CBDC will ultimately determine its impact on financial stability (Barrdear and Kumhof 2022; Syarifuddin and Bakhtiar 2022).

Further, the role of monetary policy in preserving financial system stability has been the subject of recent discussion. According to the "leaning-against-the-wind" argument, a proactive monetary policy, particularly through active interest rate adjustments, can mitigate financial instability and prevent crises (Cecchetti et al. 2002). This theory highlights the risk-taking channel as a key mechanism through which monetary policy influences financial stability (White 2009). As such, effective interest rate policies can help reduce instability and avert financial crises; however, the effects of CBDCs on bank stability and the monetary policy stance, especially in emerging economies, remain largely unexplored. Therefore, our study is the first of its kind to examine the relationship between adopting CBDC and financial stability and to uncover the role of monetary policy in the PRC and India. The PRC has been a frontrunner in CBDC research since 2014 and has conducted pilot studies in several cities and regions since 2020, while India started its research on CBDC in 2020 and launched its pilot projects in 2022. Thus, we focus on banks from these two emerging countries and compare the implications of adopting CBDC for bank stability.

In addition, our study contributes methodologically to the construction of the bank stability index. Most studies employ Z-scores to assess bank stability; however, this approach is limited and fails to capture various risk-related factors (Huljak 2015; Lapteacru 2016). Gulati (2023) raises important concerns regarding other measures of bank stability, cautioning against the use of principal component analysis when dealing with small samples or minimal variation among indicators. Consequently, this study adopts a novel approach to constructing a bank stability index, as first suggested by Gulati (2023), in utilizing the optimization-based constrained benefit-of-the-doubt method, which allows a data-driven weighting scheme and is robust in small samples, initially introduced by Melyn and Moesen (1991). We validate our results through various robustness tests. Finally, we analyze the relationship using a dynamic panel model, a two-step system generalized method of moments (GMM). Our findings underscore the potential of adopting CBDC for enhancing financial stability when carefully managed alongside appropriate monetary policy.

The study is organized as follows: Sect. 6.2 presents a review of the literature and hypothesis development; Sect. 6.3 elaborates on data and variable construction; Sect. 6.4 covers the model specification and results; Sect. 6.5 concludes; and Sect. 6.6 discusses the policy implications and limitations of the study.

6.2 Literature Review and Hypothesis Development

The growing literature on CBDC discusses various possibilities and risks associated with its adoption. As CBDC is still in its early launch stages, its implications for financial stability are unclear. Fiedler et al. (2019) describe the theory of the monetary system with a CBDC and conclude that bank deposits could lose their attractiveness with the adoption of CBDC, thereby affecting bank stability (see Fig. 6.1). Since deposits are one of the largest sources of funding, any substitution with CBDC would require banks to reassess their business models and strategies with a view to maintaining stability. According to the existing literature, CBDCs may pose threats to financial stability either by hastening bank runs (Shen and Hou 2021) or by reducing the demand for bank deposits (Temperini et al. 2024). Schilling et al. (2024) point out that if a central bank is involved in financial intermediation, such as the adoption of CBDC, it can lead to a trilemma where it cannot achieve three targets (i.e., socially efficient allocation, price, and financial stability) simultaneously. According to Dhaou and Rohman (2018), the overall advantages of CBDC for financial stability are more complex than those for output and price stability, and the possibility of mishandling the shift to a new monetary system represents a risk to financial stability. Thus, policymakers must be extremely cautious when considering adopting CBDC. Based on the above, we develop our first hypothesis:

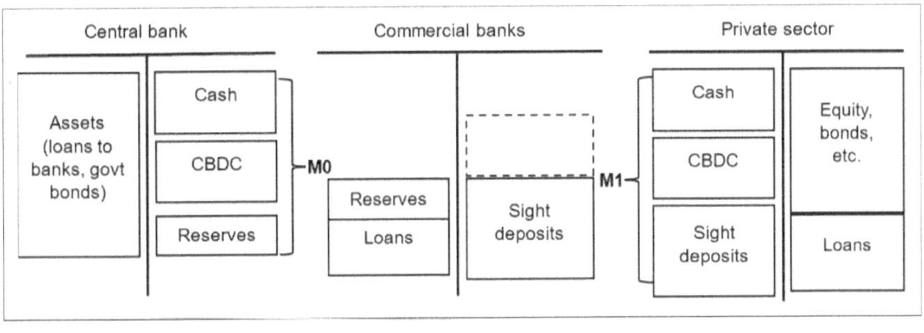

Fig. 6.1 Monetary system with CBDC. *Source* Fiedler et al. (2019)

H01: CBDC Adoption May Threaten Bank Stability

Notwithstanding, some studies suggest that adopting CBDC would not present a risk to financial stability. Brunnermeier and Niepelt (2019) state that adopting CBDC would not jeopardize financial stability if it had the same liquidity characteristics as deposits, and a swap would be liquidity neutral. According to Hoang et al. (2023), CBDCs present no risk to monetary or financial stability, as it is doubtful that they would fully replace fiat currencies. Tercero-Lucas (2023) argues that in order to ensure that a central bank avoids bank runs, it is essential to adopt CBDC, as without it, financial stability could be at risk. Similarly, Luu et al. (2023) found that banks enjoyed increased lending and asset quality after adopting CBDC, with a more favorable influence on emerging markets than on advanced ones. Therefore, our second hypothesis is as follows:

H02: CBDC Adoption May Not Threaten Bank Stability

Most researchers suggest that CBDCs enhance the transparency and efficiency of the monetary policy framework, and Belke and Beretta (2020) state that CBDCs can speed up the passthrough from the policy changes, thereby strengthening the interest rate channel. According to Fegatelli (2022), CBDC is a reliable instrument for maximizing the flow of liquidity in the system, strengthening the bank lending channel. Yang and Zhou (2022) posit that introducing CBDC favors monetary policy goals and can effectively manage the banking system. Additionally, it makes real-time monitoring of price levels possible and swiftly regulates open-market operations. Qian (2019) explains that real-time transmission via CBDC activation would permit a targeted money supply and improve forward guidance, while studies by Belke and Beretta (2020), Duarte (2019), Xin and Jiang (2023), and Shen and Hou (2021), among others, suggest that a CBDC could impose negative interest rates and thus overcome the zero lower bound. According to Chen and Siklos (2022), the McCallum rule is a better policy tool, as it can integrate CBDC and permit changes in the direction of monetary policy through an increased money supply. Using McCallum's policy rule on money growth, Rehman et al. (2023) claim that CBDCs do not increase inflation or endanger financial stability. Ngotran (2020) speculates that central banks can simultaneously use digital currency to modify the money supply and interbank rate and are, therefore, more able to meet the inflation objective and lessen the negative short-term effects of rate increases. Research by Meng et al. (2024) found that the pilot launch of the digital yuan positively impacted financial stability, with financial technology being a significant and crucial moderator. On the other hand, Yang et al. (2024) found that the efficacy of the monetary policy would be hampered, leading to increased costs resulting from policy formulation if CBDC were adopted completely. M'bakob and Tchounga (2024) show that having too much confidence in CBDC may lead to liquidity risks and restrictions on loans and deposits and could affect bank activity overall.

Further, monetary policy is significant in preserving financial stability. According to the "leaning-against-the-wind" argument, an aggressive monetary policy, especially through active adjustment of interest rates, can reduce financial instability and prevent crises (Cecchetti et al. 2002). The theory emphasizes that one important

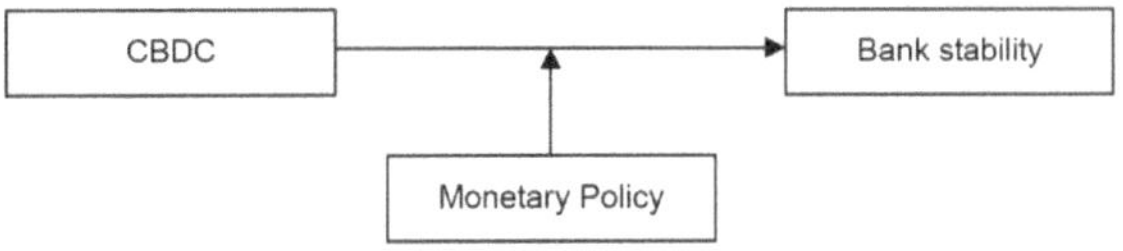

Fig. 6.2 Monetary policy as a moderator. *Source* Authors' own

way in which monetary policy affects financial stability is through the risk-taking channel (White 2009), which implies that effective interest rate policies can reduce instability and avert financial crises. Other theories suggest that CBDCs can weaken the lending and interest rate channels of monetary policy when households and businesses convert their cash and deposits to CBDCs in substantial amounts, as the deposit substitution would restrict credit availability and bank liquidity. This lessens central banks' control of the money supply in the banking sector. Thus, Ozili (2024) suggests effective and strong coordination between CBDC and monetary policy. Therefore, we augment our econometric model by introducing an interaction between monetary policy and CBDC adoption to analyze the moderating role of monetary policy (Fig. 6.2). This interaction can help us to explore how the impact of adopting CBDC on bank stability varies under different monetary policy stances. In other words, we can discover whether monetary policy moderates the effect of CBDC on stability. If it does, we can analyze whether it is stronger during an accommodative or tightening policy stance. Hence, we develop the third hypothesis, which is as follows:

H03: Monetary Policy Plays a Significant Moderating Role in Determining Bank Stability

Most studies are inconclusive and simply state that the design choice of a CBDC will determine how it affects financial stability. Some studies suggest that an account-based and interest-bearing CBDC will prove beneficial in overcoming the zero lower bound, obtaining the inflation target, and effectuating monetary policy. According to Barrdear and Kumhof (2022) and Syarifuddin and Bakhtiar (2022), a CBDC with an interest rate can be employed as a tool for policy and to improve the efficacy of monetary policy; it might, however, put pressure on bank deposits (Yamaoka 2023). On the other hand, Kesavaraj et al. (2022) suggest that by providing a variety of payment choices, a CBDC without interest rate could encourage financial inclusion. Dionysopoulos et al. (2023) emphasize that the most critical components of a CBDC are that it can be applicable to retail as well as wholesale, it can be universally available, it can bear both negative and positive interest rates, and it can be converted into other forms of financial exchanges. Bas et al. (2024) analyzed the connectedness of CBDCs with cryptocurrencies and various measures of financial stability, finding a bidirectional connectedness between financial stability and CBDC, and suggesting being careful with the design choice for CBDC, as it has the potential to influence overall financial stability. Further, Auer et al. (2022) reviewed the monetary policy and financial stability implications of CBDC and demanded empirical evidence as many questions remain unresolved. Overall, we found that the literature is mainly optimistic about introducing CBDCs.

In practice, most central banks that have launched a CBDC or initiated pilot projects have adopted a token-based and noninterest-bearing design. Ironically, we find that most studies have investigated the implications of interest-bearing CBDCs and linked them to financial instability by portraying CBDCs as competitors to bank deposits. However, central banks have not preferred to adopt interest-bearing CBDCs until now. Further, based on our knowledge garnered from the literature, the study by Luu et al. (2023) is one of the first to have empirically researched the CBDC implications for financial stability by constructing a CBDC index for 86 emerging and advanced economies from 2010 to 2021. As the CBDC is still in its initial phase, the rest of the literature is dominated by discussions, surveys, theoretical models, and arguments. This study extends the work of Luu et al. (2023) by incorporating the moderating role of monetary policy in the analysis and comparing the impacts of adopting CBDC on financial stability between India and the PRC.

6.3 Data and Variable Construction

6.3.1 Sample Selection

The study uses various databases to extract data on variables of interest. Bank-level data on 74 banks (30 from India and 44 from the PRC) were retrieved from the Bloomberg database. We included publicly listed banks in our study, as Bloomberg only provides data on these banks. We finally chose only those banks with at least three years of consecutive information. According to the CBDC tracker (2024), the PRC has been carrying out its research since 2014 and has conducted pilot studies in several cities and regions since 2020. India initiated research on CBDC recently, in 2020, and started its pilot projects in 2022. According to the World Bank's classification, while both India and the PRC are middle-income countries, the former is categorized as a lower-middle-income country and the latter as an upper-middle-income one. By analyzing these two of the largest emerging economies, we can compare the implications for financial stability post-CBDC adoption. Accordingly, the sample period of 2013–2022 was chosen for two main reasons. First, these economies began their research on CBDC within this period, with the PRC being the first to start after 2013. Second, the influence of the financial crisis of 2008 declined during this time, so the shocks from the crisis will not influence our analysis. Then, we manually selected the data on CBDC adoption stages from an online database, CBDC Tracker, which provides real-time information on various countries involved in CBDC research. Data on monetary policy rates are taken from the Bank for International Settlements, which provides key policy rates for all countries. The data were in the form of the effective date, so we converted the data into years by taking averages. Data on macroeconomic variables (GDP and inflation) are taken from the World Bank's World Development Indicators.

6.3.2 Construction of Indices (CBDC Adoption Index (CBDCI) and Bank Stability Index (BSI))

To measure the CBDC adoption index (CBDCI), we follow the methodology proposed by Luu et al. (2023), a pioneering study in this area. CBDC Tracker provides data on the stages of CBDC adoption for various countries. One of the first central banks to work on digital currencies was the People's Bank of China, which began its research in 2014 and launched its first pilot project in 2019. On the other hand, the research on CBDC by India's central bank began in 2020, followed by a pilot project in 2022. CBDC Tracker provides data on adoption in four stages: research, proof of concept, pilot, and launch. Following these stages, we compute an index that captures time-varying CBDC adoption stages for India and the PRC from 2013 to 2022, where 0 indicates no involvement in CBDC research, 1 indicates the early research stage, 2 indicates the proof-of-concept stage, 3 indicates the pilot stage, and 4 indicates fully launched.

Further, the study adopts a novel approach to constructing a bank stability index by using the optimization-based constrained benefit-of-the-doubt (BoD) approach (Gulati 2023). This method is particularly suitable for small samples and minor differences among indicators. Researchers using the BoD model often refer to it as an augmentation of the data envelopment analysis (DEA) technique, introduced by Melyn and Moesen (1991) and then advanced by Cherchye et al. (2004) and Cherchye et al. (2006). The index construction in the multiplier form of DEA models uses the given linear programming problem (LPP):

$$\left.\begin{array}{c} I_{Ak} = \max\left(v_{A1}, D_{A1,k} + v_{A2}, D_{A2,k}, \dots v_{As}, D_{As,k}\right) \\ \text{subject to :} \\ v_{A1,1}, D_{A1,1} + v_{A2,1}, D_{A2,1}, \dots v_{As,1}, D_{As,1} \leq 1, \\ v_{A1,2}, D_{A1,2} + v_{A2,2}, D_{A2,2}, \dots v_{As,2}, D_{As,2} \leq 1, \\ \vdots \\ v_{A1,n}, D_{A1,n} + v_{A2,n}, D_{A2,n}, \dots v_{As,n}, D_{As,n} \leq 1, \\ v_{A1}, v_{A2}, \dots v_{As} \geq 0 \end{array}\right\} \begin{array}{c}\text{General form of} \\ \text{LPP for two-step} \\ \text{aggregation approach}\end{array} \quad (6.1)$$

$$\alpha \leq \frac{v_{rj} D_{r,j}}{\sum_{r=1}^{s} v_{r,j} D_{r,j}} \leq \beta \cdots \quad (6.2)$$

This is a two-step aggregation approach in which the initial step involves the construction of each dimension using "s" indicators, and the next step involves the computation of the bank stability index using the dimensions extracted from the first step. In the given set of LPP Eq. 6.1, ($v_{A1,\,1}$, $v_{A2,\,1} \dots v_{As,\,k}$) are the weights assigned to each indicator (in the first step)/dimension (in the second step), ($D_{A1,\,k}$, $D_{A2,\,k}$, $\dots D_{As,\,k}$)/ ($I_{A1,\,k}$, $I_{A2,\,k}$, $\dots I_{As,\,k}$), to construct the dimension-specific/bank stability index, I_{Ak}/ BSI_{Ak}, for the kth bank from "n" banks. These steps are repeated to construct all five dimensions for different years and countries from the selected 13 indicators. In the second step, the same procedure is followed, but in place of indicators, we now have dimensions, and with these, we construct the final bank stability index. The second equation is the weight constraint, providing the lower and upper limits on indicators/dimensions in the constrained BoD model. These restrictions help to avoid the disproportionate emphasis on extreme values or outliers of indicators/dimensions. If the lower limit is $\alpha\%$, then the upper limit will be $100 - [(s - 1) * \alpha]\%$. We set the lower limit of 10%, as found consistently by Gulati (2023). Additionally, we performed a sensitivity analysis on 16 different lower-bound limits and found that, on average, there is no qualitative difference in the prioritization of stability dimensions. Table A1 in the appendix shows the average weights of dimensions. Before constructing the dimensions, we first winsorized and normalized the data following the techniques developed by Cherchye et al. (2011), Vidoli and Fusco (2018), and Gulati (2023), and then we computed the bank stability index.

We selected five dimensions and 13 indicators from the literature and financial soundness indicators from the IMF. These dimensions (indicators) include capital adequacy (tier-1 capital ratio, tier-1 common equity ratio, and total risk-based capital ratio), asset quality (NPL ratio and loan loss coverage ratio), profitability and earnings (return on equity, return on assets, and net interest margin), liquidity (liquidity coverage ratio, demand deposits to total assets, earning assets to interest-bearing liabilities), and efficiency (efficiency ratio and loan-deposit ratio). The computation of each indicator and their expected relationship with bank stability is elaborated in Table 6.1.

6.3.3 *Variable Description*

Table 6.2 describes the computation of variables employed in subsequent analysis, along with their respective sources. BSI and CBDCI construction have already been explained in Sect. 6.3.2. The key policy rate[2] is employed as a key representative of the monetary policy stance as it serves as a widely used instrument for open-market operations and a benchmark rate that central banks adjust to regulate liquidity in the banking system (Reserve Bank of India, n.d.). Bank-specific variables include bank size (calculated as the natural log of total assets), capital (calculated as the logarithm of the equity to assets ratio), deposit growth (calculated as the deposits to asset ratio), and LLP (calculated as the ratio of loan loss provisions to loans). We winsorized the LLP ratio at the tenth percentile because it showed outliers in the data. For country-control variables, we used GDP per capita, measured as the logarithm of per capita

[2] Monetary policy tools in both countries are highly heterogeneous. For instance, in India, the cash reserve ratio (CRR) is uniformly applied across all banks, whereas the PRC employs a required reserve ratio that varies across bank types (large, medium, and small). Moreover, the CRR remained constant at 4% from 2013 to 2020. This lack of variability limits its effectiveness for year-wise estimation from 2013 to 2022. Given the study's comparative scope covering both countries, we adopt a key policy rate as a proxy for monetary policy stance. This choice ensures consistency, minimizes biases, and reduces noise in our econometric estimations (Baltagi 2021).

Table 6.1 Dimensions and their Indicators for BSI

Dimension	Indicators	Computation	Expected sign
Capital adequacy	Risk-based capital ratio	Risk-based capital/assets (risk-weighted)	+
	Ratio of tier-1 capital	Capital (tier-1)/assets (risk-weighted)	+
	Ratio of tier-1 common equity	Common equity capital (tier-1)/assets (risk-weighted)	+
Asset quality	Nonperforming loans ratio	Nonperforming loans/total loans	−
	Loan loss provision coverage ratio	(Pretax income + loan loss provisions)/ actual loan losses	+
Profitability and earnings	Return on assets	(Net income/average of total assets) × 100	+
	Return on equity	(Net income for shareholders/average of total common equity) × 100	+
	Net interest margin	((Net interest income + taxable equivalent adjustment)/(earning assets + earning assets of prior year)/2) × 100	+
Liquidity	Liquidity coverage ratio	(Liquid assets of high quality/net cash outflows of 30 days) × 100	+
	Demand deposits to total assets	(Demand deposits/assets in total) × 100	+
	Earning assets to interest-bearing liabilities	(Earning assets/liabilities that are interest-bearing) × 100	+
Efficiency	Efficiency ratio (cost-to-income ratio)	(Operational expense/((net interest income + earnings from fees and commissions + other operational losses (income) + profits from trading account (losses) + gain/loss on investments/ loans + other losses (income) − fees and commissions paid) + net revenue or taxable equivalent adjustment − net paid commissions) × 100	−
	Loans to deposit ratio	(Loans/deposits) × 100	+

The expected signs show the positive (+) or negative (−) relationship of indicators with bank stability
Source Bloomberg

Table 6.2 Definition of variables

Variables	Definition	Data sources
BSI	Bank stability index constructed by using the constrained BoD method	Bloomberg
CBDCI	Stages of adoption with 1, 2, 3, and 4, respectively, for research, proof of concept, pilot project, and fully launched	CBDC Tracker
MP	Monetary policy key rate	BIS
Moderator	Interaction between CBDCI and MP = CBDCI × MP	CBDC Tracker, BIS
lnAss	Total assets (using log-natural)	Bloomberg
lnCap	Log of equity to assets in total	Bloomberg
Dep_gr	Growth of deposits to assets in total (year-on-year)	Bloomberg
LLP	Loan loss provision to total loans	Bloomberg
lnGDP	Log of GDP per capita	WDI
Inf	Percentage change in consumer price index	WDI
Dummy	Dummy = 1 if country = India, otherwise 0	–
Dummy_int	Dummy interaction variable = Dummy × CBDCI	–
Covid_dummy	Dummy for the COVID-19 pandemic for the years 2019 and 2020	–

BIS refers to Bank for International Settlements, WDI = World Development Indicators

GDP. This variable captures the average economic output or income per individual, providing a better reflection of the living standards of individuals and their impact on bank stability than real GDP growth, which focuses solely on the overall economic expansion. Next, we used the inflation rate and proxied it by the percentage change in the consumer price index, which is a standard measure of inflation in both India and the PRC. Finally, to capture the remaining unobserved heterogeneity between the countries, we introduce dummies (0 for the PRC and 1 for India) to quantify the country-specific effects of CBDC on bank stability. These country-specific dummies are easier to include in the model and account for country-specific factors that are not easily quantifiable, such as differences in the monetary policy and macroprudential frameworks of both countries and variations in payment systems and supervisory frameworks, among others.

6.3.4 Preliminary Analysis

Table 6.3 summarizes statistically the variables in our dataset. The dependent variable, bank stability constructed utilizing the constrained benefit-of-the-doubt method, has an average of 0.946, which indicates that most banks in the sample have high stability scores. The standard deviation is low (i.e., 0.043), demonstrating minimal variation in stability scores, ranging from 0.789 to 1. The key explanatory variable in our model is CBDC adoption, with a mean value of 1.035, indicating that the countries, on average, are in the initial stages of adoption. The highest value is 3, meaning that they have at least reached the pilot stage. The monetary policy rate ranges between 3.679 and 8, implying moderate variations in policy stance with a standard deviation of 1.321. We expect a positive relationship between monetary policy and bank stability as tighter policies restrict lending and enhance stability. For bank controls, the mean of deposit growth is 0.095, showing modest growth in bank deposits and high variability across sampled banks, ranging from −0.854 to 1.604. A higher deposit growth is expected to enhance stability by expanding funds and liquidity for banks. The capital ratio has a low mean value of −2.614, ranging between −3.881 and 0.208, and is expected to improve stability as it provides resilience to banks. Similarly, bank size, as proxied by the log of total bank assets, averages 11.416 and is expected to enhance bank stability because larger banks have better infrastructure and resources. The LLP ratio, which is the provision of the total loan loss to loans ratio, averages 1.409 and is negatively associated with bank stability. The log of GDP per capita averages 8.455, indicating a moderately high GDP, and the inflation rate has an average value of 3.296, exhibiting moderate inflation levels. We anticipate that bank stability will respond positively to GDP per capita and negatively to the inflation rate.

Pearson's correlation coefficients for the variables of interest in our study are shown in Table 6.4. A highly significant and positive correlation exists between the bank stability index and CBDC adoption. This indicates that a higher CBDC adoption

Table 6.3 Summary statistics

Variables	Observations	Mean	Standard deviation	Min	Max
Dependent variable					
BSI	740	0.946	0.043	0.789	1
Variable of Interest					
CBDCI	740	1.035	1.020	0	3
Control variables					
MP	740	5.217	1.321	3.679	8
Bank-control variables					
Dep_gr	655	0.095	0.126	−0.854	1.604
lnCap	728	−2.614	0.305	−3.881	0.208
lnAss	730	11.416	1.716	7.395	15.563
LLP	696	1.409	0.690	0.564	2.761
Country-control variables					
lnGDP	740	8.455	0.826	7.247	9.355
Inf	740	3.296	2.070	0.180	7.833

See Table 6.2 for the definition of variables

is associated with better financial stability. A negative and highly significant correlation between the bank stability index and monetary policy suggests that a tighter monetary policy is associated with lower financial stability. A strong positive and highly significant correlation between stability and assets indicates that banks with more assets are more financially stable. A positive and highly significant correlation between stability and deposits indicates that higher deposits are associated with better financial stability. A strong negative and highly significant correlation between stability and the LLP ratio indicates that higher loan loss provisions are associated with poorer financial stability. Lastly, GDP per capita is positively and significantly correlated with stability, while the inflation rate is negatively correlated. Further, the VIF values indicate a high degree of multicollinearity if >10. However, in our study, the VIF values have a mean of 2.45, which is very low and well below 10, indicating that multicollinearity is not a concern.

6.4 Model Specification and Results

6.4.1 Econometric Model Specification

A dynamic two-step system GMM panel regression model is used to analyze the impact of adopting CBDC on bank stability:

$$\begin{aligned} BSI_{ijt} = \alpha_0 + \alpha_1 BSI_{ijt-1} + \alpha_2 CBDCI_{jt-1} + \alpha_3 Moderator_{jt-1} \\ + \alpha_4 MP_{jt-1} + \alpha_5 BankCont_{jt-1} + \alpha_6 MacroCont_{jt-1} \\ + Dummy_j + Dummy_j * CBDC_{jt-1} + \varepsilon_{ijt} \cdots \end{aligned} \tag{6.3}$$

where $i, j, and\ t$ denote bank, country, and year, respectively. There are two specific reasons for choosing the two-step system GMM. First, it addresses the endogeneity problem through instrumental variables determined from the model. Upon applying the Durbin-Wu-Hausman test for endogeneity, we find that the model suffers from endogeneity issues. Second, the method is efficient for data with short periods and large cross sections (Roodman 2009). While the dependent variable lies in a certain range, the existing literature supports the use of the system GMM. For instance, Jha (2019) employed this method to analyze the corruption index, a dependent variable also constrained within a limited range. BSI_{ijt} is the bank stability index, measured using the constrained BoD method. $CBDCI_{jt-1}$ is the adoption index. MP_{jt-1} is the monetary policy rate. $Moderator_{jt-1}$ is the interaction between monetary policy and CBDCI. $BankCont_{ijt-1}$ includes bank deposits (ratio of growth in deposits to assets in total), capital (ratio of equity to assets), size (log of assets), and loan loss provisions (ratio of provisions to loan loss and loans). Country control variables ($MacroCont_{jt-1}$) are per capita GDP and inflation rate. Slope ($Dummy_j * CBDC_{jt-1}$) and intercept ($Dummy_j$) dummies are introduced to compare the impacts of CBDCI

Table 6.4 Correlation coefficients

	1	2	3	4	5	6	7	8	9	VIF
1	1									
2	0.199***	1								2.20
3	−0.263***	−0.728***	1							3.60
4	0.349***	0.189***	−0.174**	1						1.12
5	0.194***	0.020	−0.109***	0.104***	1					1.07
6	0.245***	0.357***	−0.424***	−0.022	0.016	1				1.49
7	−0.491***	−0.121***	−0.003	−0.072*	−0.167***	−0.174***	1			1.36
8	0.482***	0.546***	−0.703***	−0.001	0.120***	0.556***	−0.315***	1		5.83
9	−0.387***	−0.386***	0.470***	0.036	−0.124***	−0.439***	0.251***	−0.803***	1	2.90

1 – BSI, 2 – CBDCI, 3 – MP, 4 – lnCap, 5 – Dep_gr, 6 – lnAss, 7 – LLP, 8 – lnGDP, 9 – Inf. *** = 1% significance level, ** = 5% significance level, and * = 10% significance level. See Table 6.2 for the definition of variables

between India and the PRC. The explanatory variables are lagged by one year as their instantaneous effect on stability is not expected. ε_{ijt} is the error term.

6.4.2 Results

In this section, we interpret the results from a dynamic panel data estimation method, the two-step system GMM. The bank stability index is the dependent variable. The two key independent variables are CBDC adoption and the moderating variable, which is the interaction between CBDC adoption and monetary policy. Further, we include country-specific and bank-specific variables that may influence the relationship between CBDCI and bank stability as controls. Lastly, we include dummy variables to compare the relationships in two countries, namely India and the PRC.

The results in Model 1 (Table 6.5) reveal that the coefficient for CBDCI is positive and highly significant at the 1% significance level. This implies that adopting CBDC can lead to increased bank stability, confirming the results of Luu et al. (2023). While the impact is significant, it is marginally small, which reflects the early-stage effects of CBDC adoption, as both India and the PRC are still in the pilot stages and have not yet fully launched it. The result supports our second hypothesis that CBDCs may not threaten bank stability, while rejecting the first one, which hypothesizes the opposite.

Surprisingly, we find a significant and negative moderating role of monetary policy in bank stability. This implies that in a tight monetary policy, when banks offer higher interest rates to attract deposits, the stabilizing effect of CBDC is diminished, reflecting competition between bank deposits and CBDC holdings. On the other hand, in an accommodative monetary policy stance (when policy rates are lower), the positive impact of CBDC on bank stability is enhanced, due to the increased control of central banks over the money supply and overall payment system, coupled with CBDC-aided transparency. Thus, we accept the third hypothesis that monetary policy plays a significant moderating role in determining bank stability and conclude that central banks can improve stability by adopting CBDC, especially in an accommodative monetary policy stance.

Further, we find a positive and significant impact of monetary policy on bank stability, meaning that higher policy rates tend to bring such stability. This aligns with the argument of the risk-taking channel, which states that a tightening monetary policy stance improves bank stability (Albertazzi et al. 2020). For bank controls, we find that deposit growth is negatively related to bank stability. This is contrary to our expectation; however, it may be due to increased liquidity risk because of increasing deposits and the vulnerability of banks to sudden withdrawals (Diamond and Dybvig 1983). Conversely, capital positively and highly significantly determines bank stability. This supports the existing notion that banks with higher capitalization seem more stable and are better risk absorbers (Ghenimi et al. 2017). The loan

Table 6.5 Baseline regression results

Variables	Model 1	Model 2
BSI(t-1)	0.694*** (0.020)	0.625*** (0.018)
Key independent variables		
CBDCI	**0.050*** (0.010)**	**0.031*** (0.006)**
Moderator	**−0.013*** (0.003)**	**−0.008*** (0.002)**
Control variables		
MP	0.005*** (0.002)	0.003** (0.001)
Bank-control variables		
Dep_gr	−0.042*** (0.007)	−0.019*** (0.007)
ln_Cap	0.0183*** (0.003)	0.022*** (0.004)
Ln_Ass	−0.0002 (0.0005)	−0.0005 (0.0005)
LLP	−0.005*** (0.001)	−0.002** (0.001)
Country-control variables		
lnGDP	0.141*** (0.0337)	0.024*** (0.002)
Inf	0.001 (0.001)	0.003*** (0.0003)
Dummy	0.190*** (0.060)	–
Dummy_int	0.017*** (0.001)	–
Year	−0.008*** (0.002)	−0.002*** (0.0006)
Constant	15.913*** (3.842)	3.468*** (1.213)
Observations	552	552
Arellano-Bond test for AR (2) in first differences (p-value)	0.243	0.336
Hansen test (p-value)	0.215	0.062

Note Model 1 shows the coefficients with country-wise dummy variables, and Model 2 presents the aggregate results for India and the PRC. These are the estimates for the two-step system GMM. Standard errors in parenthesis. Bold numerals indicate the key variables of interest. *** = 1% significance level. ** = 5% significance level. See Table 6.2 for the definition of the variables loss provisions, which represent the level of credit risk, negatively impact bank stability (Fang et al. 2013). For country-control variables, we find a positive and significant impact of GDP per capita on bank stability, implying that GDP per capita improves financial stability, which is consistent with the existing literature (Vo et al. 2020).

Further, the intercept dummy variable for India shows that this country's intercept is 0.190 units higher than that of the PRC. Also, the interaction dummy shows that the effect of CBDC on bank stability increases by 0.017 for every unit change in the adoption of CBDC in India compared to the PRC. We note that the effect is more pronounced in India than in the PRC. This may be due to differences in monetary policy frameworks, digitalization levels, and economic structures in the two countries. The People's Bank of China is more centrally controlled and has an obligation to implement both monetary and fiscal objectives in support of the State Council (Maher 2024), while comparatively, the Reserve Bank of India is solely focused on conducting monetary policy without playing a direct role in the formulation of fiscal policy. Second, the financial system in the PRC is much bigger and more mature than that in India (Farrell and Lund 2006). The PRC had introduced its digital payment systems, such as Alipay and WeChat Pay, years before India launched its Unified Payment Interface (UPI). As the PRC has an advanced digital ecosystem, therefore, the incremental stability benefits from adopting CBDC may be less pronounced in the PRC than in India. Lastly, the Indian economic structure is more cash-dependent than that in the PRC, so adopting CBDC, which allows cash to be converted into digital form, will have a more transformative impact in India. The coefficients of Model 2, which does not include country-wise dummy variables, show an aggregate impact of all banks from the two countries. This aggregate impact also shows a positive and significant influence of CBDC adoption on bank stability and a negative and significant moderating effect of monetary policy.

6.4.3 Robustness Testing

To confirm the findings of our model and test their sensitivity, we run a few robustness tests (Tables 6.6–6.8). In Table 6.6, we utilize static panel models. The coefficients of Models 1 and 2 are the estimates of the fixed effect model with country-wise effect and the aggregate effect of all banks of the two countries, respectively. In both models, CBDCI positively and significantly impacts bank stability, with a negative and significant moderating role of monetary policy, in line with the baseline model. Moreover, the interaction dummy for country in Model 1 shows that the impact of CBDCI on bank stability increases by 0.019 for every unit change in the CBDC adoption for India, compared to the PRC. Next, given that the dependent variable lies in the range of 0–1, we run the panel Tobit model. Models 3 and 4 report the Tobit model results of country-wise dummy and aggregate levels, respectively. Further, to analyze the impact of the COVID-19 pandemic, we introduced a dummy variable for 2019 and 2020 (Model 5) and found a positive and significant impact of the pandemic on bank stability. This positive impact can be attributed to various fiscal policy measures and proactive monetary policy interventions taken by central banks during the crisis that shielded the banking stability of both countries (Gulati et al. 2023). The coefficients in all the columns are consistent with the baseline regression model for CBDC adoption and the moderating variable confirming that CBDCI positively impacts bank stability, with a more pronounced effect in India than in the PRC.

Additionally, we analyzed the impact of CBDCI on the bank stability of different sizes of banks (small, medium, and large). To classify the size of banks, we divided the sample of the log of assets into terciles. Table 6.7 reports the results, and we found that CBDCI has a positive and significant impact on large and medium banks but an insignificant effect on small ones. This implies that large and medium banks have better resources and infrastructure than small banks, which can cushion them from any challenges arising from the adoption of CBDC.

Further, we reestimate the model by replacing the BSI with another measure, the Z-score, which is a widely adopted measure in literature (Degl'Innocenti et al. 2018; Uddin et al. 2020; Luu et al. 2023). The Z-score is the ratio of the sum of the capital ratio and the return on assets to the return on assets' standard deviation. Here, a greater value implies greater stability for banks. The Z-score for bank i in country j for year t is calculated as:

$$Z\_Score_{ijt} = \frac{Capital\_Ratio_{ijt} + ROA_{ijt}}{\sigma ROA_{ijw}}$$

where capital ratio is equity capital to total assets, ROA implies return on assets, and the ROA's standard deviation is computed using three-year rolling windows, w. Table 6.8 shows the coefficients of the fixed effect model by taking the Z-score as a measure for bank stability and lagging all dependent variables to check the one-year lagged impact of CBDCI on stability. In Models 1 and 2, we introduce dummy interaction for country variables. In Model 1, we exclude country controls and add them in Model 2. In Model 3, we exclude country dummies to analyze the impact of aggregate banks. We find that CBDCI positively impacts bank stability, and the moderating role of monetary policy is also negative and significant across all three model specifications. Further, the country dummy for India (Model 1) shows that the impact of CBDCI on the stability of banks increases by 0.539 for every unit change in the adoption of CBDC for India, compared to the PRC. The results are in accordance with the baseline model; thus, we find a robust impact of adopting CBDC on, and a significant moderating role of monetary policy in, the stability of banks.

Table 6.6 Various model specifications

Variables	Model 1	Model 2	Model 3	Model 4	Model 5
Key independent variables					
CBDCI	**0.097***** (**0.023**)	**0.072***** (**0.018**)	**0.092***** (**0.020**)	**0.050***** (**0.013**)	**0.014**** (**0.006**)
Moderator	**−0.019***** (**0.005**)	**−0.011***** (**0.003**)	**−0.020***** (**0.005**)	**−0.007***** (**0.002**)	**−0.002*** (**0.001**)
Control variables					
MP	−0.006 (0.004)	−0.004 (0.004)	−0.014*** (0.003)	−0.015*** (0.003)	−0.002 (0.001)
Bank-control variables					
Dep_gr	0.016* (0.009)	0.021** (0.009)	0.016* (0.009)	0.020** (0.009)	0.007 (0.008)
lnCap	0.028*** (0.013)	0.030** (0.012)	0.038*** (0.005)	0.040*** (0.005)	0.026*** (0.006)
lnAss	−0.000 (0.010)	0.001 (0.010)	0.0005 (0.002)	0.001 (0.002)	−0.0001 (0.005)
LLP	−0.006** (0.002)	−0.006** (0.002)	−0.008*** (0.002)	−0.008*** (0.002)	−0.007*** (0.002)
Country-control variables					
lnGDP	−0.219** (0.094)	−0.303*** (0.09)	−0.006 (0.009)	−0.008 (0.009)	−0.082*** (0.017)
Inf	−0.007*** (0.002)	−0.003 (0.002)	−0.007*** (0.003)	−0.001 (0.002)	−0.001 (0.001)
Dummy_int	0.019** (0.008)	–	0.025*** (0.009)	–	–
Covid_dummy	–	–	–	–	0.008*** (0.002)
Constant	2.935*** (0.791)	3.581*** (0.770)	1.247*** (0.0890)	1.233*** (0.089)	1.734*** (0.130)
Observations	624	624	624	624	624
R-squared	0.210	0.221	–	–	0.163
Year effects	Yes	Yes	Yes	Yes	–
Bank effects	Yes	Yes	Yes	Yes	Yes

Models 1 and 2 present the results from the fixed effects model (with robust standard errors) with country-wise dummy and aggregate levels, respectively. Models 3 and 4 present the results from the panel Tobit model with country-wise dummy and aggregate levels, respectively. Model 5 shows the COVID-19 impact in a fixed effect model (with robust standard errors). Standard errors in parenthesis. Bold numerals indicate the key variables of interest. *** = 1% significance level, ** = 5% significance level, and * = 10% significance level. See Table 6.2 for the definition of the variables

Table 6.7 Impact of CBDC adoption on small, medium, and large banks

Variables	Small	Medium	Large
Key independent variables			
CBDCI	**0.022 (0.018)**	**0.065*** (0.021)**	**0.045*** (0.011)**
Moderator	**−0.007 (0.005)**	**−0.016*** (0.005)**	**−0.012*** (0.003)**
Control variables			
MP	−0.002 (0.003)	0.003 (0.004)	0.011** (0.005)
Bank-control variables			
Dep_gr	−0.010 (0.010)	0.016 (0.024)	0.010 (0.013)
lnCap	0.029* (0.017)	0.050*** (0.011)	0.029 (0.025)
lnAss	−0.023 (0.017)	0.007 (0.012)	0.027 (0.039)
LLP	−0.004 (0.004)	−0.009** (0.004)	0.001 (0.005)
Country-control variables			
lnGDP	−0.003 (0.042)	−0.145*** (0.037)	−0.065** (0.033)
Inf	−0.0002 (0.002)	−0.0002 (0.001)	−0.001 (0.001)
Dummy_int	0.010 (0.011)	0.019** (0.008)	0.026*** (0.008)
Constant	1.278*** (0.275)	2.254*** (0.303)	1.214*** (0.443)
Observations	200	199	225
R-squared	0.015	0.145	0.089
Bank effects	Yes	Yes	Yes

Models employ fixed effect estimation with robust standard errors in parenthesis. Bold numerals indicate the key variables of interest. *** = 1% significance level, ** = 5% significance level, and * = 10% significance level. See Table 6.2 for the definition of the variables

6.5 Conclusion

This study is an attempt to comprehend the moderating role of monetary policy while analyzing the impact of CBDC adoption on financial stability; hence, it makes various contributions to the literature. First, it adopts a novel and more comprehensive approach to constructing the bank stability index. Second, it provides empirical evidence on the implications of CBDC for financial stability. Third, it analyzes the

Table 6.8 Z-score as a proxy for bank stability

Variables	Model 1	Model 2	Model 3
Key independent variables			
CBDCI	**3.304*** (1.069)**	**1.089** (0.551)**	**0.890* (0.473)**
Moderator	**−0.629*** (0.164)**	**−0.269* (0.138)**	**−0.209* (0.118)**
Control variables			
MP	0.260* (0.143)	0.159* (0.089)	0.096 (0.063)
Bank-control variables			
Dep_gr	−0.050 (0.450)	−0.274 (0.433)	−0.147 (0.391)
lnCap	0.369 (0.310)	0.459 (0.279)	0.473* (0.259)
lnAss	−0.432 (0.339)	−0.230 (0.328)	−0.217 (0.245)
LLP	−0.180 (0.119)	−0.209* (0.116)	−0.204** (0.094)
Country-control variables			
lnGDP	–	2.142** (0.871)	1.997** (0.824)
Inf	–	0.016 (0.026)	0.038 (0.034)
Dummy_int	0.539* (0.285)	0.141 (0.096)	–
Constant	7.169** (3.195)	−12.080** (6.272)	−10.745* (6.326)
Observations	555	555	555
R-squared	0.016	0.296	0.298
Year effects	Yes	Yes	No
Bank effects	Yes	Yes	Yes

Model 1 presents the estimates of the fixed effect model with robust standard errors, excluding country controls and introducing country-wise dummy variables. Model 2 presents the estimates of the fixed effect model with robust standard errors, including country controls and country-wise dummy variables. Model 3 presents the aggregate results for India and the PRC. Standard errors in parenthesis. Bold numerals indicate the key variables of interest. *** = 1% significance level, ** = 5% significance level, and * = 10% significance level. See Table 6.2 for the definition of the variables moderating role of monetary policy. Finally, it compares the effects on India and the PRC. The study finds that adopting CBDC has a positive impact on financial stability. However, the impact of such adoption on banking stability is negatively and significantly moderated by monetary policy. This negative interaction implies that when policy rates increase, the impact is reduced as banks raise their interest rates to attract more deposits, thereby creating competition between traditional deposits and CBDC holding. On the other hand, the stabilizing impact of CBDC is enhanced when policy rates are lower. Therefore, in an accommodative stance of monetary policy in which banks' profitability and liquidity increase, the adoption of an advanced payment system, i.e., CBDC, can better manage risks and thus overall financial stability. The study validates two out of three hypotheses, leading to the conclusion that CBDCs may not threaten bank stability and that monetary policy plays a significant moderating role in this relationship. Other findings reveal that the monetary policy rate is positively related to financial stability, implying that a tighter monetary policy can curb excess liquidity in the banking system and promote financial stability. Furthermore, control variables such as bank capital, deposits, the loan loss provisions ratio, and GDP per capita significantly impact financial stability. Notably, the study finds that the positive impact of adopting CBDC on financial stability is more pronounced in India than in the PRC. When analyzing bank types, large and medium-sized banks exhibit a significant impact on bank stability, whereas small banks demonstrate an insignificant impact. Additionally, the study finds that the COVID-19 pandemic crisis had a surprisingly positive influence on bank stability, reflecting the effectiveness of prompt measures taken by central banks during the crisis. These findings remain consistent with robustness tests and align with the findings of Luu et al. (2023), who also reported a positive influence of CBDC adoption on financial stability.

6.6 Policy Discussion and Limitations of the Study

Based on the results, the following policy approaches may help in managing risks better and maintaining overall financial stability. First, despite the positive impacts shown, the findings should be interpreted with caution, mainly due to the limited data available on CBDC, as most countries are still in the nascent stage of development. Therefore, central banks should carefully expand pilot projects and thoroughly assess the outcomes before implementing them fully. Second, with regard to the moderating role of monetary policy, policymakers must be aware that while conventional monetary tightening helps curb excess liquidity, it also moderates the stability gains from adopting CBDC. To address this, policymakers should use CBDCs to complement macroprudential measures and examine the resilience of banks by conducting stress testing under various monetary policy conditions. Finally, central banks should design CBDCs appropriately to ensure effective liquidity management that can create a balance between bank deposits and CBDC holdings, thus eliminating any competitive tensions, particularly under tight monetary conditions. Furthermore, as the impact is more pronounced in India, the Reserve Bank of India should follow a more gradual implementation and accurately assess any risks to banks due to deposit displacements while conducting pilot studies. On the other hand, the PRC's digital infrastructure is already well developed and equipped with digital innovation; therefore, it should focus more on analyzing the risks due to its multiple projects on CBDCs, especially the uncertainties related to cross-border CBDCs. Other countries in the Asia and the Pacific region should first analyze the key motivations and their countries' needs before launching their own digital currency. For example, countries like the Philippines and Fiji have delayed or canceled the implementation of CBDC as they do not consider its issuance an immediate necessity for their countries. The primary focus of central banks that are still exploring the possibilities of CBDCs should be to make their existing payment system efficient and learn from the adoption processes of those who are in advanced stages of implementation. Therefore, our study recommends careful adoption of CBDC.

This is a first-of-its-kind research study that examines the moderating role of monetary policy in empirically assessing the implications of CBDCs for financial stability. However, this study has certain limitations, the most significant of which is the fact that the CBDC has not yet been fully implemented. Therefore, the findings will be more reliable once the CBDC has been fully adopted. The study was also not able to include the bank-level variations of CBDCs to capture the bank-variant CBDC index because of data limitations, as it requires information on the extent to which the banks are exposed to CBDC. In addition, as large-scale implementation takes place and more countries reach the full-launch stage of CBDC, it will become possible to incorporate stage-specific variables or interaction terms to better capture the distinct effects of pilot and full-launch phases. Moreover, future research can empirically examine the asymmetric impacts of CBDC on bank stability under different monetary policy conditions identified in this study. To examine this, long panel data would be required that sufficiently capture the changing regimes of monetary policy. Such an analysis would bring more evidence on how bank stability is affected under changing policy regimes. Further, the study has not accounted for the effects of a policy mix. Future research can explore the moderating impacts of various macroeconomic policies of different countries to uncover the conditions under which adopting CBDC most benefits financial stability. Such inclusions in future studies can provide more comprehensive insights into the interplay between digital currency initiatives and the overall policy environment, ultimately guiding more informed decision-making for financial stability.

Appendix A

Table A1 reports the average dimensional weights under different lower-bound restrictions.

Table A1 Sensitivity analysis for BSI by varying lower-bound restrictions on weights

Dimensional weights→lower bounds (%) ↓	$\overrightarrow{w_A}$	$\overrightarrow{w_B}$	$\overrightarrow{w_C}$	$\overrightarrow{w_D}$	$\overrightarrow{w_E}$
0	0.131	0.432	0.071	0.178	0.188
5	0.120	0.400	0.102	0.173	0.205
6	0.118	0.395	0.107	0.172	0.207
7	0.128	0.386	0.107	0.172	0.207
8	0.127	0.369	0.117	0.173	0.213
9	0.133	0.355	0.124	0.174	0.214
10	0.139	0.340	0.128	0.175	0.218
11	0.143	0.324	0.136	0.178	0.219
12	0.148	0.307	0.143	0.181	0.221
13	0.154	0.291	0.149	0.184	0.222
14	0.161	0.274	0.157	0.188	0.220
15	0.169	0.260	0.164	0.192	0.215
16	0.176	0.246	0.170	0.197	0.211
17	0.182	0.231	0.178	0.202	0.208
18	0.189	0.216	0.184	0.207	0.204
19	0.195	0.206	0.192	0.206	0.202
20	0.200	0.200	0.200	0.200	0.200

$\overrightarrow{w_A}$, $\overrightarrow{w_B}$, $\overrightarrow{w_C}$, $\overrightarrow{w_D}$, and $\overrightarrow{w_E}$ stand for average dimensional weights for capital adequacy, asset quality, profitability and earnings, liquidity, and efficiency, respectively

References

Albertazzi, U., F. Barbiero, D. Marques-Ibanez, A. A. Popov, C. Rodriguez D'Acri, and T. Vlassopoulos. 2020. Monetary policy and bank stability: The analytical toolbox reviewed. *SSRN Electronic Journal*. https://doi.org/10.2139/ssrn.3541733.

Annunziata, F., C. Hadjiemmanuil, and B. Joosen. 2025. *Central bank digital currency the birth of the digital euro*. Cham: Springer Nature Switzerland AG.

Auer, R., G. Cornelli, and J. Frost. 2020. Rise of the central bank digital currencies: Drivers, approaches and technologies. *SSRN Electronic Journal*. https://doi.org/10.2139/ssrn.3724070.

Auer, Raphael, J. Frost, L. Gambacorta, C. Monnet, T. Rice, and H. Song Shin. 2022. Central bank digital currencies: Motives, economic implications, and the research frontier. *Annual Review of Economics* 14 (1): 697–721. https://doi.org/10.1146/annurev-economics-051420-020324.

Baltagi, B. H. 2021. *Econometric analysis of panel data*. Springer Texts in Business and Economics. https://doi.org/10.1007/978-3-030-53953-5.

Barrdear, J., and M. Kumhof. 2022. The macroeconomics of central bank digital currencies. *Journal of Economic Dynamics and Control* 142:104148. https://doi.org/10.1016/j.jedc.2021.104148.

Bas, T., I. Malki, and S. Sivaprasad. 2024. Connectedness between central bank digital currency index, financial stability and digital assets. *Journal of International Financial Markets Institutions and Money* 92:101981. https://doi.org/10.1016/j.intfin.2024.101981.

Bech, M., and R. Garratt. 2017. Central bank cryptocurrencies. *BIS Quarterly Review*55–70.

Belke, A., and E. Beretta. 2020. From cash to central bank digital currencies and cryptocurrencies: A balancing act between modernity and monetary stability. *Journal of Economic Studies* 47 (4): 911–938. https://doi.org/10.1108/jes-07-2019-0311.

Bharathan, V. 2020. Central bank digital currency: The first nationwide CBDC in the world has been launched by the Bahamas. Forbes, October 22. Accessed on August 8, 2024. Available at https://www.forbes.com/sites/vipinbharathan/2020/10/21/central-bank-digital-currency-the-first-nationwide-cbdc-in-the-world-has-been-launched-by-the-bahamas/?sh=5a20b83c506e.

Bibi, S. 2023. Money in the time of crypto. *SSRN Electronic Journal*. https://doi.org/10.2139/ssrn.4373847.

Boar, C., and A. Wehrli. 2021. Ready, steady, go? Results of the third BIS survey on central bank digital currency. BIS Papers, January. Accessed on July 10, 2024. Available at https://ideas.repec.org/b/bis/bisbps/114.html.

Bordo, M. D. 2005. Gold as a commitment mechanism: Past, present and future. In *Routledge eBooks*, 35–79. https://doi.org/10.4324/9780203987643-11.

Brand, M., L. de Koker, and C. Herse. 2025. Privacy-preserving data analytics: A case study in anti-money laundering and counter terrorist and proliferation financing innovation in Australia. In *Combating financial crime: Intended and unintended consequences*, ed. D. Goldbarsht, L. de Koker, and J. Ferrill, 21–53. Cham: Springer Nature Switzerland AG.

Brunnermeier, M. K., and D. Niepelt. 2019. On the equivalence of private and public money. *Journal of Monetary Economics* 106:27–41. https://doi.org/10.1016/j.jmoneco.2019.07.004.

Cecchetti, S., H. Genberg, and S. Wadhwani. 2002. Asset prices in a flexible inflation targeting framework. https://doi.org/10.3386/w8970.

CBDC Tracker. 2024. Today's Central Bank Digital Currencies Status. Accessed on August 1, 2024. Available at https://cbdctracker.org/.

Chen, H., and P. L. Siklos. 2022. Central bank digital currency: A review and some macro-financial implications. *Journal of Financial Stability* 60:100985. https://doi.org/10.1016/j.jfs.2022.100985.

Cherchye, L., W. Moesen, and T. Van Puyenbroeck. 2004. Legitimately diverse, yet comparable: On synthesizing social inclusion performance in the EU. *JCMS Journal of Common Market Studies* 42 (5): 919–955. https://doi.org/10.1111/j.0021-9886.2004.00535.x.

Cherchye, L., W. Moesen, N. Rogge, and T. Van Puyenbroeck. 2006. An introduction to 'benefit of the doubt' composite indicators. *Social Indicators Research* 82 (1): 111–145. https://doi.org/10.1007/s11205-006-9029-7.

Cherchye, L., W. Moesen, N. Rogge, and T. Van Puyenbroeck. 2011. Constructing composite indicators with imprecise data: A proposal. *Expert Systems with Applications* 38 (9): 10940–10949. https://doi.org/10.1016/j.eswa.2011.02.136.

Degl'Innocenti, M., K. Grant, A. Šević, and N. G. Tzeremes. 2018. Financial stability, competitiveness and banks' innovation capacity: Evidence from the global financial crisis. *International Review of Financial Analysis* 59:35–46. https://doi.org/10.1016/j.irfa.2018.07.009.

Dhaou, S. I. B., and I. K. Rohman. 2018. Everything and its opposite—socio-economic implications of blockchain technology: Case of monetary policy. *ACM International Conference Proceeding Series*. doi:https://doi.org/10.1145/3209415.3209502.

Diamond, D. W., and P. H. Dybvig. 1983. Bank runs, deposit insurance, and liquidity. *Journal of Political Economy* 91 (3): 401–419. https://doi.org/10.1086/261155.

Dionysopoulos, L., M. Marra, and A. Urquhart. 2023. Central bank digital currencies: A critical review. *International Review of Financial Analysis* 91:103031. https://doi.org/10.1016/j.irfa.2023.103031.

Duarte, C. B. 2019. Alternative monetary targets, instruments and future monetary policy frameworks. *Review of Political Economy* 31 (4): 582–601. https://doi.org/10.1080/09538259.2020.1730606.

Fang, Y., I. Hasan, and K. Marton. 2013. Institutional development and bank stability: Evidence from transition countries. *Journal of Banking & Finance* 39:160–176. https://doi.org/10.1016/j.jbankfin.2013.11.003.

Farrell, D., and S. Lund. 2006. *A tale of two financial systems: A comparison of China and India*. McKinsey & Company. Accessed on October 18, 2024. Available at https://www.mckinsey.com/featured-insights/winning-in-emerging-markets/a-tale-of-two-financial-systems.

Fegatelli, P. 2022. A central bank digital currency in a heterogeneous monetary union: Managing the effects on the bank lending channel. *Journal of Macroeconomics* 71:103392. https://doi.org/10.1016/j.jmacro.2021.103392.

Fiedler, S., K.-J. Gern, and U. Stolzenburg. 2019. The impact of digitalisation on the monetary system. Monetary Dialogue Papers, November. Accessed on October 10, 2024. Available at https://www.ifw-kiel.de/fileadmin/Dateiverwaltung/IfW-Publications/Salomon_Fiedler/The_Impact_of_Digitalisation_on_the_Monetary_System/2019-11-The_Impact_of_Digitalisation_on_the_Monetary_System.pdf.

Financial Stability Report. 2010. Financial stability report, Reserve Bank of India. Mumbai. Accessed on December 14, 2024. Available at https://www.rbi.org.in.

Freiman, O. 2024. CBDC governance: Programmability, privacy and policies. Digital Policy Hub Working Paper, Centre for International Governance Innovation, Waterloo, ON. Accessed on April 4, 2026. Available at https://www.cigionline.org/static/documents/DPH-paper-Freiman.pdf.

Ghenimi, A., H. Chaibi, and M. A. B. Omri. 2017. The effects of liquidity risk and credit risk on bank stability: Evidence from the MENA region. *Borsa Istanbul Review* 17 (4): 238–248. https://doi.org/10.1016/j.bir.2017.05.002.

Gulati, R. 2023. Beyond the Z-score: A novel measure of bank stability for effective policymaking. *Journal of Public Affairs* 23 (4): https://doi.org/10.1002/pa.2866.

Gulati, R., V. Charles, M. K. Hassan, and S. Kumar. 2023. COVID-19 crisis and the efficiency of Indian banks: Have they weathered the storm? *Socio-Economic Planning Sciences* 88:101661. https://doi.org/10.1016/j.seps.2023.101661.

Huljak, I. 2015. Market power and stability of CEE banks. *Business Systems Research Journal* 6 (2): 74–90. https://doi.org/10.1515/bsrj-2015-0013.

Hoang, Y. H., V. M. Ngo, and N. B. Vu. 2023. Central bank digital currency: A systematic literature review using text mining approach. *Research in International Business and Finance* 64:101889. https://doi.org/10.1016/j.ribaf.2023.101889.

Jha, C. K. 2019. Financial reforms and corruption: Evidence using GMM estimation. *International Review of Economics & Finance* 62:66–78. https://doi.org/10.1016/j.iref.2019.03.003.

Kesavaraj, S. V., C. M. Jakhiya, and C. N. Bhandari. 2022. A study on upcoming central bank digital currency: Opportunities, obstacles, and potential FinTech solutions using cryptography in the Indian scenario. In *2022 13th International Conference on Computing Communication and Networking Technologies (ICCCNT)*, October. https://doi.org/10.1109/icccnt54827.2022.9984539.

Lapteacru, I. 2016. On the consistency of the Z-score to measure the bank risk. *SSRN Electronic Journal*. https://doi.org/10.2139/ssrn.2787567.

Luu, H. N., C. P. Nguyen, and M. A. Nasir. 2023. Implications of central bank digital currency for financial stability: Evidence from the global banking sector. *Journal of International Financial Markets Institutions and Money* 89:101864. https://doi.org/10.1016/j.intfin.2023.101864.

Maher, W. 2024. China's monetary policy framework and financial market transmission | bulletin—April 2024. Reserve Bank of Australia, April 18. Accessed on October 10, 2024. Available at https://www.rba.gov.au/publications/bulletin/2024/apr/chinas-monetary-policy-framework-and-financial-market-transmission.html.

Marmefelt, T. 2024. Central bank digital currencies and international crises: Toward an authoritarian international monetary order? *Politics and Governance* 12 (4): 1–12. https://doi.org/10.17645/pag.8540.

M'bakob, G. B., and A. Tchounga. 2024. CBDC and banking stability: Modeling cascading effects on reserves, lending, and liquidity. *Research in Economics* 78 (4): 101005. https://doi.org/10.1016/j.rie.2024.101005.

Melyn, W., and W. Moesen. 1991. Towards a synthetic indicator of macroeconomic performance: Unequal weighting when limited information is available. Accessed on July 10, 2024. Public Economics Research Paper No. 17, Leuven, January 1–24. Available at https://api.semanticscholar.org/CorpusID:157419812.

Meng, Y., J. Wu, and Y. Tu. 2024. Central bank digital currency, financial technology level and regional financial stability. *International Review of Economics & Finance* 96:103598. https://doi.org/10.1016/j.iref.2024.103598.

Ngotran, D. 2020. The E-monetary theory. *Economics* 14 (1): https://doi.org/10.5018/economics-ejournal.ja.2020-13.

Opare, E. A., and K. Kim. 2020. A compendium of practices for central bank digital currencies for multinational financial infrastructures. *IEEE Access* 8:110810–110847. https://doi.org/10.1109/access.2020.3001970.

Ozili, P. K. 2024. Central bank digital currency and the monetary policy and financial stability implications. In *Digital currency assets and challenges to financial system stability*, 52–62. IGI Global. https://doi.org/10.2139/ssrn.4659959.

Peneder, M. 2022. Digitization and the evolution of money as a social technology of account. *Journal of Evolutionary Economics* 32 (1): 175–203. https://doi.org/10.1007/s00191-021-00729-4.

Qian, Y. 2019. Central bank digital currency: Optimization of the currency system and its issuance design. *China Economic Journal* 12 (1): 1–15. https://doi.org/10.1080/17538963.2018.1560526.

RBI. 2022. Concept note on central bank digital currency. Reserve Bank of India. Accessed on July 10, 2024. Available at https://rbidocs.rbi.org.in/rdocs/PublicationReport/Pdfs/CONCEPTNOTEACB531172E0B4DFC9A6E506C2C24FFB6.PDF.

Rehman, M. A., M. Irfan, M. A. Naeem, B. M. Lucey, and S. Karim. 2023. Macro-financial implications of central bank digital currencies. *Research in International Business and Finance* 64:101892. https://doi.org/10.1016/j.ribaf.2023.101892.

Reserve Bank of India. n.d. Overview. Accessed on December 15, 2024. Available at https://www.rbi.org.in/scripts/FS_Overview.aspx?fn=2752.

Ricoy-Casas, R. M. 2022. Digital currencies: Challenges between the United States, the European Union and Asia Pacific. *Cuadernos Europeos de Deusto* 03:95–114. https://doi.org/10.18543/ced-03-2022pp95-114.

Roodman, D. 2009. How to do Xtabond2: An introduction to difference and system GMM in stata. *The Stata Journal Promoting Communications on Statistics and Stata* 9 (1): 86–136. https://doi.org/10.1177/1536867x0900900106.

Schilling, I., J. Fernández-Villaverde, and H. Uhlig. 2024. Central bank digital currency: When price and bank stability collide. *Journal of Monetary Economics* 145:103554. https://doi.org/10.1016/j.jmoneco.2024.01.007.

Shen, W., and L. Hou. 2021. China's central bank digital currency and its impacts on monetary policy and payment competition: Game changer or regulatory toolkit? *Computer Law & Security Review* 41:105577. https://doi.org/10.1016/j.clsr.2021.105577.

Syarifuddin, F., and T. Bakhtiar. 2022. The macroeconomic effects of an interest-bearing CBDC: A DSGE model. *Mathematics* 10 (10): 1671. https://doi.org/10.3390/math10101671.

Temperini, J., C. D'Ippoliti, and L. Gobbi. 2024. Is the time ripe for helicopter money? Growth impact and financial stability risks of outright monetary transfers. *Structural Change and Economic Dynamics* 69:24–36. https://doi.org/10.1016/j.strueco.2023.11.003.

Tercero-Lucas, D. 2023. Central bank digital currencies and financial stability in a modern monetary system. *Journal of Financial Stability* 69:101188. https://doi.org/10.1016/j.jfs.2023.101188.

Uddin, M. H., S. Mollah, and M. H. Ali. 2020. Does cyber tech spending matter for bank stability? *International Review of Financial Analysis* 72:101587. https://doi.org/10.1016/j.irfa.2020.101587.

Vidoli, F., and E. Fusco. 2018. Compind: Composite indicators functions based on frontiers in R (Compind package version 2.0). Accessed on August 20, 2024. Available at https://cran.r-project.org/web/packages/Compind/vignettes/Compind_vignette.pdf.

Vo, D. H., N. T. Nguyen, and L. T.-H. Van. 2020. Financial inclusion and stability in the Asian region using bank-level data. *Borsa Istanbul Review* 21 (1): 36–43. https://doi.org/10.1016/j.bir.2020.06.003.

White, W. R. 2009. Federal Reserve Bank of Dallas globalization and monetary policy institute should monetary policy "lean or clean"?. Accessed on June 23, 2024. Available at http://www.dallasfed.org/assets/documents/institute/wpapers/2009/0034.pdf.

Xin, B., and K. Jiang. 2023. Central bank digital currency and the effectiveness of negative interest rate policy: A DSGE analysis. *Research in International Business and Finance* 64:101901. https://doi.org/10.1016/j.ribaf.2023.101901.

Yamaoka, H. 2023. The future of central banking. *Accounting Economics and Law—A Convivium* 13 (2): 103–132. https://doi.org/10.1515/ael-2019-0003.

Yang, J., and G. Zhou. 2022. A study on the influence mechanism of CBDC on monetary policy: An analysis based on e-CNY. *PLoS One* 17 (7): e0268471. https://doi.org/10.1371/journal.pone.0268471.

Yang, Y., C. Zhang, and W. Hou. 2024. CBDC, cash, and financial intermediary in HANK. *Portuguese Economic Journal* 23 (3): https://doi.org/10.1007/s10258-023-00250-5.

Zhang, Z. W. 2024. CBDC Security. In *Web3 applications security and new security landscape. Future of business and finance*, ed. K. Huang, C. Parisi, L. J. Y. Tan, W. Ma, and Z. W. Zhang, 73–92. Cham: Springer Nature Switzerland AG.

Chapter 7
Monetary Policy, Prudential Regulations, and Domestic Credit: The Role of Commercial Banks in Pakistan

Muhammad Ayub Khan Mehar

Abstract The objective of this study is to test the impacts of significant devices of monetary policy and prudential regulations on banks' ability to invest and lend. The interconnectedness of the banking sector, public sector debt, and financing for private sector business activities in Pakistan is also an important concern of this study. It was presumed that the effects of prudential regulations are transformed through mandatory magnitudes of equity and cash requirements. The significant positive and robust impact of equity on investment, advances, deposits, and liquidity has been ascertained. It was concluded that prudential regulations do not discourage the lending or investment. This study is based on 5 years of data of 33 commercial banks in Pakistan and the random effect models (REM) and the seemingly-unrelated regression estimation (SURE) techniques have been adopted to estimate the parameters.

Keywords Broad money · Capital advocacy ratio · Cash reserve ratio · Deposits · Public borrowing · Statuary liquidity ratio

7.1 Introduction

Despite its large market, fertile land, strategic location, global connectivity, and rich mineral resources, Pakistan is facing severe economic challenges. Stagnant economic activities, lower GDP growth, a severe debt crisis, rapid devaluation, high interest rates, growing poverty and unemployment, and unpredictable high inflation rates have become severe economic issues that can lead to social and political unrest. To mitigate the severe negative impacts of these issues and avoid financial disasters,

M. A. K. Mehar (✉)
Employers' Federation of Pakistan, Karachi, Pakistan

R. Gulati et al. (eds.), *Emerging Challenges in Banking in Asia and the Pacific*, Economics, Law, and Institutions in Asia Pacific,
https://doi.org/10.1007/978-981-92-2144-8_7

governments in the past adopted heavy domestic and external borrowing, the objectives of which were to protect their votebanks, gain popularity, and delay the onset of crisis. Borrowing from commercial banks is one of those strategies adopted in recent years.

The theoretical debate on the role of credit from banking institutions in economic growth, investment, and trade activities has a rich history, and the role of monetary policy, credit enhancement, and investment in economic growth, employment, and inflation has been widely discussed by Phillips (1958), Friedman (1968), Tobin (1969), and Stiglitz (1985). They provided a strong theoretical foundation for determining the role of credit and monetary policies. The role of credit in trade and business activities has also been ascertained by Kindleberger (1970), Stein (1982), Montecino and Epstein (2015), and Mehar (2022). Despite the significant role of credit from banks in the promotion of economic and business activities, the government's intervention through monetary policy and prudential regulation is still a debatable issue. This study fills this gap, and the role of monetary policy and prudential regulations in investment activities, lending, and bank deposits has been tested in the context of Pakistan.

In recessions and economic crises, governments introduce monetary and fiscal measures, where banks are encouraged to sanction and enhance their lending and investment facilities for those business entities that are facing liquidity crises (Mehar 2021). However, the interconnectedness of the banking sector, public sector debt, and financing for private sector business activities is an important concern in the present scenario. Apostolik et al. (2009) explained the role of banking risks in soft credit policies; however, Carpenter and Maureen Murphy (2010) described the speculative risks attached to credit enhancement.

The transmission of monetary policy and prudential regulations in investment and lending activities has motivated the researchers to explore the mechanism of banking channels. Against this background, the objective of this study is to test the impacts of major monetary policy devices and prudential regulations on the ability of banks to invest and lend. In brief, this study examines the impacts of capital ratio (equity), liquidity, and interest rates on (1) lending from commercial banks, (2) investment by commercial banks, (3) deposits by commercial banks, (4) the liquidity of commercial banks, and (5) the return on assets of commercial banks. The next section of this paper discusses the importance of credit from banks to the private sector and the role of monetary policy, prudential regulations, and public borrowing. The mechanism and instruments of prudential regulations are explained in Sect. 7.3, while the methodology and statistical techniques used to assess the role of explanatory variables are discussed in Sect. 7.4. Section 7.5 explains the empirical pieces of evidence based on the statistical parameters, and finally, some policy implications and limitations are described in Sect. 7.6.

7.2 The Importance of Credit from Commercial Banks

Several studies have concluded that banks, through their credit policies, can play an important role in alleviating poverty and creating employment and business opportunities. Domestic credit to the private sector refers to the aggregation of lending by financial institutions, mainly commercial banks. It covers loans, purchases of nonequity securities, trade credits, and other accounts receivable, while "domestic credit to the private sector by banks" refers to financial resources provided to the private sector by deposit-taking corporations (except for central banks). This is a subset of monetary sector credit, which includes short-term securities issued by monetary authorities to the private sector (Mehar 2023), and is the main vehicle through which changes in the money supply are regulated. The central bank can regulate lending to the private sector in several ways, including adjusting the cost of refinancing facilities to commercial banks, fixing a minimum interest rate through monetary policy, and changing the reserve requirements of commercial banks to restrict their lending ability.

Various studies have established links between lending from banks and poverty (Duffy-Deno and Eberts 1991; Hideo et al. 2019), though return on investment is an important consideration of banks and other business enterprises. This consideration becomes more important in the context of Pakistan, where credit to the private sector is much lower than that in other countries in the region. The global average of domestic credit to the private sector as a percentage of GDP is 141: It is 149 in high-income countries, 140 in upper-middle-income nations, 47 in lower-middle-income economies, and 46 in South Asian countries. It is 51% in India; however, in Pakistan, it is less than 15%. Over the last decade, there has been a worldwide increasing trend in this ratio; however, it continues to decrease in Pakistan year after year. Domestic credit as a percentage of GDP in South Asian countries is lower than that in the rest of the world, and the ratio is lowest in Pakistan (apart from Afghanistan).

In the context of Pakistan, the role of commercial banks becomes more important because of the low level of domestic credit to the private sector, while the size of the nonbanking financial sector in domestic lending is almost negligible. Table 7.1 shows that more than 99% of credit to the private sector in Pakistan comes from commercial banks. The volume of credit provided by banks is derived from their deposits and regulatory parameters and bindings, including monetary policy and prudential regulations. Table 7.1 envisages that the number of borrowers per thousand people is 26 in Pakistan. This is an indicator of financial inclusion. The number is 84 in Bangladesh and 82 in lower-middle-income countries. There are multiple reasons for the lower number of borrowers in Pakistan, with qualitative controls, including guarantees and collateral, the lack of financial literacy, and high interest rates being among the more obvious ones. Indeed, Pakistan is one of the countries with the highest interest rates, with the prime rate of interest currently being 12% (it was 22% in 2023–2024). Figure 7.1 depicts the patterns of credit to the private sector from commercial banks. Notably, in high-income countries, the volume of domestic credit to the private sector is much higher because of the participation of the nonbanking financial sector in providing such credit.

Another significant indicator in Pakistan is the rapid growth in government borrowing from commercial banks to finance the fiscal deficit. Tables 7.2 and 7.3 show the growth in government borrowing from commercial banks, and the huge lending by these banks to the government can further affect the volume of domestic credit to the private sector. Figure 7.2 shows the trend of credit to the private sector and financing of the fiscal deficit of the federal government in Pakistan.

In developing countries, and particularly in Pakistan, the share of the nonbanking financial sector is almost negligible. The most important point is the flow of domestic credit from commercial banks to the federal government to finance its budget deficit. Table 7.2 shows that the share of the private sector in the expansion of the money supply (M2) is less than 5%; the remaining growth in the money supply is due to government borrowing.

7.3 Mechanism and Instruments of Prudential Regulations

Many banks and other financial institutions in various countries can control their economies, but if they fail, it can create severe consequences for the national and global economy. Because of the interconnectedness of the banking industry and the global economy, regulatory agencies need to maintain control over the standardized practices of banking institutions, which is why monetary authorities regulate the banking system through prudential regulations. The supervision of the banking system and prudential regulations in the contemporary world are based on the Basel Accords—i.e., the banking supervision mechanism issued by the Basel Committee on Banking Supervision. In 1988, the Basel Committee published a set of minimum capital requirements for banks, and then a new set of rules (Basel II) was developed and published in 2004 to supersede the Basel I Accord. In response to the financial crisis of 2007–2008, Basel III was recommended, which represented an enhancement of the previous rules. Several aspects of Basel III reflect a macroprudential approach to financial regulations (de la Torre and Ize 2009); however, Basel III does not supersede either Basel I or II. The Basel Accords are integrated into the consolidated Basel framework.

Macroprudential supervision and regulation assess how a financial institution is connected with the rest of the financial system and the real economy. A large number of instruments have been proposed for implementing the prudential regulations; however, there is no agreement on which one should play the primary role in the implementation of macroprudential policy (Clement 2010), which views the financial system as a whole, while microprudential regulations apply to individual credit institutions. The focus of microprudential regulations is the stability of individual financial institutions.

Table 7.1 Domestic credit in South Asian countries (% of GDP, unless specified)

Country/group/ region	Domestic credit to the private sector	Domestic credit to the private sector by banks	Monetary sector credit to the private sector	Borrowers from commercial banks (per 1000 adults)
2019				
Afghanistan	3.2	3.2	3.2	3.0
Bhutan	59.4	59.4	59.4	
Bangladesh	39.0	38.9	39.0	82.9
India	50.7	50.7	50.7	
Nepal	78.9	78.8	78.9	
Maldives	31.5	28.1	28.1	170.7
Pakistan	15.7	15.6	15.7	23.1
Sri Lanka	47.0	46.9	47.0	
World	131.2	88.7	89.0	155.8
Upper middle income	123.3	120.6	120.6	261.8
South Asia	46.4	46.4	46.4	23.1
Lower middle income	44.6	43.9	44.0	63.1
High income	145.3	80.3	80.7	
2022				
Afghanistan	3.1*	3.0*	3.1*	
Bhutan	67.9	67.9	67.9	
Bangladesh	39.0	38.8	39.0	84.0*
India	50.1*	50.1*	50.1*	
Nepal	94.5	94.3	94.5	
Maldives	35.3	31.0	31.0	
Pakistan	14.8	14.8	14.8	25.8*
Sri Lanka				
World	141.3	96.1	96.5	
Upper middle income	139.9	137.8	137.8	259.9*
South Asia	46.4*	46.4*	46.4*	
Lower middle income	46.7*	46.1*	46.2*	81.9*
High income	148.9	79.6	80.2	

*2021

Source Author's presentation based on World Bank (2024)

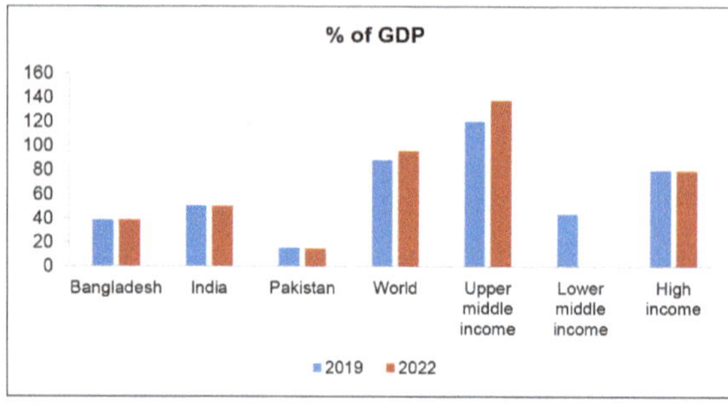

Fig. 7.1 Domestic credit from commercial banks. *Source* Author's own based on World Bank (2024)

Table 7.2 Net change in broad money (M2) (PKR billion)

Year/ causative factor	Public sector borrowing (including autonomous bodies and PSEs)	Credit to the private sector	Others	Net foreign assets	Change in money supply (M2)
2019	2482.7	693.5	−76.2	−1298.7	1801.3
2020	2313.9	196.4	−391.6	990.9	3109.6
2021	1693.6	766.2	−311.0	1240.9	3389.7
2022	3609.4	1329.7	−156.3	−1478.0	3304.8
2023	4538.6	208.3	1108.1	−1934.5	3920.5
2024 (Mar)	3744.3	187.9	−2245.7	529.7	2216.2

Source Author's presentation based on State Bank of Pakistan (2024b)

Table 7.3 Causative factors associated with broad money (M2) (PKR billion)

Year/ causative factor	Public sector borrowing (including autonomous bodies and PSEs)	Credit to the private sector	Others	Net foreign assets	Change in money supply (M2)
2019	13,743	6667	−1104	−1507	17,799
2020	16,057	6863	−1496	−516	20,908
2021	17,751	7629	−1807	725	24,298
2022	21,360	8959	−1963	−753	27,603
2023	25,899	9167	−855	−2688	31,523
2024 (Mar)	29,643	9355	−3100	−2158	33,740

Source Author's presentation based on State Bank of Pakistan (2024b)

The overall purpose of prudential regulations is to ensure that banks are viable and resilient. These regulations impose certain requirements, restrictions, and guidelines set by monetary authorities. To protect the depositors (Federal Deposit Insurance Corporation 2011), reduce the risk of disruption resulting from adverse trading conditions for banks causing major bank failures, reduce the risk of banks being

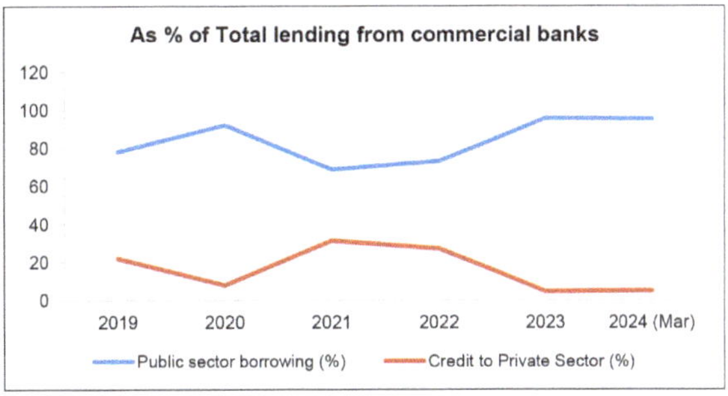

Fig. 7.2 Share of public and private sectors in lending from commercial banks. *Source* Author's own based on State Bank of Pakistan (2024d)

used for criminal purposes, protect banking confidentiality, direct credit to priority sectors, treat customers fairly and having corporate social responsibility are the most common objectives of prudential regulations.

Prudential regulations and supervision require banks to control risks and hold adequate capital as defined by capital requirements, liquidity requirements, the imposition of concentration risk limits, related reporting and public disclosure requirements, and supervisory controls and processes (Morris 2019). Other components of prudential regulations include supervision for consumers' protection and anti-money laundering. One of the reasons to maintain the regulations of banking institutions is the concern over the global repercussions that could result from a bank's failure (Rochet 2009).

The prudential regulations play an important role in the resilience of commercial banks through their qualitative and quantitative restrictions. The caps on the leverage ratio, the loan-to-value ratio, and the debt-to-income ratio, the countercyclical capital requirement, the levy on noncore liabilities, the time-varying reserve requirement, the liquidity coverage ratio, liquidity risk charges that penalize short-term funding, capital requirement surcharges proportional to the size of maturity mismatch, and the minimum haircut requirements for asset-backed securities are included in the instruments used by the prudential regulations. Different types of contingent capital instruments are proposed to facilitate a bank's recapitalization in the event of a crisis (Bank of England 2009; Reinhart and Rogoff 2009).

Some analysts have discussed the theoretical and empirical evidence on the effects of prudential regulations and their relation with investment and lending activities, while some theoretical studies indicate that macroprudential policies may make a positive contribution to long-run average growth. Jeanne and Korinek (2011) show that in a model with externalities of crises that occur under financial liberalization, well-designed macroprudential regulation both reduces crisis risk and increases long-run growth as it mitigates the cycles of boom and bust. Popov and Smets (2012) recommend that macroprudential tools should be employed more forcefully during costly booms driven by overborrowing, targeting the sources of externalities but preserving the positive contribution of financial markets to growth. Using data from the UK, Aiyar et al. (2011) find that unregulated banks in the UK have been able to partially offset changes in the credit supply induced by time-varying minimum capital requirements over the regulated banks. Hence, they highlight a potential leakage in macroprudential regulation of bank capital. Most of the central banks' authorities believe that such regulations effectively contributed to the resilience of their domestic financial systems in the wake of the financial crisis of the late 2000s (Popov and Smets 2012). In analyzing the costs of higher capital requirements implied by a macroprudential approach, Hanson et al. (2011) report that the long-run effects on loan rates for borrowers should be quantitatively small.

As far as the impact of the Basel Accords on the credit from commercial banks to the private sector is concerned, it is evident that the Basel framework has not affected negatively the credit to the private sector, as depicted in Table 7.4. A growing trend in the credit to the private sector is a worldwide phenomenon, except in Pakistan, and the reasons for the decline in such credit in this country are explored in this study.

Due to major fundamental changes in the scope and orientation of the financial system in Pakistan, prudential regulations were adopted in 1992 (State Bank of Pakistan 2024a). In this country, prudential regulations apply to banks and development finance institutions (DFIs) only. Nonbanking finance companies (NBFCs) are governed separately by the Securities and Exchange Commission of Pakistan under

Table 7.4 Credit to the private sector by commercial banks

Year	Bangladesh	India	Pakistan	South Asia	World	Lower–middle-income countries	High-income countries
Before Basel framework							
1987	13.2	25.4	27.6	24.5	75.6	22.6	83.7
1988	14.4	25.3	26.4	24.4	80.4	22.6	88.9
After Basel I							
1989	16.0	26.6	24.9	25.3	83.2	23.3	89.8
1990	16.1	24.9	24.2	23.9	79.1	21.9	89.7
Implementation of Basel framework in Pakistan							
1993	15.3	23.8	24.4	22.7	81.9	21.5	89.7
1994	16.3	23.6	23.8	22.7	82.0	22.0	91.1
After Basel II							
2005	29.0	40.1	21.6	36.6	77.0	32.8	83.3
2006	30.9	43.6	22.7	39.6	79.3	34.1	86.4
After Basel III							
2010	40.8	50.6	19.2	46.0	82.2	40.0	88.4
2011	42.3	51.3	16.7	46.4	81.0	39.8	86.4
Recent past							
2021	39.0	50.1	15.3	46.4	94.7	46.1	81.9
2022	38.8		14.8		96.1		79.6
2023	37.5		11.9		95.6		75.8

Source Author's presentation based on World Bank (2025)

a distinct set of regulations. During the last 5 years, it has been noted that the capital ratios of Pakistani banks have ranged between 1.5% and 50%. For the majority of commercial banks, it has been less than 4%, if we ignore the negative capital ratios for a few banks including the Industrial Development Bank of Pakistan, which is a public sector entity and specialized commercial bank. It should be noted that the capital ratio is different from the capital adequacy ratio (CAR). In calculating the capital ratio, capital is measured as an aggregation of paid-up capital and reserves as reported in the balance sheet, while assets mean the assets reported therein. However, the CAR is a legal requirement, for which the capital and the risk-weighted assets are calculated in a prescribed manner. The prudential regulations set a minimum requirement for the capital adequacy ratio (CAR), which is calculated by dividing a bank's capital by its risk-weighted assets. Currently, the minimum ratio of capital to risk-weighted assets is 8% under Basel II, while it is 10.5% under Basel III (which includes a 2.5% conservation buffer). In implementing the current capital requirement, the State Bank of Pakistan requires all banks to maintain a minimum capital adequacy ratio (CAR) of 11.50%.

7.4 Methodology to Capture the Impacts of Prudential Regulations

To examine the impacts of monetary policy and prudential regulations on banks' lending, investment, deposits, and profitability, it is assumed that public borrowing, the capital adequacy ratio, the statutory liquidity requirement, and the cash reserve ratio will affect owners' equity, and their cash in banks. Subsequently, owners' equity and cash will affect investment, lending, deposits, and profitability, as explained in Fig. 7.3. Bank capital indicates the shareholders' investment in the bank. A bank that has sufficient capital can cover customers' deposits in the case of bad debts and a drop in the value of the bank's assets. The cash reserve ratio (CRR) and statutory liquidity ratio (SLR) are key instruments for measuring the liquidity position of a bank, with the latter being the minimum percentage of deposits that a commercial bank has to maintain in the form of liquid cash, gold, or other securities. By adjusting the CRR and statutory liquidity ratio (SLR), the central banks can regulate the amount of money that is available for lending. The capital adequacy ratio and various measures used to maintain a bank's liquidity are the main instruments in the prudential regulations. Most of the rules described in these regulations are transformed in the magnitude of the capital and liquidity positions of the commercial banks. The effects of prudential regulations on commercial banks are reflected in their equity, cash, and cash equivalence. The capital ratio refers to equity as a percentage of total assets. The minimum capital adequacy ratio (CAR) of 11.50% set by the State Bank of Pakistan fulfills the Basel III requirements for 6% total Tier 1 capital, 8% total capital, and an additional 2.5% countercyclical buffer. It is presumed in this study that banking regulations, future investment plans, and extra safety consciousness influence the magnitude of equity, while equity is an explanatory variable in determining the advances, investment, and liquidity, which limits the banks' ability to create money or advances for their clients. As advances and investments are parts of assets, in order to maintain the capital ratio with growing advances and investments, the banks have to increase their equity. Notably, banks often hold government securities as part of their asset portfolio, and they may also have loans or deposits with the central bank. These claims are considered low-risk and are used to manage liquidity and meet regulatory requirements. The government claims are the financial assets of the commercial banks; these assets refer to government securities (bonds, bills, notes), treasury bills and bonds, central bank deposits, loans to the government, refundable taxes, and government guarantees. This is why this study has attempted to ascertain the role of equity, liquidity, the interest rate, and government borrowing from commercial banks. The process of transforming prudential regulations into credit to the private sector is explained in Fig. 7.3, which simplifies the scope and limitations of this study. However, to test the falsification and quantify the net impacts of explanatory variables, some control variables have also been adopted in the study. In determining the advances, investment, and return on assets, government borrowing, equity, and liquidity are the main explanatory variables. The dummy variables to incorporate the effects of COVID-19 and the types of the banks are also included as independent variables, while the real interest rate, exchange rate, industrial growth rate, and, in some cases, deposits are applied as other control variables.

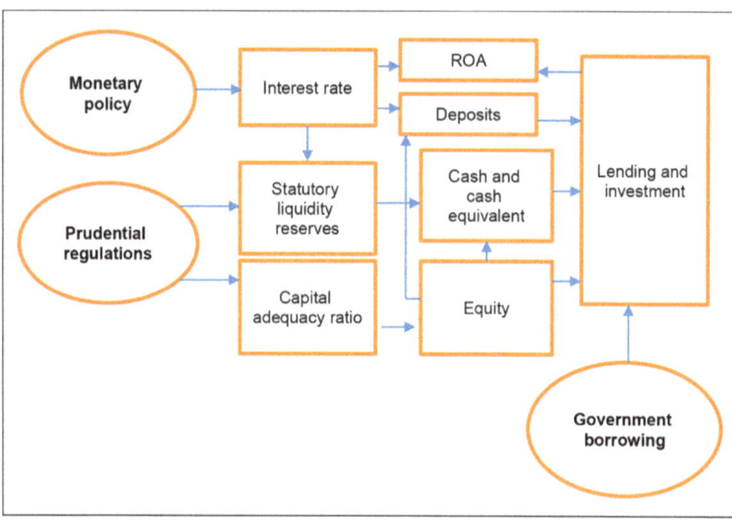

Fig. 7.3 Effects of monetary policy and prudential regulations on investment and lending. * Oval shapes indicate influence by public policy or regulations. *Source* Author's depiction

This study is based on 5 years of data from 33 commercial banks in Pakistan, five of which are owned by the public sector (federal or provincial governments). Four foreign commercial banks operate in Pakistan, although their head offices are located abroad. Four more foreign commercial banks are listed as scheduled banks in Pakistan. Twenty commercial banks are owned by the private sector, and the activities of four specialized banks, namely the Industrial Development Bank of Pakistan (IDBP), the Punjab Provincial Cooperative Bank, SME Bank Limited, and Zarai Tarqiati (Agriculture Development) Bank Limited, target the financing of some specific sectors. Islamic banks are another category of commercial banks in Pakistan. Out of the above-mentioned 20 private banks, six are full-fledged Islamic banks. These banks operate under Shariah guidance (Islamic laws) in their investment and lending activities. They cannot lend money at a fixed interest rate, and they participate in the risk and profit of borrowers' business and assets valuation. Moreover, because of the prohibition on fixed interest rates, they cannot get involved with, or lend money to, any businesses that are anti-Islamic or prohibited by Islam on moral and ethical grounds, which restricts their ability to lend and invest. They have to incur additional costs for verifying and exploring the types of businesses of their clients. Because of these restrictions, they charge a slightly higher markup rate. Similarly, they cannot pay high markups to their depositors, so their interest rate spread is higher than that of other commercial banks (Table 7.5).

The aggregate value of total assets of these 33 banks was recorded at PKR35.7 trillion in 2022, while their aggregate lending was PKR12.7 trillion, investment PKR18.3 trillion, and deposits PKR23.4 trillion in the same year. The magnitude of aggregate equity was PKR1.9 trillion, and liquidity was PKR2.9 trillion. Table 7.6 shows the componential breakdown of these variables.

In this research, the explanatory factors of advances from banks, investment by banks, banks' liquidity position, banks' deposits, and return on assets are explained. It is supposed that equity affects banks' advances and investment in direct and indirect ways; it directly affects investment and advances because of the enhancement in the capital base, while its indirect effect on advances and investment is transformed through deposits. The direct and indirect effects of equity on lending and advances can be expressed as follows:

$$\frac{dADVNC}{dEQTY} = \frac{\partial ADVNC}{\partial EQTY} + \frac{\partial ADVNC}{\partial DPSTS} \cdot \frac{\partial DPSTS}{\partial EQTY}$$

$$\frac{dINVS}{dEQTY} = \frac{\partial INVS}{\partial EQTY} + \frac{\partial INVS}{\partial DPSTS} \cdot \frac{\partial DPSTS}{\partial EQTY}$$

The lending from commercial banks to the public and private sector is indicated by "ADVNC," while "INVS" indicates investment by commercial banks in various types of businesses. "DPSTS" is the total deposits of a commercial bank, "EQTY" is shareholders' equity including paid-up capital and retained earnings, "CASH" is cash and cash equivalent in commercial banks, "RELINT" is the real interest rate, "IND-GRW" is the rate of industrial sector growth, "EXCHRAT" is the number of Pakistani

Table 7.5 List of banks

Public Sector Commercial Banks
1. First Women Bank Ltd.
2. National Bank of Pakistan
3. Sindh Bank Limited
4. The Bank of Khyber
5. The Bank of Punjab
Foreign Banks
1. Citibank N.A.
2. Deutsche Bank AG
3. Industrial and Commercial Bank of China Limited
4. Bank of China Limited
Specialized Scheduled Banks
1. The Punjab Provincial Co-operative Bank
2. Industrial Development Bank Limited (IDBL)
3. SME Bank Limited
4. Zarai Taraqiati Bank Limited
Private Local Banks
1. Allied Bank Limited
2. Albarka Bank Pakistan Limited*
3. Askari Bank Limited
4. Bank Al Falah Limited
5. Bank Al Habib Limited
6. BankIslami Pakistan Limited*
7. Dubai Islamic Bank Pakistan Limited*
8. Faysal Bank Limited*
9. Habib Bank Limited
10. Habib Metropolitan Bank Limited
11. JS Bank Limited
12. MCB Bank Limited
13. MCB Islamic Bank*
14. Meezan Bank Limited*
15. Samba Bank Limited
16. Silk Bank Limited
17. Soneri Bank Limited
18. Standard Chartered Bank (Pakistan) Limited
19. Bank Makramah Limited (Formerly Summit Bank Limited)
20. United Bank Limited

* Full-fledged Islamic bank

Source State Bank of Pakistan (2024c)

Table 7.6 Componential breakdown of business variables (averages in PKR billion)

Component/variable	Total assets	Advances	Investment	Deposits	Equity	Liquidity
Overall	804.9	307.2	382.2	569.3	47.2	89.6
Total assets ≤1000 billion	292.5	122.3	123.6	199.8	17.9	36.3
Total assets >1000 billion, but ≤2000 billion	1437.0	552.1	648.4	1054.4	85.1	159.7
Total assets >2000 billion	2994.8	1052.3	1513.6	2104.3	170.3	310.8
Public sector banks	617.6	231.4	309.2	422.1	33.7	62.4
Specialized banks	77.6	39.7	25.1	17.3	5.6	3.5
Foreign banks	206.0	24.5	140.8	77.1	19.2	58.9
Islamic banks	562.4	265.4	182.2	428.9	30.8	83.8

Source Author's computation based on the State Bank of Pakistan (2024c)

rupees to one US dollar, "SPRD" is the interest rate spread, and "GBWR" is government borrowing from commercial banks to finance its budget deficit. "ISLAMIC," "PUBLIC," "FOREIGN," and "SPECIALIZED" are the types of commercial banks mentioned in Table 7.5 above. The short names of these variables are explained in Tables 7.7, 7.8, 7.9, and the statistical results in Tables 7.10, 7.11, 7.12, 7.13 and 7.14 include these. The data on commercial banks' variables are s in thousand PKR, except for ratios; however, government borrowing from commercial banks to finance its budget deficit is in billion Pakistani rupees (PKR). The descriptive statistics and correlation among the variables are mentioned in Tables 7.8 and 7.9, respectively.

To reduce the variation in the magnitude of parameters, the data of these variables have been transformed into natural logarithmic form. The impacts of explanatory factors on commercial banks' advances (ADVNC), investment (INVS), deposits (DPSTS), liquidity (LQDTY), and return on assets (ROA) are explained in the following equations:

$$\begin{aligned} ADVNC_{it} = \propto_i &+ \beta_1 EQTY_{it} + \beta_2 CASH_{it} + \beta_3 GBWR_{it} \\ &+ \beta_4 DPSTS_{it} + \beta_5 ISLAMIC_i + \beta_6 PUBLIC_i \\ &+ \beta_7 FOREIGN_i + \beta_8 SPECIALIZED_i + \beta_9 COVID_t + \varepsilon_{it} \end{aligned} \quad (7.1)$$

$$\begin{aligned} INVST_{it} = \propto_i &+ \beta_1 EQTY_{it} + \beta_2 CASH_{it} + \beta_3 GBWR_{it} \\ &+ \beta_4 DPSTS_{it} + \beta_5 ISLAMIC_i + \beta_6 PUBLIC_i \\ &+ \beta_7 FOREIGN_i + \beta_8 SPECIALIZED_i + \beta_9 COVID_t + \varepsilon_{it} \end{aligned} \quad (7.2)$$

$$\begin{aligned} DPSTS_{it} = \propto_i &+ \beta_1 EQTY_{it} + \beta_2 RELINT_{it} + \beta_3 INDGRW_{it} \\ &+ \beta_4 EXCHRAT_{it} + \beta_5 ISLAMIC_i + \beta_6 PUBLIC_i \\ &+ \beta_7 FOREIGN_i + \beta_8 SPECIALIZED_i + \varepsilon_{it} \end{aligned} \quad (7.3)$$

Table 7.7 List of variables

Variable	Description
ADVNC	Lending in thousands of PKR
CASH	Cash and balance with the State Bank of Pakistan (thousands of PKR)
COVID	Dummy variable is equal to 1 for 2020 and 2021 (the COVID-19 period) and 0 otherwise
DPSTS	Total deposits in thousands of PKR
EQTY	Total equity (head office capital account in the case of a foreign bank) including paid-up capital and all retained earnings (in thousands of PKR)
EXCHRAT	PKR per USD
FOREIGN	The dummy variable is equal to 1 if the head office of a commercial bank is abroad and 0 otherwise
GBWR	Government borrowing to finance budget deficit (in billion PKR)
INDGRW	Industrial growth rate (%)
INVST	Investment in businesses in thousands of PKR
ISLAMIC	The dummy variable is equal to 1 if a commercial bank is a full-fledged Islamic bank and 0 otherwise
LQDTY	Cash and balance with financial institutions in thousands
PUBLIC	The dummy variable is equal to 1 if a commercial bank is a public sector entity and 0 otherwise
RELINT	Real interest rate (%)
ROA	Return on assets before tax in %
SPECIALIZED	The dummy variable is equal to 1 if a commercial bank provides specialized services only and '0' otherwise
SPRD	Interest rate spread (%)

Source Author's presentation

Table 7.8 Descriptive statistics

Parameter/variable	TOTAST	EQTY	DPSTS	INVST	ADVNC	LIQDTY
Mean	804.9	47.2	569.3	382.2	307.2	89.6
Median	408.4	19.7	229.6	175.7	155.5	38.9
Standard deviation	981.5	58.6	700.9	516.5	348.3	118.3
Minimum	4.3	−25.9	0.1	0.4	0.1	0.4
Maximum	5240.4	257.9	3234.2	3477.4	1709.4	614.2

Source Author's computation based on the State Bank of Pakistan (2024c)

$$
\begin{aligned}
LQDTY_{it} = \propto_i + \beta_1 EQTY_{it} + \beta_2 RELINT_{it} + \beta_3 GBWR_{it} \\
+ \beta_4 ISLAMIC_i + \beta_5 PUBLIC_i + \beta_6 FOREIGN_i \\
+ \beta_7 SPECIALIZED_i + \varepsilon_{it}
\end{aligned}
\quad (7.4)
$$

Table 7.9 Correlation matrix

	TOTAST	EQTY	DPSTS	INVST	ADVNC	LIQDTY
TOTAST	1.000					
EQTY	0.954	1.000				
DPSTS	0.985	0.941	1.000			
INVST	0.979	0.935	0.940	1.000		
ADVNC	0.977	0.923	0.984	0.920	1.000	
LIQDTY	0.863	0.834	0.882	0.784	0.847	1.000

Source Author's computation based on the State Bank of Pakistan (2024c)

$$\begin{aligned} ROA_{it} = {} & \propto_i + \beta_1 INVST_{it} + \beta_2 SPRD_{it} + \beta_3 GBWR_{it} \\ & + \beta_4 EXCHRAT_{it} + \beta_5 ISLAMIC_i + \beta_6 PUBLIC_i \\ & + \beta_7 FOREIGN_i + \beta_8 SPECIALIZED_i + \beta_9 RELINT_{it} + \varepsilon_{it} \end{aligned} \quad (7.5)$$

A priori sign of estimated betas of public borrowing (GBWR) and cash reserves in banks (CASH) in the determination of advances (ADVNC) and investment (INVST) should be negative, while deposits (DPSTS) should affect advances (ADVNC) and investment (INVS) positively. In the determination of liquidity (LQDTY), the role of real interest (RELINT) and banks' equity (EQTY) should be positive. A higher inflow of workers' remittances is expected in the case of depreciation of the Pakistani rupee, in which case they will build more assets in Pakistan. Devaluation attracts the inflow of foreign exchange through workers' remittances and growth in exports, a large part of which is deposited in commercial banks. So, the expected effect of the exchange rate (EXCHRAT) on banks' deposits (DPSTS) should be positive. The exchange rate (EXCHRAT) has also been taken as a control variable in the determination of profitability (ROA).

Advances cover the lending from commercial banks to private and public sectors, including the lending to government for financing the fiscal deficit and public sector entities. The credit to the private sector covers lending to industry, consumers (credit cards and personal loans), housing, and car financing, and the lending for fixed assets and working capital is also included in the advances from banks. Investment indicates the banks' direct participation in business, including participation in private business entities, investment in the capital market, and project financing. Liquidity is defined as the sum of cash and balance with the State (Central) Bank of Pakistan, balance with other commercial banks, and lending to other financial institutions. Deposits include all kinds of public deposits in commercial banks, including both time and demand deposits. The government borrowing to finance its budget deficit was included in the explanatory factors of return on investment, and it is hypothesized that government borrowing from commercial banks improves the latter's profitability. It is a common perception that investing in gilt-edged securities is the safest investment from the lenders' point of view, while the acceptable interest rates on these securities are decided in open-market operations.

Table 7.10 Dependent variable: Ln (ADVNC)

Independent variables/ method	Panel EGLS (cross-sectional random effects)[##]			PLS (Cross-sectional Seemingly Unrelated Regression Estimation)		
	1	2	3	4	5	6
	Coefficients (t-Statistics)	Coefficients (t-Statistics)	Coefficients (t-Statistics)	Coefficients (t-Statistics)	Coefficients (t-Statistics)	Coefficients (t-Statistics)
Constant	3.857*** (3.582)	3.058*** (3.251)	0.335 (0.304)	3.892*** (7.021)	2.302 (1.393)	0.641 (0.884)
Ln (DPSTS)	0.795*** (13.826)	1.060*** (9.418)	1.085*** (10.051)	0.792*** (44.652)	1.222*** (4.662)	1.111*** (10.467)
ISLAMIC	0.041 (0.177)	0.067 (0.448)	0.171 (1.147)	0.039* (1.921)	0.093 (1.435)	0.150*** (3.710)
PUBLIC	−0.188 (−0.753)	−0.107 (−0.631)	−0.056 (−0.345)	−0.190*** (−7.969)	−0.139*** (−3.610)	−0.073*** (−2.659)
FOREIGN	−1.605*** (−5.308)	−1.239*** (−5.399)	−0.969*** (−4.008)	−1.469*** (−10.875)	−0.947*** (−3.038)	−0.903*** (−6.867)
SPECIALIZED	1.124*** (2.833)	2.214*** (5.439)	1.698*** (3.351)	1.111*** (15.994)	3.007*** (3.254)	1.793*** (6.534)
COVID	−0.088** (−2.109)	−0.081 (−1.612)	−0.133** (−2.459)	−0.044 (−0.949)	−0.031 (−0.418)	−0.093* (−1.772)
Ln (GBWR)	−0.036 (−0.558)	−0.059 (−0.754)	−0.085 (−1.021)	−0.034 (−0.598)	−0.158* (−1.655)	−0.096 (−1.405)
Ln (LNDGFI)		0.002 (0.101)	−0.002 (−0.094)		0.038 (1.299)	0.020 (0.669)
Ln (CASH)		−0.249** (−2.229)			−0.382* (−1.731)	
Ln (EQTY)			−0.108 (−1.043)			−0.173 (−1.523)
Goodness of Fit						
Adjusted R-squared	0.731***	0.847***	0.862***	0.899***	0.938***	0.939***
F-statistic	63.931	82.504	87.538	207.799	224.121	212.270
Testing for Common/Random/Fixed Effect (Lagrange Multiplier Test)						
Breusch-Pagan	160.756***	13.004***	23.572***			
Honda	12.678***	3.606*	4.855*			
King-Wu	12.678***	3.606*	4.855*			
Criteria for Model Selection						
Akaike Inf. Criterion				1.662	1.108	0.979
Schwarz Criterion				1.814	1.326	1.206
H-Q Criterion				1.724	1.196	1.072
Stationary Property (Augmented Dickey-Fuller Test), Null: Panel Unit root						

(continued)

Table 7.10 (continued)

Independent variables/ method	Panel EGLS (cross-sectional random effects)##			PLS (Cross-sectional Seemingly Unrelated Regression Estimation)		
	1	2	3	4	5	6
	Coefficients (t-Statistics)	Coefficients (t-Statistics)	Coefficients (t-Statistics)	Coefficients (t-Statistics)	Coefficients (t-Statistics)	Coefficients (t-Statistics)
ADF Test: Fisher Chi-square	44.629					
Residual Cross-Sectional Dependence Test (Null hypothesis: No cross-sectional dependence in residuals)						
Pesaran CD	1.298	NA	NA			

T-Statistics in parenthesis
Swamy and Arora estimator of component variances
$^{*}p < 0.1$; $^{**}p < 0.05$; $^{***}p < 0.01$
Source Author's estimations

As well as these measures reflecting banking strength, the profitability of a commercial bank is also important, and the study identifies the key factors of this profitability For this purpose, the return on assets (ROA) has been taken as a measure of a commercial bank's profitability. Though the return on equity is also a good measure of profitability, it is not appropriate for commercial banks because equity represents a smaller part of their capital.

Liquidity (LQDTY) is defined as the sum of cash and balance with the State Bank of Pakistan (CASH), balance with other commercial banks (BNLBAL), and lending to other financial institutions (LNDGFI). Total equity is the sum of paid-up capital (head office capital account in the case of a foreign bank), reserves, unappropriated profits (unremitted profits in the case of a foreign bank), and other retained earnings. The interest rate spread for a bank is calculated by dividing the difference between interest income and interest expenditure by interest income. It is different from the interest rate spread that is calculated in macroeconomic analysis, which is the difference between the weighted average rate of lending and the weighted average rate of deposits.

Before estimating the parameters, the stationary property in the dependent and independent variables was tested through the Augmented Dickey-Fuller (ADF) test for panel data. The regression estimators are considered inefficient if the variables in panel data are nonstationary. The Augmented Dickey-Fuller test (Fisher chi-square) was applied to test the stationarity. A lower ADF statistic than the critical values (p-value is below a certain threshold) indicates that the time series is stationary (no unit root).

Due to the nature of the data, the random effects model (REM) technique was adopted to estimate the parameters. The appropriateness of the random effects model (REM) was determined through the Breusch-Pagan Lagrange multiplier test, while estimated parameters of Honda and King-Wu Lagrange multiplier tests were also reported. However, the seemingly unrelated regression estimation (SURE) technique

Table 7.11 Dependent variable: Ln (INVST)

Independent variables/ method	Panel EGLS (Cross-sectional random effects)##			PLS (cross-sectional seemingly unrelated regression estimation)		
	1	2	3	4	5	6
	Coefficients (t-statistics)	Coefficients (t-statistics)	Coefficients (t-statistics)	Coefficients (t-statistics)	Coefficients (t-statistics)	Coefficients (t-statistics)
Constant	−2.633*** (−2.648)	−5.164*** (−5.939)	−4.786*** (−4.985)	−2.358** (−2.408)	−4.323*** (−5.006)	−4.267*** (−4.436)
Ln (DPSTS)	0.987*** (20.350)	1.179*** (12.587)	1.205*** (13.758)	0.974*** (34.559)	1.089*** (10.897)	0.904*** (9.700)
ISLAMIC	−0.621*** (−3.271)	−0.524*** (−3.480)	−0.577*** (−4.154)	−0.629*** (−8.192)	−0.616*** (−7.666)	−0.631*** (−9.611)
PUBLIC	0.132 (0.651)	0.124 (0.726)	0.084 (0.550)	0.122** (2.306)	0.067 (1.186)	0.059 (1.137)
FOREIGN	0.425* (1.685)	0.889*** (3.989)	0.860*** (3.922)	0.483*** (4.500)	0.782*** (5.440)	0.508*** (3.976)
SPECIALIZED	0.442 (1.351)	2.902*** (7.452)	2.792*** (6.442)	0.390** (2.112)	2.392*** (8.761)	1.916*** (7.318)
COVID	0.096** (1.965)	0.124*** (3.009)	0.133*** (3.219)	0.091 (1.172)	0.144** (2.056)	0.161** (2.266)
Ln (GBWR)	0.308*** (4.085)	0.200*** (3.055)	0.205*** (3.107)	0.305*** (2.651)	0.199** (1.891)	0.252** (2.323)
Ln (LNDGFI)		−0.043** (−2.091)	−0.051** (−2.477)		0.029 (0.915)	0.019 (0.593)
Ln (CASH)		0.009 (0.104)			−0.001 (−0.008)	
Ln (EQTY)			−0.033 (−0.395)			0.194* (1.927)
Goodness of Fit						
Adjusted R-squared	0.853***	0.901***	0.873***	0.944***	0.962***	0.941***
F-statistic	134.047	132.968	94.056	389.830	376.646	219.028
Testing for Common/Random/Fixed Effect (Lagrange Multiplier Test)						
Breusch-Pagan	92.895***	50.527***	31.812***			
Honda	9.638***	7.108**	5.640**			
King-Wu	9.638***	7.108**	5.640**			
Criteria for Model Selection						
Akaike Inf. Criterion				1.342	0.830	0.766
Schwarz Criterion				1.495	1.049	0.995
H-Q Criterion				1.404	0.919	0.859
Stationary Property (Augmented Dickey-Fuller Test), Null: Panel Unit root						

(continued)

Table 7.11 (continued)

Independent variables/ method	Panel EGLS (Cross-sectional random effects)##			PLS (cross-sectional seemingly unrelated regression estimation)		
	1	2	3	4	5	6
	Coefficients (t-statistics)	Coefficients (t-statistics)	Coefficients (t-statistics)	Coefficients (t-statistics)	Coefficients (t-statistics)	Coefficients (t-statistics)
ADF Test: Fisher Chi-square	69.748					
Residual Cross-Sectional Dependence Test (Null hypothesis: No cross-sectional dependence in residuals)						
Pesaran CD	7.415***	NA	NA			

T-Statistics in parenthesis
Swamy and Arora estimator of component variances
*p < 0.1; **p < 0.05; ***p < 0.01
Source Author's estimations

was also adopted to tackle the cross-sectional dependency (CD) in the variables. The parameters of these tests are reported in Tables 7.10, 7.11, 7.12, 7.13 and 7.14.

7.5 Results and Empirical Findings

The statistical results and estimated parameters are reported in Tables 7.10, 7.11, 7.12, 7.13 and 7.14. The estimations are based on 5 years of data from 33 banks (cross section), which provide 165 balanced observations. To test the robustness of the estimated parameters, each equation has been estimated in three alternative scenarios, adding and subtracting some additional variables. The conclusion has been drawn that the estimated parameters of the main variables are robust in all alternative scenarios, thereby improving the reliability of the statistical results.

After estimating the random effects model (REM), the Pesaran test was performed to test the cross-sectional dependence (CD) in all the equations. Significant cross-sectional dependence (CD) was found in some cases where the p-value was lower than 0.05 (threshold level), while its calculation was not reported in some cases because of a perfect cross-sectional correlation. So, the null hypothesis of "No cross-sectional dependence" was rejected. The seemingly unrelated regression estimation (SURE) model allows for correlation between the residuals of different cross-sectional units. So, to address the issue of cross-sectional (CS) dependence, the seemingly unrelated regression estimators (SURE) have been estimated and are reported in Tables 7.10, 7.11, 7.12, 7.13 and 7.14.

For comparison purposes, the SURE results for each equation are presented with its panel EGLS results. This technique further validated the robustness of the parameters, because no major change in the estimated parameters was observed in SURE. There is no change in the direction and significance of the explanatory variables in

Table 7.12 Dependent variable: Ln (DPSTS)

Independent variables/ method	Panel EGLS (Cross-sectional random effects)##			PLS (Cross-sectional seemingly unrelated regression estimation)		
	1	2	3	4	5	6
	Coefficients (t-statistics)	Coefficients (t-statistics)	Coefficients (t-statistics)	Coefficients (t-statistics)	Coefficients (t-statistics)	Coefficients (t-statistics)
Constant	3.747** (2.029)	3.656* (1.979)	3.734** (2.073)	−0.531 (−0.102)	−0.669 (−0.123)	1.093 (0.288)
Ln (EQTY)	0.444*** (7.141)	0.448*** (7.245)	0.505*** (9.992)	1.092*** (9.465)	1.106*** (9.083)	0.905*** (8.563)
RELINT	0.282*** (2.553)	0.281*** (2.547)	0.272** (2.466)	0.061 (0.232)	0.055 (0.200)	0.127 (0.689)
INDGRW	0.014*** (3.121)	0.014*** (3.113)	0.014*** (3.006)	0.008 (0.756)	0.007 (0.715)	0.010 (1.317)
Ln (EXCHRAT)	1.412*** (5.063)	1.407*** (5.047)	1.344*** (4.858)	0.180 (0.258)	0.146 (0.201)	0.546 (1.133)
ISLAMIC		0.230 (0.595)	−0.470* (−1.881)		0.452*** (6.165)	−0.141 (−1.147)
PUBLIC			−0.612** (−2.297)			−0.296** (−2.444)
FOREIGN			−2.054*** (−7.003)			−1.508*** (−8.019)
SPECIALIZED			−2.594*** (−6.075)			−2.466*** (−26.891)
Goodness of Fit						
Adjusted R-squared	0.585***	0.582***	0.696***	0.646***	0.656***	0.869***
F-statistic	54.054	42.851	44.059	69.506	58.422	125.727
Testing for Common/Random/Fixed Effect (Lagrange Multiplier Test)						
Breusch-Pagan	193.930***	184.406***	143.452***			
Honda	13.925***	13.579***	11.977***			
King-Wu	13.925***	13.579***	11.977***			
Criteria for Model Selection						
Akaike Inf. Criterion				2.779	2.755	1.809
Schwarz Criterion				2.879	2.875	1.988
H-Q Criterion				2.820	2.804	1.882
Stationary Property (Augmented Dickey-Fuller Test), Null: Panel Unit root						
ADF Test: Fisher Chi-square	73.112					

(continued)

Table 7.12 (continued)

Independent variables/ method	Panel EGLS (Cross-sectional random effects)##			PLS (Cross-sectional seemingly unrelated regression estimation)		
	1	2	3	4	5	6
	Coefficients (t-statistics)	Coefficients (t-statistics)	Coefficients (t-statistics)	Coefficients (t-statistics)	Coefficients (t-statistics)	Coefficients (t-statistics)
Residual Cross-Sectional Dependence Test (Null hypothesis: No cross-sectional dependence in residuals)						
Pesaran CD	NA				NA	NA

T-Statistics in parenthesis
Swamy and Arora estimator of component variances
*p < 0.1; **p < 0.05; ***p < 0.01
Source Author's estimations

explaining the investment and liquidity. The changes in the magnitudes of parameters are negligible. Similarly, the improvement in the goodness of fit (adjusted R-square and F-statistics) in SURE is obvious.

According to the statistical results in Tables 7.10 and 7.11, the magnitude of equity and deposits positively affects the advances and investment, while cash in banks negatively impacts lending. These results capture the effect of prudential regulations that determine the parameters of capital (owners' equity) and cash reserve requirement (CRR). However, the role of government is not consistent and significant. The results apply to all kinds of banks, and the type of bank is insignificant in the case of the size of advances and investment. However, in the case of SURE, the effect of public sector banks on advances is negative and significant.

Tables 7.12 and 7.13 indicate that the size of banks' equity (EQTY), industrial growth (INDGRW), interest rate (RELINT), and exchange rate (EXCHRAT) are important factors of banks' deposits (DPSTS), while the liquidity (CASH) of banks is highly dependent on their equity (EQTY). The effects of equity on deposits are the same in the case of the random effects model (REM) and seemingly unrelated regression estimations (SURE), but the effects of the real interest rate, exchange rate, and industrial growth are insignificant in the case of SURE.

Strangely, interest rate spread (SPRD) and public borrowing (GBWR) are significantly important determinants of banks' profitability (Table 7.14), contrary to financial inclusion. Public borrowing is not considered a good practice for growth in private investment. Similarly, a higher spread depicts the transfer of financial benefits to bankers instead of depositors and investors.

The seemingly unrelated regression estimators (SURE) show the negative impact of the exchange rate on the return on banks' assets (ROA).

The positive effect of the interest rate (RELINT) on deposits and banks' profitability (ROA) is quite obvious and justifiable; however, the impact of the interest rate (RELINT) on lending and investment cannot be quantified in the case of Pakistan because of the diversification in the types of banks and their clients. The lending rates are determined based on clients and the types of banks. Lending to the public sector

Table 7.13 Dependent variable: Ln (LQDTY)

Independent variables/ method	Panel EGLS (Cross-sectional random effects)##			PLS (Cross-sectional seemingly unrelated regression estimation)		
	1	2	3	4	5	6
	Coefficients (t-statistics)	Coefficients (t-statistics)	Coefficients (t-statistics)	Coefficients (t-statistics)	Coefficients (t-statistics)	Coefficients (t-statistics)
Constant	6.136 (1.573)	5.518 (1.341)	8.375 (1.446)	1.656 (0.724)	1.702 (0.630)	3.875 (1.068)
Ln (EQTY)	1.596*** (7.289)	1.569*** (7.026)	1.539*** (6.756)	1.852*** (14.680)	1.852*** (14.597)	1.849*** (14.441)
ISLAMIC	0.003 (0.005)	−0.014 (−0.023)	−0.034 (−0.055)	0.256 (0.687)	0.256 (0.684)	0.255 (0.682)
PUBLIC	0.294 (0.429)	0.291 (0.427)	0.283 (0.408)	0.297* (1.843)	0.297* (1.835)	0.296** (1.816)
FOREIGN	−0.064 (−0.086)	−0.092 (−0.123)	−0.126 (−0.167)	0.235 (0.579)	0.235 (0.576)	0.233 (0.573)
SPECIALIZED	−2.729* (−1.675)	−2.785* (−1.714)	−2.856* (−1.737)	−2.835*** (−24.786)	−2.832*** (−20.048)	−2.901*** (−18.095)
Ln (GBWR)		0.145 (0.496)	−0.076 (−0.170)		−0.006 (−0.032)	−0.209 (−0.715)
RELINT			−0.220 (−0.665)			−0.194 (−0.881)
Goodness of Fit						
Adjusted R-squared	0.319***	0.312***	0.300***	0.636***	0.633***	0.631***
F-statistic	12.831	10.540	8.737	45.167	37.328	31.799
Testing for Common/Random/Fixed Effect (Lagrange Multiplier Test)						
Breusch-Pagan	45.618***	45.605***	45.731***			
Honda	6.754**	6.753**	6.762**			
King-Wu	6.754**	6.753**	6.762**			
Criteria for Model Selection						
Akaike Inf. Criterion				3.655	3.671	3.685
Schwarz Criterion				3.790	3.828	3.864
H-Q Criterion				3.710	3.735	3.758
Stationary Property (Augmented Dickey-Fuller Test), Null: Panel Unit root						
ADF Test: Fisher Chi-square	63.695					

(continued)

Table 7.13 (continued)

Independent variables/ method	Panel EGLS (Cross-sectional random effects)##			PLS (Cross-sectional seemingly unrelated regression estimation)		
	1	2	3	4	5	6
	Coefficients (t-statistics)	Coefficients (t-statistics)	Coefficients (t-statistics)	Coefficients (t-statistics)	Coefficients (t-statistics)	Coefficients (t-statistics)
Residual Cross-Sectional Dependence Test (Null hypothesis: No cross-sectional dependence in residuals)						
Pesaran CD	NA	NA	NA			

T-Statistics in parenthesis
Swamy and Arora estimator of component variances
*p < 0.1; **p < 0.05; ***p < 0.01
Source Author's estimations

and large clients is usually considered a part of the economic package at the subsidized interest rate, while the share of consumer financing and lending to small and medium enterprises (SMEs) is much lower in the case of Pakistan than in the rest of the world. Indeed, the lending to small and medium enterprises from commercial banks is less than 5% in Pakistan. In this case, a direct effect of the interest rate (RELINT) on lending (ADVNC) cannot be tested; however, the higher interest rate spread (SPRD) in Pakistan provides a good opportunity for commercial banks to make attractive profits, as is demonstrated in this study.

It was presumed that the effects of prudential regulations are transformed through mandatory magnitudes of equity and cash requirements. The effects of cash and equity on investment, advances, deposits, liquidity position, and return on assets have been tested in this study, and the significant positive and robust effects of equity on investment, advances, deposits, and liquidity have been ascertained. The equity directly affects the investment and advances, while its indirect effect on advances and investment is channelized through deposits.

A negative association between cash and advances has also been ascertained, and the higher real interest rate induces the deposits. This conclusion is confirmed with all alternative scenarios. Another important finding is the positive effect of real interest rates on the liquidity positions of commercial banks, as higher interest rates discourage borrowers. Consequently, the cash in banks, interbank lending, and lending to financial institutions may be higher.

However, it is noted that government borrowing for deficit financing is positively correlated with banks' investment in businesses. The effects of government borrowing from commercial banks are insignificant in determining the banks' liquidity position because this is largely determined by regulation and managerial requirements.

Notably, estimated betas indicate the effects of explanatory variables. In interpreting the higher magnitude of estimated betas, it is interesting that data on banks'

Table 7.14 Dependent variable: ROA

Independent variables/ method	Panel EGLS (Cross-sectional random effects)##			PLS (Cross-sectional seemingly unrelated regression estimation)		
	1	2	3	4	5	6
	Coefficients (t-statistics)	Coefficients (t-statistics)	Coefficients (t-statistics)	Coefficients (t-statistics)	Coefficients (t-statistics)	Coefficients (t-statistics)
Constant	−0.139*** (−4.361)	−0.140*** (−4.342)	−0.158*** (−2.535)	−0.148*** (−6.639)	−0.137*** (−5.813)	−0.157*** (−3.033)
Ln (INVST)	0.004*** (4.508)	0.004*** (3.255)	0.004*** (3.252)	0.004*** (10.671)	0.002*** (4.496)	0.003*** (4.479)
SPRD	0.079*** (10.26)	0.083*** (10.649)	0.083*** (10.649)	0.085*** (21.683)	0.093*** (24.771)	0.093*** (24.704)
Ln (EXCHRAT)	−0.020 (−1.387)	−0.019 (−1.381)	−0.017 (−0.993)	−0.017** (−2.124)	−0.017** (−2.186)	−0.015 (−1.281)
Ln (GBWR)	0.016** (2.366)	0.018** (2.483)	0.0175** (2.460)	0.017*** (4.036)	0.019*** (4.622)	0.018*** (4.675)
ISLAMIC		−0.002 (−0.368)	−0.002 (−0.371)		−0.005*** (−2.778)	−0.005*** (−2.769)
PUBLIC		−0.002 (−0.296)	−0.002 (−0.296)		−0.003 (−1.631)	−0.003 (−1.625)
SPECIALIZED		−0.004 (−0.486)	−0.004 (−0.489)		−0.012** (−2.433)	−0.012** (−2.425)
FOREIGN		0.0101 (1.5105)	0.0101 (1.514)		0.008 (1.624)	0.008 (1.621)
RELINT			0.001 (0.344)			0.001 (0.426)
Goodness of Fit						
Adjusted R-squared	0.405***	0.430***	0.428***	0.636***	0.666***	0.664***
F-statistic	28.276	16.148	14.34	71.132	40.942	36.181
Testing for Common/Random/Fixed Effect (Lagrange Multiplier Test)						
Breusch-Pagan	47.662***	28.093***	33.905***			
Honda	6.904**	5.300**	5.823**			
King-Wu	6.904**	5.300**	5.823**			
Criteria for Model Selection						
Akaike Inf. Criterion				−5.568	−5.629	−5.617
Schwarz Criterion				−5.472	−5.457	−5.426
H–Q Criterion				−5.529	−5.559	−5.539
Stationary Property (Augmented Dickey-Fuller Test), Null: Panel Unit root						

(continued)

Table 7.14 (continued)

Independent variables/ method	Panel EGLS (Cross-sectional random effects)##			PLS (Cross-sectional seemingly unrelated regression estimation)		
	1	2	3	4	5	6
	Coefficients (t-statistics)	Coefficients (t-statistics)	Coefficients (t-statistics)	Coefficients (t-statistics)	Coefficients (t-statistics)	Coefficients (t-statistics)
ADF Test: Fisher Chi-square	67.4742					
Residual Cross-Sectional Dependence Test (Null hypothesis: No cross-sectional dependence in residuals)						
Pesaran CD	3.917***	3.701***	3.834***			

T-Statistics in parenthesis
Swamy and Arora estimator of component variances
*p < 0.1; **p < 0.05; ***p < 0.01
Source Author's estimations

deposits, advances, investment, and liquidity are in thousands of Pakistani rupees (PKR), while public borrowing is in billion rupees (PKR). However, their data in logarithmic form minimized the variations in betas associated with the independent variables.

The implications of the types of commercial banks are also an important consideration. Surprisingly, foreign commercial banks are reluctant to provide more lending and attract more deposits; this may be because of their concentrated operations in just a few selected cities and a small number of branches. The low contribution of Islamic banks in terms of investment was noted. The return on assets in specialized commercial banks is lower than that of other commercial banks because they focus on achieving specific targets and objectives, and they have fewer options in which to invest their available funds. Industrial growth must be a significant reason for the growth in banks' deposits.

7.6 Policy Implications and Limitations

This research will help in identifying the primary causes of lower levels of domestic credit being provided to the private sector in Pakistan. It is found that prudential regulations do not discourage lending or investment; rather, it is the monetary and fiscal policies that lead to a decline in the provision of credit to the private sector. One of the most important findings in this analysis is that almost all of the domestic credit provided to the private sector in Pakistan comes from commercial banks, and the share of the nonbanking financial sector is negligible.

Unfortunately, the prudential regulations cannot limit the public borrowing from commercial banks. Seeing lending to the government as a haven is just an illusion. A government with a high debt-to-GDP ratio and continuous growth in borrowing to repay previous loans seems strange to lenders, and it becomes even stranger if GDP growth is lower than the required growth and the tax base cannot be increased. Oddly enough, the debt liability of the government is ultimately repaid by the private sector through additional taxes or the withdrawal of subsidies or public services. In this situation, lending to the government can be riskier than advances to private businesses, where the earning capacity is visible and assets can be pledged by the lenders.

Policymakers and international financial institutions should consider the important point that borrowing from commercial banks to repay public sector debt is a dangerous way of financing, as these debts can further damage businesses.

It is important in deriving conclusions and interpreting the results that this study does not cover up the effects of cyclical fluctuation and global trends, which a dynamic analysis could do. The 5 years of data in this study cannot capture the time trend and business cycle effects; however, the trends of the banking sector in Pakistan are not affected by the global cyclical fluctuation due to the smaller size of the financial sector in the country and the very high dependency on lending to the government and public enterprises.

This research does not cover the effects of financial inclusion, which is an important expansion factor in the credit provided to the private sector. Similarly, due to the limited data availability, it cannot segregate the role of small and medium enterprises (SMEs) in domestic credit and the hindrances in terms of the provision of credit to such enterprises in Pakistan. The number of individuals and firms financed by banks are important determinants of the provision of domestic credit to the private sector, but unfortunately, the data on these variables are not consistently available for Pakistan, and analysis on the insufficient number of observations cannot be performed.

References

Aiyar, S., C. Calomiris, and T. Wieladek. 2011. Does macro-pru leak? Evidence from a UK policy experiment. NBER Working Papers 17822, National Bureau of Economic Research.

Apostolik, R., C. Donohue, and P. Went. 2009. *Foundations of banking risk*, 62–63. Hoboken, New Jersey: Wiley.

Bank of England. 2009. The role of macroprudential policy. Bank of England Discussion Paper, November.

Carpenter, D. H., and M. Maureen Murphy. 2010. The "Volcker rule": Proposals to limit "speculative" proprietary trading by banks. Congressional Research Service, 2010.

Clement, P. 2010. The Term "Macroprudential": Origins and Evolution. *BIS Quarterly Review*, March, 59–67.

de la Torre, A., and A. Ize. 2009. Regulatory reform: Integrating paradigms. Policy Research Working Paper 4842. The World Bank.

Duffy-Deno, K. T., and R. Eberts. 1991. Public infrastructure and regional economic development: A simultaneous equations approach. *Journal of Urban Economics* 30 (13): 329–343.

Federal Deposit Insurance Corporation. 2011. Risk management manual of exam policies, section 1.1. Available at https://www.nrc.gov/docs/ML1103/ML110320397.pdf. Accessed on 17 August 2011.

Friedman, M. 1968. The role of monetary policy. *American Economic Review* 58 (1): 1–17.

Hanson, S., A. Kashyap, and J. Stein. 2011. A macroprudential approach to financial regulation. *Journal of Economic Perspectives* 25:3–28.

Hideo, N., et al. 2019. *Principles of infrastructure: Case studies and best practices.* Tokyo: Asian Development Bank Institute and Mitsubishi Research Institute.

Jeanne, O., and A. Korinek. 2011. *Booms, bust and growth. Mimeo.* Maryland: Johns Hopkins University and the University of Maryland.

Kindleberger, C. P. 1970. *Power and money: The economics of international politics and the politics of international economics.* New York: Basic Books Inc.

Mehar, M. A. 2021. Bridge financing during COVID-19 pandemics: Nexus of FDI, external borrowing and fiscal policy. *Transnational Corporation Review* 13 (1): 109–124.

Mehar, M. A. 2022. Role of monetary policy in economic growth and development: From theory to empirical evidences. *Asian Journal of Economics and Banking* 7 (1): 99–120.

Mehar, M. A. 2023. Digital divide, credit financing and financial inclusion: Changing patterns of poverty, employment and income inequalities. *Industrial Policy* 3 (10): 21–41.

Montecino, J. A., and Epstein, G. 2015. Did quantitative easing increase income inequality? Working Paper No. 28. Institute of New Economic Thinking, New York.

Morris, C. H. R. 2019. *The law of financial services groups*, 57. Oxford: Oxford University Press.

Phillips, A. W. 1958. The relation between unemployment and the rate of change of money wage rates in the United Kingdom 1861–1957. *Economica* 25:283–299.

Popov, A., and F. Smets. 2012. On the tradeoff between growth and stability: The role of financial markets. Available at VoxEU.org. Accesssed on 3 November.

Reinhart, C., and K. Rogoff. 2009. *This time is different: eight centuries of financial folly.* Princeton University Press.

Rochet, J.-C. 2009. *Why are there so many banking crises? The politics and policy of bank regulation.* Princeton: Princeton University Press.

State Bank of Pakistan. 2024a. Prudential regulations. Available at www.sbp.org.pk. Accessed on 20 July 2024.

State Bank of Pakistan. 2024b. *Annual report: state of economy 2023–2024.* Karachi: The State Bank of Pakistan. https://www.sbp.org.pk/reports/annual/aarFY24/Complete.pdf. Accessed on 20 July 2024.

State Bank of Pakistan. 2024c. *Financial statement analysis of financial sector: 2018–2022.* Karachi: The State Bank of Pakistan. www.sbp.org.pk. Accessed on 20 July 2024.

State Bank of Pakistan. 2024d. Half-yearly report. Available at www.sbp.org.pk. Accessed on 20 July 2024.

Stein, J. L. 1982. *Monetarist, Keynesian & new classical economics.* Oxford: Blackwell.

Stiglitz, J. E. 1985. Credit markets and the control of capital. *Journal of Money, Credit, Banking* 17 (2): 133–152.

Tobin, J. 1969. A general equilibrium approach to monetary theory. *Journal of Money, Credit and Banking* 1969 (1): 15–29.

World Bank. 2024. *World development indicators.* Washington: The World Bank Group.

World Bank. 2025. *World development indicators.* Washington: The World Bank Group.

Chapter 8
Banking for Resilient and Sustainable Growth in Asia and the Pacific

Rachita Gulati, Dil B. Rahut, Sunil Kumar, and Tetsushi Sonobe

Abstract This chapter discusses a forward-looking roadmap for resilient banking systems in the Asia-Pacific. It examines key emerging challenges: macroeconomic volatility, digital disruption, the gap between financial access and usage, climate sustainability pressures, and regulatory complexity. To address these vulnerabilities, the chapter recommends strategic imperatives, including strengthening macroprudential frameworks, building interoperable digital public infrastructure, closing the financial access-usage gap, and integrating climate risks into prudential oversight. It concludes by suggesting that coordinated action among regulators, governments, financial institutions, and development partners is required to develop an innovation-enabled banking system capable of driving long-term regional prosperity.

Keywords Banking resilience · Financial inclusion · Digital transformation · Financial governance · Sustainable growth · Central bank digital currency · Regulatory complexity · Quality growth · Asia

8.1 Background

As highlighted in the introductory chapter, while the Asia and the Pacific region serves as the primary engine of global economic expansion, it must navigate a complex nexus of persistent institutional vulnerabilities and evolving macro-financial risks

R. Gulati · D. B. Rahut · T. Sonobe
Asian Development Bank Institute, Tokyo, Japan

R. Gulati (✉)
Department of Humanities and Social Sciences, Indian Institute of Technology Roorkee, Roorkee, Uttarakhand, India

S. Kumar
Faculty of Economics, South Asian University, New Delhi, India

T. Sonobe
National Graduate Institute for Policy Studies (GRIPS), Tokyo, Japan

R. Gulati et al. (eds.), *Emerging Challenges in Banking in Asia and the Pacific*, Economics, Law, and Institutions in Asia Pacific,
https://doi.org/10.1007/978-981-92-2144-8_8

to ensure systemic resilience. The region accounts for approximately 46% of global gross domestic product (GDP) and comprises a diverse mix of advanced and emerging economies. It remains highly susceptible to external shocks, increasing inequalities, and climate risks. To navigate this complex landscape, characterized by the lingering lessons of the Asian financial crisis (AFC) and the global financial crisis (GFC), as well as the rapid onset of digital transformation, development strategies must pivot toward quality growth, that is, resilient, inclusive, productive, and environmentally sustainable. Economies must be resilient to withstand systemic shocks, such as those observed during financial contagion and global pandemics such as the coronavirus disease (COVID-19); inclusive to ensure that the benefits of economic expansion and digitalization reach all households and firms; productive to drive economies beyond the development frontier; and environmentally sustainable, incorporating environmental, social, and governance (ESG) regulation to align banking activities with net-zero emissions targets.

The banking system plays a pivotal role in enabling quality growth, serving as the primary mediator to mobilize savings and efficiently channel resources toward productive investment. An efficient, well-functioning, and growth-driven banking system must be characterized by resilience to shocks, inclusive innovation, and a deep alignment with environmental sustainability. Building such a system requires drawing lessons from past crises while remaining adaptive to increasingly complex regulatory environments, digital disruption, and the imperative of the Sustainable Development Goals (SDGs). In the context of Asia and the Pacific, recent currency depreciations and interest rate volatility have renewed concerns about regional stability and the risk of a repeat of the AFC experience. As documented in Chapter 2, Southeast Asian currencies (including the Indonesian rupiah, Thai baht, Malaysian ringgit, Vietnamese dong, and Philippine peso) depreciated by approximately 5% in the first half of 2024, while the Japanese yen plunged to about ¥160 per US dollar, its lowest level since 1990. However, unlike with the AFC in 1997, the region now confronts these pressures with stronger institutional defense lines. The recent real estate crisis of the People's Republic of China (PRC), triggered by the collapse of property giants like Evergrande, did not lead to a "Lehman moment" precisely because of the strengthened financial governance mechanisms developed since the AFC. Similarly, Japan's central bank managed the yen's sudden appreciation in August 2024 through timely interest-rate adjustments.

Simultaneously, digital transformation presents a dual-edged trajectory. While advances in digitalization, fintech, and nonbank financial institutions (NBFIs) hold the potential to bridge financing gaps for micro, small, and medium-sized enterprises (MSMEs) and the underserved, they can introduce systemic instability if regulatory perimeters are not adequately expanded. Specific innovations, such as central bank digital currencies (CBDCs), also have the potential to enhance banking stability when supported by conducive monetary policies. Therefore, these advances must be coupled with well-informed prudential measures to balance the gains of inclusion against the potential risks. Additionally, banking operations must pivot toward sustainable practices, as the region's acute vulnerability to climate risk directly threatens the asset quality and long-term resilience of the financial sector.

This chapter draws on the preceding chapters to present emerging challenges and a forward-looking roadmap for banking systems that support resilience, inclusion, innovation, and sustainability in the Asia and the Pacific region. The chapter underscores the importance of regulatory governance reform at the national, regional, and global levels to strengthen the financial system's lines of defense. It also emphasizes the need to calibrate risk management frameworks, prudential measures, and policy designs to leverage emerging technologies while mitigating systemic risks effectively. In addition, the chapter highlights the imperative of closing gaps in information and communication technology (ICT) infrastructure to bridge the divide between digital access and meaningful usage, alongside concerted efforts to improve financial and digital literacy in the region. Finally, it calls for a cautious approach to the adoption of digital assets, coupled with the systematic integration of ESG considerations into the supervisory mandates.

8.2 Emerging Challenges in the Banking Landscape in Asia

8.2.1 Macroeconomic Volatility and Crisis Risks

The banking system plays a significant role in driving economic growth, particularly in low- and middle-income countries characterized by underdeveloped capital markets, weak creditor rights, and issues with contract enforcement and transparency. Economies exhibiting these characteristics tend to have a bank-dominated financial system because financial intermediaries serve a critical "monitoring function" when information on borrowers is scarce. By building long-term relationships, banks can screen borrowers and enforce repayment more effectively than arm's-length markets, contributing to better allocation of financial resources (Allen et al. 2018). Consequently, in developing economies such as Pakistan, the share of the nonbanking financial sector is negligible, with more than 99% of private sector credit provided by commercial banks.

Despite this capacity to mobilize resources, the banking systems in the region remain highly vulnerable to macroeconomic volatility. The region faces a convergence of risks, including geopolitical tensions, climate change, and growing interconnectedness with NBFIs. Chapter 2 by Yang and Kijkasiwat documents that recent currency depreciations and high interest rates have renewed concerns regarding regional stability. The chapter provides detailed case studies of how Thailand, Indonesia, Malaysia, and the Republic of Korea managed the AFC through distinct strategies. While the region is better positioned than it was during the 1997 AFC, persistent vulnerabilities, such as liquidity stress transmission, governance gaps, and data asymmetries, continue to challenge financial stability. These vulnerabilities are often rooted in weak institutional frameworks, limited supervisory capacity, and inadequate enforcement of prudential regulations, which impede the early detection of risks. Middle-income and small open economies are particularly at acute risk, where shallow capital markets amplify the impact of capital flow reversals and external shocks. These vulnerabilities can undermine investment, credit allocation, and productivity growth, which are the key foundations of quality growth in the region.

Furthermore, a critical structural vulnerability in the region is the distortion of credit markets caused by fiscal imbalances. While prudential regulations are essential for stability, they are not the primary constraints on private sector lending. Instead, the interaction between monetary and fiscal policies plays a decisive role, as documented in Chapter 7. Empirical evidence from Pakistan reveals a phenomenon of fiscal dominance, where excessive government borrowing from commercial banks to finance budget deficits severely crowds out private-sector investment. A study of 33 Pakistani commercial banks reveals that the share of the private sector in money supply (M2) expansion is less than 5%, with the remaining growth absorbed by government borrowing. Pakistan's domestic credit to the private sector as a percentage of GDP stands at less than 15%, far below the global average of 141% and the South Asian average of 46%. The number of borrowers per 1000 people is only 26 in Pakistan, compared to 84 in Bangladesh and 82 in lower-middle-income countries. This heavy reliance on banks for public sector financing creates an "illusion" of safety for lenders but absorbs liquidity that would otherwise support MSMEs, effectively weakening the banking sector's ability to drive genuine economic growth.

Therefore, to mitigate these internal distortions and external shocks, policymakers must strengthen financial governance across the three "lines of defense", outlined in Chapters 2 and 7. The first line of defense: the national financial system requires not only robust regulatory and prudential frameworks to improve corporate governance, transparency, and risk management, but also fiscal discipline to prevent the crowding out of private credit. Macroprudential measures must ensure that banks are well capitalized, liquid enough to support domestic credit flows, and well prepared to respond to systemic stress. Resolution frameworks must also be strengthened to limit the spread of uncertainty in the banking system. Beyond the national level, the region must leverage the second line of defense through regional safety nets, such as the Chiang Mai Initiative Multilateralization (CMIM) and the ASEAN+3 Macroeconomic Research Office (AMRO), to provide liquidity support and surveillance independent of global institutions. Finally, the third line of defense involves enhancing global coordination through platforms such as the G20 and the Financial Stability Board to manage cross-border contagion and align supervisory standards.

8.2.2 Digital Disruption and Cybersecurity

The past few decades have witnessed a period of "creative destruction," with the rapid proliferation of digital transformation through fintech adoption, CBDCs, and artificial intelligence (AI)-driven banking models. These innovations offer transformative opportunities to bridge the gap between financial access and usage. However, they introduce a complex new risk landscape that requires building banking resilience.

Empirical evidence from the region suggests that the relationship between digitalization and stability is not uniform and varies significantly between private fintech innovations and central bank-backed digital currencies. Chapter 4 by Koirala provides rigorous empirical evidence of a "speed-stability trade-off" using panel data from 21 economies in Asia and the Pacific (including the PRC, India, Japan, the Republic of Korea, Singapore, Malaysia, Thailand, Viet Nam, Bangladesh, and the Philippines) spanning 2000–2021. Regarding these innovations, Chapter 4 by Koirala finds that while financial inclusion enhances banking stability by diversifying credit portfolios and increasing access to stable retail deposits, fintech adoption is likely to decrease banking stability in the region. The study finds that fintech exerts pressure on the stabilizing effects of financial inclusion. This instability stems from a "speed-stability trade-off": while fintech improves credit monitoring and risk management capabilities, it often leads to rapid credit expansion and initial operational inefficiencies that outpace the regulatory capacity. Therefore, fintech adoption can improve efficiency and reach, but competition dynamics, regulatory perimeter expansion, and operational risk need to be calibrated to protect bank stability. Without robust regulatory frameworks to manage over-leveraging and repayment discipline, fintech integration dampens the resilience benefits usually gained from broadening financial access.

Cryptocurrency, for instance, is one of the most significant innovations in recent years, reaching a market capitalization of $2.8 trillion in 2021 (Feyen et al. 2022), and has the potential to enhance financial inclusion, reduce transaction costs, and increase transparency. However, they also have the potential to threaten financial system stability because of their volatility, regulatory uncertainty, cybersecurity (Joshi 2025), liquidity, market, credit, operational, capital flow, and disintermediation risks (BIS 2023). In an attempt to reduce these risks, central banks worldwide are actively exploring and piloting their own versions of cryptocurrencies, known as central bank digital currencies (CBDCs). As CBDCs are a relatively new innovation, many aspects remain uncertain, particularly regarding how they interact with traditional central bank policies, including monetary policy transmission and financial regulation.

Chapter 6 (Gupta, Gulati, and Chahal) provides evidence that CBDC adoption can positively influence banking stability, particularly in emerging economies, such as India and the PRC. Using a novel multidimensional bank stability index constructed through the constrained benefit-of-the-doubt optimization method (encompassing 13 indicators across five dimensions: capital adequacy, asset quality, profitability, liquidity, and efficiency) and analyzing bank-level data from 74 banks (30 Indian banks and 44 Chinese banks) between 2013 and 2022, the study employs a two-step generalized method of moments (GMM) system to address endogeneity. The CBDC adoption index captures time-varying stages from no involvement (0) to research (1), proof-of-concept (2), pilot (3), and fully launched (4). The PRC began CBDC research in 2014 and launched pilots in 2019, while India began research in 2020 and pilots in 2022. However, this positive impact is heavily dependent on its design and the monetary policy environment. The authors find that monetary policy plays a significant negative moderating role: in a tight monetary policy environment (high interest rates), the stabilizing effect of the CBDC is diminished as it competes with commercial bank deposits for funding. Conversely, under an accommodative monetary stance, CBDCs enhance stability by improving their liquidity and transparency. The more pronounced stability effects in India than in the PRC are attributed to variations in economic structures (India as a lower-middle-income country and the PRC as an upper-middle-income country), digital ecosystem maturity, and monetary policy frameworks. Therefore, the experiences from India and the PRC CBDC pilots underscore that design choices, not the CBDC itself, determine the outcomes for financial stability. This suggests that CBDC implementation must be carefully calibrated to macro-financial conditions to avoid disintermediation risks.

As banking systems become increasingly digitized and interconnected, these innovations have elevated cyber risk from an operational concern to a macro-financial stability risk. The potential for cyber attacks to trigger systemic disruptions requires enhanced cybersecurity frameworks and regular stress testing of operational resilience. Ultimately, the region's digital transition requires a two-pronged approach: strengthening the regulatory perimeter to mitigate fintech-driven volatility while designing CBDCs that complement, rather than cannibalize, the commercial banking system (see Box 8.1).

Box 8.1 CBDC design choices: Stability implications

Central bank digital currencies (CBDCs) represent a fundamental innovation, but their impact on banking stability depends critically on design choices rather than on the technology itself. CBDCs can enhance payment efficiency and financial inclusion; however, poorly designed CBDCs may pose risks to bank funding and financial stability. Policymakers must consider several critical risks: (i) if CBDC interest rates are too attractive, deposits may flow from commercial banks to the central bank, reducing bank funding and lending capacity, leading to disintermediation risk; (ii) during stress periods, CBDCs could enable rapid deposit flight, accelerating bank runs and amplifying liquidity pressures; and (iii) CBDC design choices, such as whether to implement wholesale versus retail models, affect the effectiveness of interest rate policy and credit channel mechanisms. To address these concerns, several design features can be deployed: (i) tiered remuneration with different interest rates for different CBDC holding amounts to discourage excessive holdings; (ii) caps on CBDC balances to prevent excessive disintermediation; (iii) wholesale versus retail design choices that limit CBDC access or use cases to specific segments; and (iv) two-tier distribution models where central banks issue CBDCs and commercial banks distribute them, thereby preserving the intermediation role of the banking system.

Exemplary cases of India's and the PRC's CBDC pilots, as presented in Chapter 6, demonstrate that the monetary policy stance significantly moderates the impact of CBDC on bank stability. When designed with appropriate safeguards, including careful attention to interest rate structures, holding limits, and distribution mechanisms, CBDCs can enhance payment efficiency and financial inclusion without undermining the stability of the banking system. Therefore, the design details, not the CBDC concept itself, determine whether CBDCs will strengthen or weaken financial stability. Policymakers must prioritize careful pilot testing and iterative design refinement before full-scale implementation.

Source CBDC Tracker. https://cbdctracker.org/ (accessed 15 January 2026)

8.2.3 *Financial Inclusion Gaps*

Despite expanded access through digital channels, critical gaps in usage, trust, affordability, and financial capability persist, particularly for women-led MSMEs and rural households across the region. While account ownership rates have increased, persistent gaps in access (to accounts or internet connectivity), meaningful usage, and trust limit the developmental impact of digital finance and weaken bank-customer relationships, thereby reducing the effectiveness of financial deepening. Chapter 3 by Haini and Hashim provides empirical evidence of this "uneven digital divide" through a case study of Brunei Darussalam. Although Brunei Darussalam possesses digital infrastructure with 95.6% internet penetration, which places it ahead of many ASEAN peers, financial inclusion remains moderate due to a stark "usage gap." The study reveals that while 65.7% of the population holds a bank account, online banking penetration is only 35.9%, and debit card penetration is 51.1%.

The analysis identifies a critical structural barrier that drives the exclusion gap. Because most digital payment services (such as QR code platforms) require users to link to an existing bank account or debit card, the unbanked population is inherently excluded from the benefits of fintech innovations. Furthermore, the study finds that while the volume of digital transactions has grown, the average transaction value per user has shown a declining or moderate trend. This signals that digital availability has not yet translated into deep, meaningful engagement and that usage remains uneven or superficial for many users. Chapter 3 documents Brunei Darussalam's policy response: the central bank established a fintech office in 2017 to encourage digital financial technologies; the Digital Payment Roadmap 2019–2025 advocates technologies such as QR codes, biometric solutions, and Association of Southeast Asian Nations (ASEAN) payment system integration; a regulatory sandbox was introduced to test new financial products; and the Digital Economy Masterplan 2025 aims to create a "Smart Nation" with a National Digital Payment Hub and national QR payment system, expected by late 2025. Despite these initiatives, the urban-rural divide persists: Brunei-Muara (capital district) has 36 bank branches and 85 ATMs, while remote Temburong has only two branches and no multifunction machines. These findings underscore that digital infrastructure alone is insufficient; bridging the digital divide requires targeted regulatory efforts to decouple digital finance from legacy banking prerequisites and enhance financial literacy. Box 8.2 explores why this gap persists and what it means for policymakers.

Box 8.2 From access to usage: Why digital financial inclusion still falls short

Despite impressive gains in account ownership and digital payment infrastructure across Asia and the Pacific, a gap persists between access and meaningful usage of digital services. Increased access to digital finance does not automatically translate into meaningful financial inclusion. Five critical barriers prevent financial access from becoming meaningfully inclusive: (i) account dormancy, where many newly opened accounts see minimal or no activity after initial opening (similar concerns were observed under Pradhan Mantri Jan Dhan Yojana (PMJDY) in India)[1]; (ii) digital literacy barriers, as having a smartphone or account does not equal confident, effective use of financial services; (iii) trust deficits, where security concerns, past fraud experiences, and lack of transparency deter active usage; (iv) affordability constraints, as transaction fees, minimum balance requirements, and service charges exclude poor people; and (v) product misalignment, where available products often do not match user needs, particularly for rural households and MSMEs.

What Sustainable Inclusion Requires

Access-focused metrics, such as account ownership rates, ATM density, and mobile money registration, may overstate the inclusion outcomes. Moving beyond access to meaningful inclusion requires (i) regular and productive usage of financial services rather than dormant accounts; (ii) quality products that serve real needs and create value for users; (iii) consumer confidence in the financial system's security and fairness; and (iv) the financial capability to make informed decisions. Banks play a central role in translating digital access into productive credit and savings. Without active usage, access alone cannot drive development outcomes or contribute to quality growth. Shifting from access to effective usage is essential for financial inclusion to contribute meaningfully to shared prosperity and quality of growth.

Addressing the access-usage gap requires not only behavioral and educational interventions but also the development of foundational infrastructure. Box 8.3 examines how well-designed digital public infrastructure can support this transition, drawing lessons from small, high-income economies.

[1] As of August 2025, approximately 23% (130.4 million) of the total 560.4 million PMJDY accounts were considered inoperative or dormant.

Box 8.3 Digital public infrastructure (DPI): What works in small, high-income economies

Brunei Darussalam's experience, as presented in Chapter 3 (Haini and Hashim), offers valuable lessons for economies in Asia and the Pacific for building digital financial infrastructure. A well-designed digital public infrastructure (DPI), consisting of shared, interoperable rails for digital identity, payments, and data sharing, supports innovation, inclusion, and resilience, with particularly high payoffs in small and developing economies.[2] First, interoperability built on open standards (e.g., ISO 20022, harmonized application programming interfaces (APIs)) reduces fragmentation and enables cross-provider and cross-border transactions, amplifying network effects and lowering costs (BIS 2024; OECD 2025). Second, public–private collaboration, combining public digital rails with private innovation, and clear governance structures covering roles, funding, and accountability are essential, along with privacy by design, data protection, cybersecurity, and effective redress mechanisms to maintain trust. Third, proportionate, risk-based regulation (tiered know your customer (KYC), sandboxes, competition policy) prevents undue compliance burdens while managing risks and keeping markets contestable (World Bank 2023a, 2023b).

For small states and Small Island Developing States, shared DPI lowers fixed costs, supports resilience, and attracts investment when paired with connectivity and skills programmes (UNDP 2024; WEF 2024). Evidence from India, Brazil, Europe, Japan, and the United Kingdom shows that DPI can accelerate financial inclusion, service efficiency, and private-sector innovation, yielding fiscal savings and productivity gains; however, outcomes depend on the foundations: affordable connectivity, digital skills, and consumer protection (IMF 2023). Interoperability mandates should also be paired with coverage incentives to avoid underinvestment in rural last-mile infrastructure (Brunnermeier et al. 2023). When combined with strong governance, cybersecurity standards, and proportionate regulation, DPI accelerates financial inclusion without undermining stability, which is a model for achieving quality growth through digital transformation. With these safeguards, economies in Asia and

[2] Refer to OECD (2024) for other exemplary cases globally and in the region, including India Stack (Aadhaar/UPI/DEPA; PIX/receipts), GOV.UK OneLogin, European Digital Identity Wallet, Japan's Co-operation Network System for Personal Information, among others.

the Pacific, many of which have already adopted interoperability and API standards, such as the Philippines through its National Retail Payment System and QR Ph framework, and India through UPI and Account Aggregator (APIs), can treat DPI as a high-return reform to drive quality growth in finance and beyond (OECD 2025).

Low- and middle-income countries benefit from establishing DPI, with an estimated increase in their GDP by 1%–1.4% points by 2030, as documented in a study by the OECD (2024). The initial cost of establishing a DPI can be high, but once the system is in place, the marginal cost of providing additional services becomes low. For instance, the Aadhaar digital ID system in India cost approximately $1.5 billion to establish, but the Indian government was able to reduce the cost of verifying a customer's identity from $10–$12 to about $0.2. Moreover, the government saved more than $42 billion by reducing fraud, errors, and leakage in public benefit programmes (Jain 2025).

8.2.4 Climate and Sustainability Pressures

Beyond digital disruptions, climate-related financial risks pose increasingly material threats to banking system stability in Asia and the Pacific. Both physical risks, such as typhoons, flooding, sea-level rise, and droughts, and transition risks associated with the shift away from fossil fuels, directly impact bank balance sheets. Physical risks affect borrower's repayment capacity and collateral values. For example, agricultural loans become riskier as weather patterns become more unpredictable, while coastal property values face pressure from rising sea levels. Transition risks emerge as economies decarbonize: banks with significant exposure to coal, oil, or high-emission industries face potential loan losses as these sectors decline (Calice and Miguel 2021; Gulati et al. 2025). As documented in Chapter 5 by Ghosh, topic modelling of 1815 central bank documents reveals an increasing SDG-driven policy orientation, particularly in climate resilience and sustainable development. The study demonstrates that policy shocks, including the implementation of SDGs in 2015, have been game changers in shaping central bank's commitment to sustainability. SDG 13 (Climate Action) has seen particularly remarkable growth in central bank policy discourse since 2015, reflecting the region's growing recognition of climate risks as systemic threats to financial stability. However, the translation of policy discourse into concrete action remains uneven across the region. The operationalization of climate risk assessment in the financial sector relies on a spectrum of methodologies that vary in granularity, data requirements, and modelling (Campiglio et al. 2018). Specifically, addressing climate risk requires an inclusive and sustainable approach that integrates green finance, climate-aligned banking systems, and proper green taxonomy to identify green activities.

The key elements of climate risk integration include:

- *Climate stress testing.* Scenario analysis of loan portfolios under various climate pathways (e.g., 1.5°C vs. 3°C warming scenarios) to assess potential credit losses and capital adequacy under different future states
- *Enhanced disclosure standards.* Requiring borrowers to report climate risk exposures, including physical vulnerabilities (location of assets in flood-prone or coastal areas) and transition exposures (revenue dependence on fossil fuels)
- *Green taxonomy convergence.* Developing clear, harmonized definitions of environmentally sustainable activities to guide lending decisions and prevent greenwashing
- *Risk-adjusted pricing.* Incorporating climate risk assessments into lending decisions, collateral valuation, and loan loss provisioning
- *Sector-specific guidance.* Providing targeted supervisory guidance for high-risk sectors (coal mining, coastal real estate, and agriculture in drought-prone regions).

Scaling up green finance is equally essential. This includes promoting instruments, such as green bonds, sustainability-linked loans, and blended finance mechanisms, that combine concessional public funding with commercial funds. The region must also develop robust measurement frameworks to track progress and ensure that green finance flows support genuine environmental outcomes, rather than superficial compliance. Climate risk integration and green finance scaling are not merely regulatory compliance issues; they are fundamental to long-term banking stability and the region's quality growth trajectory.

8.2.5 Regulatory Complexity

As financial innovation blurs the traditional boundaries among banks, fintech firms, and NBFIs, regulators face increasing complexity in defining their supervisory boundaries and ensuring comprehensive risk oversight. Regulatory fragmentation across institutions, jurisdictions, and instruments creates arbitrage opportunities that financial entities can exploit, potentially concentrating risks outside the regulated banking system.

First, the *proliferation of fintech platforms* performing bank-like functions (credit extension, payment services, deposit-taking) without full banking licenses poses significant regulatory challenges. Similarly, NBFIs, including peer-to-peer (P2P) lending platforms, digital wallets, and cryptocurrency exchanges, may escape traditional prudential oversight despite performing intermediation functions that create systemic linkages in the financial system. This regulatory arbitrage can lead to shadow banking risks, where credit creation and maturity transformation occur outside the regulated perimeter, making it difficult for authorities to monitor and manage aggregate leverage and liquidity risk.

Second, the *capacity constraints* challenge is particularly acute for lower-income and middle-income economies in the region, where limited supervisory capacity slows the pace of rapid financial innovation and the operationalization of climate risk assessment. Many regulators face constraints in terms of (i) technical and climate expertise needed to evaluate complex evolving fintech and sustainable business models, (ii) sufficient data infrastructure to monitor real-time activity across diverse platforms, (iii) flexible legal frameworks sufficient to support innovation safely, and (iv) resources for ongoing training and technology upgrades for effective supervision. Consequently, innovation often progresses more rapidly than regulation, creating gaps in oversight. This regulatory lag increases consumer risk, fraud, and financial instability.

Third, *cross-border spillovers* arise from the rapid expansion of fintech platforms and digital financial services across multiple jurisdictions, complicating enforcement and crisis management. Chapter 2 documents how the lack of a coordinated regional response during the AFC (when the IMF's crisis resolution was criticized for failing to differentiate between the economic, political, and sociocultural contexts of various nations) prompted the creation of regional mechanisms. However, even today, cross-border operations raise questions about supervisory coordination and information sharing, legal jurisdiction in the event of failures or consumer disputes, regulatory harmonization to prevent race-to-the-bottom competition, and crisis-resolution mechanisms when firms operate across multiple markets. The lack of harmonized regulatory standards across ASEAN, the South Asian Association for Regional Cooperation, and the broader Asia and the Pacific region compounds these challenges, increasing compliance costs for firms operating in the region and limiting the effectiveness of supervisory oversight.

Overall, addressing the regulatory complexity requires a multifaceted approach. Drawing on the evidence from Chapters 2–7, six priority areas have emerged. First, implementing risk-based regulatory approaches tailored to institutional size, complexity, and systemic importance, rather than "one-size-fits-all" frameworks, as Brunei Darussalam has done with its Regulatory Sandbox introduced by the central bank. Second, establishing controlled testing environments (regulatory sandboxes) where innovations can be piloted under temporary regulatory relief, allowing regulators to learn and adapt to the frameworks. Third, leveraging supervisory technology (RegTech/SupTech) to enhance monitoring capabilities, automate compliance checking, and analyze large datasets for early risk detection is recommended. Fourth, working through regional associations (such as ASEAN and the Executives' Meeting of East Asia-Pacific Central Banks) and other forums to develop common regulatory standards (such as the ASEAN Taxonomy for Sustainable Finance) and reduce arbitrage opportunities and compliance costs. Fifth, technical assistance and knowledge-sharing platforms should be provided for resource-constrained regulators, potentially through regional development institutions. Sixth, regulating activities rather than entities, ensuring that "same risk, same regulation" principles apply regardless of institutional form. Drawing on comparative evidence across Asia, regulatory fragmentation and uneven supervisory capacity remain binding constraints on effective risk oversight, which is mandatory for harnessing the benefits of financial innovation while safeguarding stability.

8.3 Strategic Imperatives for Prosperity and Quality Growth

To achieve high-income status, policymakers must strengthen and calibrate reforms to build a resilient banking sector. Some of the recommendation are listed below:

1. *Strengthen Macroprudential Frameworks, Crisis Management Protocols, and Regional Resilience*: Strengthen macroprudential frameworks, crisis management protocols, and regional safety nets to ensure that the banking system can withstand shocks. This requires upgrading capital and liquidity requirements, improving bank resolution mechanisms, and deepening regional mechanisms, such as the Chiang Mai Initiative Multilateralization (CMIM). Early warning systems must be enhanced to detect vulnerabilities, including excessive credit growth, asset price bubbles, and cross-border contagion risks, before they escalate into full-blown crises. Regional cooperation on supervisory information sharing and joint stress testing can help strengthen collective resilience.
2. *Promote Digital Public Infrastructure, Interoperable Payment Systems, and Secure CBDC Design*: Promote digital public infrastructure, interoperable payment systems, and secure CBDC designs to harness technology for inclusion and efficiency. As demonstrated by Brunei Darussalam's experience (Chapter 3) and discussed in Box 8.3, a well-designed DPI can accelerate financial inclusion without compromising stability when combined with strong governance and proportionate regulation. Interoperable payment systems, including QR code-based platforms (such as QR Ph in the Philippines and UPI in India), should be prioritized to reduce transaction costs and expand merchant acceptance. For economies considering CBDCs, careful design is paramount (see Box 8.1). Tiered remuneration, holding limits, and two-tier distribution models can mitigate disintermediation risks while preserving the benefits of enhanced payment efficiency and monetary policy transmission.
3. *Advance Inclusive Finance for MSMEs, Women, and Underserved Populations*: Expanding MSME credit access, developing gender-sensitive financial products, and scaling financial and digital literacy programmes are recommended. As Boxes 8.2 and 8.3 emphasize, true financial inclusion requires moving beyond account ownership metrics to ensure meaningful usage and consumer confidence in the financial system. Chapters 3 and 4 together reveal a critical policy insight: expanding access (accounts and connectivity) without addressing usage barriers and regulatory frameworks can be counterproductive. The finding in Chapter 4 that the combined effect of fintech and financial inclusion may destabilize banking if "not properly managed" underscores the need for holistic approaches. This demands targeted interventions, such as credit guarantee schemes to de-risk MSME lending, alternative credit scoring using digital footprints, gender-disaggregated data collection to identify specific barriers, and comprehensive financial education programs delivered through digital channels. Chapter 7 provides evidence that addressing financing gaps in MSMEs requires both supply-side interventions (reducing collateral requirements and developing

MSME-focused products) and demand-side programs (financial literacy and business formalization support). Closing the usage gap is essential for financial inclusion to contribute to shared prosperity and quality of growth.

4. *Integrate Climate Risk and Scale Green Finance*: Integrate climate risk into supervision and scale green-finance solutions. This requires implementing climate stress tests, enhancing disclosure standards, developing harmonized green taxonomies, and incorporating climate considerations into prudential frameworks. Chapter 5's analysis demonstrates that SDG 13 (Climate Action) has seen remarkable growth in policy discourse since 2015, but that discourse must translate into supervisory action. Specific steps include: mandating climate risk disclosure aligned with Task Force on Climate-Related Financial Disclosures (TCFD) recommendations; incorporating climate scenarios into bank stress tests; developing region-wide green taxonomy building on the ASEAN Taxonomy for Sustainable Finance; and requiring banks to report financed emissions and set decarbonization targets. Green financing initiatives, including green bonds, sustainability-linked loans, and blended finance mechanisms, must be scaled up dramatically. As Chapter 5 demonstrates, central banks across the region have increasingly prioritized SDG 13 (Climate Action) in their policy discourse; this commitment must now be translated into concrete supervisory practices and measurable green finance flows. Finally, long-term resilience and quality growth require the systematic integration of climate considerations into all aspects of banking supervision and finance.

8.4 Call to Action for Stakeholders

Achieving sustainable futures, shared prosperity, inclusiveness, and poverty reduction can be challenging. A robust, resilient, inclusive, and well-regulated banking system can contribute to achieving these objectives by allocating resources to the most productive investments. However, fostering a well-regulated and resilient banking system that withstands diverse shocks requires coordination among all stakeholders to fulfil their roles.

8.4.1 For Governments and Central Banks

The government and central banks play complementary roles in ensuring economic and financial stability. Therefore, it is imperative to ensure coordination between monetary policy and other government policies to achieve synergy and fully leverage the potential to strengthen financial system stability. Coordinated monetary-prudential governance is essential, as demonstrated in Chapter 7, where the interaction between monetary policy and prudential regulations significantly shapes domestic credit flows, particularly for MSMEs. Climate integration into monetary policy frameworks and the development of inclusive digital payment rails are also priorities. Moreover, as the financial system becomes more complex and interconnected, it is necessary to enhance risk oversight of emerging disruptions and strengthen regional cooperation, which is increasingly important. This can be achieved through the harmonization of regulatory frameworks, data sharing, and cross-border pilot projects. Regional cooperation, building on existing mechanisms such as the CMIM, ASEAN+3, and the Executive's Meeting of East Asia–Pacific Central Banks, will be critical to managing shared risks and scaling successful innovations. A harmonized regulatory framework will help reduce costs and improve efficiency, facilitating cross-border investment. At the same time, data sharing can improve oversight and risk detection, while cross-border pilot projects can strengthen cooperation and trust among authorities.

8.4.2 For Financial Regulators

To ensure that financial regulators are prepared to address potential shocks and uncertainties, it is important to modernize the regulatory framework by incorporating innovations that enhance risk monitoring, safeguard consumer's rights, and improve financial inclusion. It is essential to expand the regulatory perimeter proportionately through activity-based regulation, where the principle of "same risk, same regulation" applies across all institutional forms. Further, incorporating new innovations, such as SupTech, is imperative to enhance risk monitoring, which would allow regulators to detect emerging vulnerabilities at an early stage. Moreover, clear consumer protection regulations are needed to safeguard consumer data privacy and enhance transparency, particularly as financial services are introduced to underserved groups through advances in digitalization. These can help build trust, protect consumers, and reduce risks to the banking system. Regulatory sandboxes can facilitate controlled experimentation with innovations while managing the associated risks. A clear regulatory framework is also needed to oversee the growing role of fintech and NBFIs and limit the risks they pose to the banking system. These institutions are often new, and many developing countries still lack the necessary regulations and capacity to oversee their roles. Additionally, to ensure financial inclusion without compromising stability, financial regulators should implement proportional regulations, where regulations are applied based on the individual risk posed by institutions.

8.4.3 For Private and Non-bank Financial Sector and Development Partners

The private and non-bank financial sectors, as well as development partners, also play significant roles in ensuring a robust banking system. The private sector plays an important role in selecting innovations that are secure through investment decisions. As investors provide capital to firms, they often carefully evaluate risks before investing to protect their capital. This process encourages firms to evaluate their risk exposure to secure investments. Simultaneously, the presence of NBFIs increases market competition, providing consumers with more options for financial products and services. This will compel providers to offer more transparent pricing and better products to remain competitive and attract customers to their services. The proliferation of NBFIs also improves financing for underserved groups, such as MSMEs. However, as discussed in Sect. 8.2.5, the growth of NBFIs requires careful regulatory oversight to prevent shadow banking risks. Additionally, development partners can provide a platform for regional dialogue, technical support, and funding for cross-border pilot programmes to enhance regional cooperation and strengthen banking system resilience. Multilateral development banks, including the Asian Development Bank, the World Bank, and regional institutions, play a crucial role in providing technical assistance, facilitating knowledge exchange, and supporting capacity building in resource-constrained jurisdictions.

Building a crisis-ready, digitally inclusive, climate-conscious, and innovation-enabled banking system is central to shaping prosperity through quality growth in Asia and the Pacific. The region's ability to convert disruption into opportunity will depend on coordinated action across governments, regulators, financial institutions, and development partners. Strengthening banking systems today is not merely a response to past crises and a cushion for future shocks; it is an investment in the region's long-term productivity, resilience, and growth.

References

Allen, F., X. Gu, and O. Kowalewski. 2018. Financial structure, economic growth, and development. In *Handbook of finance and development*, edited by T. Beck and R. Levine, 31–62. Edward Elgar Publishing. Available at https://www.e-elgar.com/shop/gbp/handbook-of-finance-and-development-9781785360503.html?srsltid=AfmBOooB1Tb0uk6TOz1_C84KGZiN8UaIUVYhuF0qgW2kPT_6uR6oqlyC

Bank for International Settlements (BIS). 2023. *Financial stability risks from cryptoassets in emerging market economies*. Basel: BIS, Bank for International Settlements, Monetary and Economic Department. Ciudad de México, Mexico.

Bank for International Settlements (BIS). 2024. Committee on Payments and Market Infrastructures. Press release: CPMI reports to G20 on fast payment system interlinking and APIs, October 15. Available at https://www.bis.org/press/p241015.htm. [accessed 15 Jan 2026].

Brunnermeier, M. K., N. Limodio, and L. Spadavecchia 2023. Mobile money, interoperability, and financial inclusion. NBER Working Paper No. 31696, National Bureau of Economic Research. Available at https://www.nber.org/system/files/working_papers/w31696/w31696.pdf. [accessed 4 Jan 2026].

Calice, P., and F. Miguel. 2021. *Climate-related and environmental risks for the banking sector in Latin America and the Caribbean: A preliminary assessment*. Washington, DC: World Bank. Available at https://doi.org/10.1596/1813-9450-9694.

Campiglio, E., Y. Dafermos, P. Monnin, J. Ryan-Collins, G. Schotten, and M. Tanaka. 2018. Climate change challenges for central banks and financial regulators. *Nature Climate Change* 8 (6): 462–468. Available at https://www.nature.com/articles/s41558-018-0175-0. [accessed 12 Dec 2025].

Feyen, E. H. B., Y. Kawashima, and R. Mittal. 2022. *Crypto-assets activity around the world: Evolution and macro-financial drivers*. The World Bank. Available at https://doi.org/10.1596/1813-9450-9962.

Gulati, R., D. B. Rahut, and S. Kumar. 2025. Banking for climate change: South Asia initiatives. *Wiley Interdisciplinary Reviews: Climate Change* 16 (5): e70021. Available at https://doi.org/10.1002/wcc.70021.

International Monetary Fund (IMF). 2023. Stacking up the benefits: Lessons from India's digital journey. IMF Working Paper 2023/078. Available at https://www.imf.org/en/publications/wp/issues/2023/03/31/stacking-up-the-benefits-lessons-from-indias-digital-journey-531692. [accessed 12 Dec 2025].

Jain, S. 2025. Digital public infrastructure's road to economic growth. Gates Foundation, April 16. Available at https://www.gatesfoundation.org/ideas/articles/inclusive-economies-digital-public-infrastructure. [accessed 4 Jan 2026].

Joshi, P. 2025. Cryptocurrency vs traditional banking: A financial stability perspective. SSRN 5337259. Available at https://papers.ssrn.com/sol3/papers.cfm?abstract_id=5337259. [accessed 15 Jan 2026].

Organisation for Economic Cooperation and Development (OECD). 2024. Digital public infrastructure for digital governments. OECD Public Governance Policy Papers, No. 68, OECD. Available at https://www.oecd.org/content/dam/oecd/en/publications/reports/2024/12/digital-public-infrastructure-for-digital-governments_11fe17d9/ff525dc8-en.pdf. [accessed 15 Jan 2026].

Organisation for Economic Co-operation and Development (OECD). 2025. Government at a glance 2025: Digital public infrastructure (section 7.2). Available at https://www.oecd.org/en/publications/government-at-a-glance-2025_0efd0bcd-en/full-report/digital-public-infrastructure_1cee4220.html. [accessed 15 Jan 2026].

United Nations Development Programme (UNDP). 2024. Small island digital states: How digital can catalyse SIDS development. Available at https://www.undp.org/sites/g/files/zskgke326/files/2024-04/undp-small-island-digital-states-how-digital-can-catalyse-sids-development.pdf. [accessed 12 Dec 2025].

World Bank. 2023a. Creating digital public infrastructure for empowerment, inclusion, and resilience. Available at https://projects.worldbank.org/en/results/2023/10/12/creating-digital-public-infrastructure-for-empowerment-inclusion-and-resilience. [accessed 12 Dec 2025].

World Bank. 2023b. G20 policy recommendations for advancing financial inclusion and productivity gains through DPI. Available at https://documents1.worldbank.org/curated/en/099092023121016458/pdf/P178703046f82d07c0bbc60b5e474ea7841.pdf. [accessed 12 Dec 2025].

World Economic Forum (WEF). 2024. Bridging the digital divide by putting the focus on people. World Economic Forum, December 19.

Index

R. Gulati et al. (eds.), *Emerging Challenges in Banking in Asia and the Pacific*, Economics, Law, and Institutions in Asia Pacific,
https://doi.org/10.1007/978-981-92-2144-8

FSC
www.fsc.org
MIX
Papier | Fördert
gute Waldnutzung
FSC® C083411

Kolibri 360 GmbH
Ferdinand-Jühlke-Straße 7
99095 Erfurt, Deutschland
produktsicherheit@kolibri360.de